Praise for Marion Pastor's
Psychospiritual Explorations

… a compelling and entertaining first person inner adventure story told by someone who for 50 years has been on the front lines of the psychospiritual growth scene. A seeker after truth, Marion Pastor---with insight and wisdom--- shares her amazing journey with many of the most influential pioneers of the human potential movement, from the 1950s through today's leading spiritual teachers.

Ron Luyet,
author of *Radical Collaboration: Five Essential Skills to Overcome Defensiveness and Build Successful Relationships*

… Marion delves deeply into the many mysteries of how to become a happy and fulfilled human being. In pursuit of healing herself, she generously and frankly takes us on her 50-year journey of exploring the twentieth century's multiple sources of spiritual and psychological guidance. The narrative flows beautifully and the book has been put together with such honesty---to me she is the wandering seeker. From her, we learn that there are no easy solutions but the exploration is fun and fascinating.

Serena Steir,
author of *Deadly Illumination: A Gilded Age Mystery*

I was amazed by the precise and vivid memories of Marion's long life, and by her complete openness in sharing her inner life. Detailing all the methods she explored to change her negative childhood programming, the book becomes a fabulous resource for learning something about almost every important psycho-spiritual practice to come on the horizon from Marion's adolescence in the 1930's, up into today. It demonstrates how to use these methods in your life or in helping others.

Freda Morris,
author of *Self-Hypnosis in Two Days*

… a great read: a very personal portrait of a remarkable woman on a remarkable journey. It tells the story of Marion's search for meaning and wholeness after a childhood that left her "emotionally numb, socially ignorant, badly educated, fearful and often sullen." Furthermore, it is a participant's picture of the Personal Growth/Human Potential Movement in the latter half of the twentieth century. It paints with a broad brush the many and varied methods of personal and spiritual growth that Marion explored. Beginning with Mary Baker Eddy's Christian Science in her childhood, she became deeply involved in Subud, Gestalt, Arica, the Fischer/Hoffman Process, *A Course in Miracles*, EMDR, Avatar, and Michael Brown's *The Presence Process,* among others. As a licensed Psychotherapist, she used what she learned to help her clients as well as herself.

Beth Glick-Rieman,
author of *Peace Train to Beijing and Beyond.*

Psychospiritual Explorations

A Personal Journey

By Marion Pastor, Ph.D.
2011

3

ISBN-10: 1449991645
ISBN-13/EAN-13: 9781449991647

psychospiritualexplorations@gmail.com

to my mother and my father;
my daughter and son;
and
all my remarkable teachers and dear friends.

Contents

Preface

During my lifetime of almost ninety years, my passionate interest has been investigating and experiencing the many different psychospiritual teachings that were available to me. I was involved in some of these teachings for weeks; some for months; and some for years. My pursuit was not only intellectual and professional, but was also deeply personal. My childhood left me confused, unhappy, angry a lot of the time and blaming others (mainly my parents) and, most of all, disappointed with myself and mired in self-hatred. The methods I have studied (and sometimes taught) were my fervent attempt to grow beyond the person created by that childhood.

I was a Psychiatric Social Worker and Field Instructor at UCLA; and a licensed psychotherapist. I earned a Ph.D. in Philosophy and Religion from the California Institute of Integral Studies (CIIS). I was also a certified teacher of Gestalt Therapy; Hypnosis and Guided Imagery; the Fischer/Hoffman Process; EMDR (Eye Movement Desensitization and Reprocessing); and Avatar. I have been deeply involved in teachings with different backgrounds: Subud (Moslem); the Arica Training (esoteric wisdom); A Course In Miracles (Christian); the Diamond Heart Approach of H.A. Almaas (Sufi-Buddhist); Adyashanti (Zen Buddhist); and the Presence Process of

Michael Brown (many sources). I've also participated in and studied more than fifty other remarkable psychological and spiritual methods.

Much of this book is a condensation of intimate journals and notes that I kept during the many years of my involvement with these myriad approaches. The first two chapters of the book, however, are culled from my memories of the precarious childhood and chaotic early adulthood that ushered in my search to become more than I was. To the best of my personal knowledge and research, the descriptions I've given of each approach are accurate.

I have been living peacefully in the Puget Sound area across the water from Seattle since 2008, although coping with some of the physical limitations of old age. When I left my long-time home in Berkeley two years ago, I retired from my professional psychotherapy practice. Now I enjoy my little condominium overlooking the beautiful bay shown on the cover, and living near my daughter.

∞ ∞ ∞ ∞ ∞

I want to gratefully acknowledge and thank my dear friend, Lee Olivier, who chose to bring her editing skills to all of these pages. I also want to gratefully acknowledge and thank my beloved daughter, Laana Fishman, for doing everything else necessary to turn my manuscript into a book.

Chapter 1   Early Learnings

Many of us have come to know how profoundly important to our lives are the learnings of our early years. This wasn't very widely understood during the first half of my life and certainly not in 1921, when I was born. This book is about my lifetime attempt to explore, often blindly, what else there might be to me beyond my tendency to feel and think and act in both the positive and the negative ways I learned from my parents, and from the surroundings in which I grew up.

When my mother, Paula Elise Hansen-Olson, was born in Hamburg, Germany in 1884, their most prestigious authority on child rearing had just pronounced that unless the spirit of a child was broken before it was two years old, that child would grow up to be little better than a wild beast. My mother's upbringing (and therefore mine in turn) was greatly influenced by this attitude toward children, and also by the fact that she was the third girl born to her parents who had greatly wanted a boy this time. (The long-awaited son arrived two years later.) She didn't tell me much about her early life and even less about how she felt during that time. She did say that her family lived in a big flat in an upper middle-class district, where her father wouldn't let the girls take piano lessons because it might disturb the neighbors.

My mother shared her brother Neil's bedroom until he was six, and then she was given a bed in her older sisters' room, much to their displeasure. Once she was pretending to sleep when her sisters came home from a party. They stopped to look at her. One (it must have been Mai, who later brought her so much cruel grief) commented, "It's a pity she's so ugly. She has no eyebrows or eyelashes." Her oldest sister, Amelia, wouldn't have said that. Amelia was the one who sent us the only really nice Christmas presents I can remember getting during my childhood. We sent her boxes of dried fruit for Christmas in the early days of World War II in Europe, until she and her husband were killed in the bombings.

In her youth my mother worked at a prestigious jewelry store and eventually became assistant manager. For ten years she was semi-engaged to a medical student whose mother would not permit them to marry, feeling that Paula's bourgeois background made her an unsuitable wife for a doctor. On her deathbed, his mother exacted a promise from her son that he would not marry Paula, or so he told her. She was then twenty-nine years old, virtually an old maid at that time. Both of her parents (with whom she still lived) died within months of each other that same year.

In 1913 there was already talk of war in Europe. She had studied English and dreamed of going to America. Friends introduced her to the man who became my father, Charles Augustus Stich, solid-looking and self-assured, a mechanical engineer who was ten years her senior. His father owned a shipyard and was Polish-Russian. His mother, who was reputed to have kept her girlish figure all her life despite bearing twelve children (two of whom later committed suicide) was German. Charles had become an American citizen some years before. He wrote to her soon after he returned to the United States and asked her to join him. She agreed. They were married without ceremony in a Boston judge's chambers and moved into a small apartment in the area. Following his work, they moved to New York, to Pennsylvania and then back to Boston.

By this time, World War I had begun in Germany. Paula's brother, an immaculately dressed and very sober-faced young man in the one photo she had of him, was sure he would be killed if he was conscripted. He bicycled up hills for weeks trying to strain his heart to become medically unfit for military service. His heart however did not become strained. He died on a train that was blown up within days after he was conscripted and sent to the front. In less than two years my mother had lost the man she'd thought of as her future husband, both her parents and her only brother, and she was living in a foreign country at war with her homeland, knowing nobody here but the relative stranger she had married.

My father was an inventor as well as a mechanical engineer. (One of his inventions, a mammoth metal working machine, was still in use in an East Coast factory when my brother Charlie found the nametag in the nineteen-fifties.) My father also worked for years on a perpetual motion machine, which the then head of the U.S. Patent Office believed could actually be done. (My mother spoke of her hands becoming raw from sandpapering the wooden wheel to absolute smoothness.) In those early years, our family was occasionally wealthy for a while, but it never lasted. Apparently every time my father invented something useful, his business partners ended up with most of the profits.

I was three years old in 1924, when my mother moved with her three children to Plymouth, Wisconsin. We children were told that my father had a new job awaiting him in Plymouth, and he was going to join us as soon as he had completed the one he was working on in New York. We went ahead so that my brothers, Walter and Charlie, who were six and nine, could start the fall school term there. But my father never joined us, though Mama assured us for months and years afterward that he would come soon. I never questioned how it came to be that we waited for him for three years. Only when I was an adult did I realize that I hadn't been told all of the truth, but there was no one left alive by that time to tell me what had really happened.

I have only a few memories of my father before we moved to Wisconsin. One was the Christmas before my third birthday. Papa had built a little wooden slide in the basement for us. My brothers and I had so much fun with it that Mama had to tell us to quiet down. But when it was my turn, a splinter ran into my behind and I shrieked with pain. Then I was upside down on Papa's lap, and he pulled down my panties as if he was going to spank me, but instead he took out the splinter. I sobbed with pain and relief and gratitude.

I also vaguely remember living in a beautiful big brown house with white window frames. There was a creek along one side of the front yard that ended in a shallow little pool surrounded by rocks. I was pretending to fish in the pool with my toy fishing rod, proud of my pretty pink dimity dress and of the shiny new patent leather shoes that I

14

must not get dirty, waiting for Papa to take us for a ride in his beautiful big new touring car. It was the first car on our street, though that must have been something my mother told me later, when there was no longer a beautiful big house or a new touring car or even a Papa.

Another memory of my early childhood has stayed with me. When I was about five, distant relatives passing through Wisconsin on vacation invited us to drive out with them to picnic at one of the beautiful lakes not far from the city. As we rode off in their gleaming, black touring car, the three grown-ups sat in the wide front seat and talked in German. I understood them because Mama always spoke German to us when we were alone, but I didn't pay much attention. I heard the unusual happiness in her voice as the countryside rushed by, and I felt happy, too.

Then we were at the big lake, and I saw the blue, blue water stretching far away into the distance. It fascinated me so much that I hardly noticed when the picnic basket, covered with a white cloth and promising all sorts of good things to eat, was brought from the car's trunk. After lunch my brothers went off to explore the nearby trees. I moved cautiously away from Mama's protection. The sun shone on my naked shoulders and legs, soft little breezes puffed against my skin. My bare feet felt grass and then sand as I approached the edge of the lake. I mustn't touch the water, of course, since we had been told that we couldn't go in until an hour after eating, but I squatted down and watched it. The tiny waves licking at the shore tugged at my heart. Finally the hour passed and the boys threw themselves into the water, making great splashes. Mama came and pinned my hair on top of my head, telling me not to get it wet.

I took my first step into the cool water. It tickled my toes and the soft mud squiggled beneath them. The lake stretched endlessly into the distance, strange and yet familiar. I took a step further. The water rose a tantalizing half-inch higher on my calf. Dreamily I took another step and another. I was now invisible up to my knees to the grown-ups on the shore. Only I could feel the smooth little stones my toes touched, investigated, passed by. With each step something in me eased and opened. The water was at my waist now. I could see the shining, gently moving surface all around me, while underneath it was this secret silence. Soon it would hide me entirely. I went on without hesitating. The waters closed over my shoulders and touched my throat, and nothing else existed. I was becoming one with the lake.

Just as the water was lapping blissfully at my chin, one of my brothers grabbed me and struggled proudly back to shore with me. The grown-ups scolded me for nearly going in over my head. None of them seemed to know anything about the secret place I had almost entered, and I had no words to explain it to them. Somewhere in my subconscious, though, I carried the memory that such an experience was possible.

I was not yet six when I first heard the tale of how difficult the births of my two older brothers were. "Sixty hours," my mother told me, her face and voice strained with the memory, "I was in labor each time for over sixty hours. The doctor said I would certainly die if I had another baby." I didn't know how to respond. Something awful and frightening had happened to her, but it had no reality for me. I'd never even been around a baby.

They hadn't intended to have another child after the doctor's warning, and she told me that they were shocked and frightened when she became pregnant again. Not knowing of any other recourse, my mother turned to fervent prayer. As the crucial time neared, a nurse was brought in to stay with her until the doctor was required. My mother described to me how she started down the hall from her bedroom one afternoon and the nurse demanded, "Where are you going?" "To the bathroom," Mama answered. The nurse yelled, "Oh, no, you are not—you are going to have that baby!" She grabbed my mother, pulled her back into her room and practically threw her on the bed. Shortly thereafter, with hardly any fuss at all, I was born. So I learned about the efficacy of prayer.

There were other things I may have learned on a far less conscious level during the months while my mother carried me. She was terrified that she would again suffer for long hours and probably die during childbirth. Recent research has shown that human babies are deeply affected by their mother's attitudes and emotions during the nine months of her pregnancy.

When I was six years old, a letter came from someone in New York. There was a funny look on Mama's face when she read it, a look I recognized that came when she was thinking of Papa. During the night I lay listening to her sobbing and clutched my teddy bear closer. The next morning she faced us over the breakfast table, looking drawn and tired. "I have prayed all night." she said solemnly. "We are going back to your father in New York." I didn't remember Papa very clearly by that time, but I had a vague memory of his mustache tickling my neck and being lifted high in the air, and his deep, warm laughter. The thought of him made my heart beat faster and little shivers run down my back.

It was a long trip by railway train, broken by staying overnight at a ramshackle hotel. I was unintentionally left alone for a little while and was molested by some "older" boys whom I thought at first were just being friendly. Though my mother was terribly upset when she heard what had happened to me, the awful teenagers had disappeared and we had no other recourse than to continue our trip.

When we got to New York, we all moved into a house in the suburbs of Staten Island: Papa who seemed like a stranger to me, Mama, Charlie and Walter and I; and Tante Mai, my mother's sister. Tante Mai had come to America almost three years before and gotten to know my father. She was taller than Mama and thinner; she went to New York City every day to her own fancy lamp shop, leaving on a streetcar with Papa each morning. She wore elegant, frilly blouses that Mama ironed along with Papa's stiff white shirts. Tante Mai sometimes brought me little gifts and promised me that someday she would take me to spend a whole day in the city with her, but I didn't really want to go. I would listen while she and my father discussed politics and business at the dinners that my mother had cooked and served, and felt that something was dreadfully wrong.

After a few months, my mother told my brothers and me that we were going to move to the country, where an old family friend was letting us live in a farmhouse he owned. We would have lots of room to play, and we could have pets. Papa's work would keep him in the city. He would come and visit us; perhaps things would change so that he could come to the country to be with us soon. I listened with quiet disbelief: last time it had been three years.

In the few photos I have from our three years in the country in Massachusetts, my brothers and I are tall and skinny, with solemn dark eyes and poorly cut dark hair. We stare into the camera, sort of scared-looking, but with something of defiance from my brothers. They would sometimes turn their defiance on our mother, to her confusion and anger. She would storm at them, "Every time you do that (whatever the latest misbehavior was) you pound another nail in my coffin!" I don't know what effect it had on them, but it terrified me. What would we do if we lost her as we had lost our father?

The farmhouse was more than a quarter mile from our nearest neighbor and three miles from the four-room school house. We walked to the school, and it was hard for me from the start. We were strangers and city folk in that farming community and therefore not liked or trusted. Also, having been allowed into the second grade after testing, I was younger than my classmates. I made only one sort-of friend in those years, another girl who was an outsider like me, but she lived too far away for us to see each other except at lunch time.

There was much that was good, however, about living in the country. In early summer I could pick bouquets of violets and lilies-of-the-valley for my mother from around our well. Sometimes I got to follow my brothers as we roamed on top of the stone walls built generations before to clear the fields for crops. Eventually we knew where to find pears, apples, peaches, plums and walnuts, as they came into season on farms that had already been abandoned in those pre-Depression days.

My brothers ran trap lines in the winter, catching muskrats and occasionally a prize raccoon for their skins, which they sold in town. They shot rabbits and squirrels for dinner, and with our neighbor's permission we ate ears of sweet corn grown for his herd of cows. One year, besides cooking and cleaning for half a dozen boarders who had come to the country to get away from the heat of New York, my mother canned over two hundred jars of fruits and vegetables to see us through the winter. She was solely responsible for herself and three growing children, overworked, overburdened and sometimes hysterical. And still I remember her raising her arms to the day, happily calling, "Ach, die liebe Sonne scheint" (Oh, the beloved sun is shining).

"Uncle Teddy" was the old gentleman who let us live in his farmhouse in return for feeding and housing his grown-up, mildly retarded son. Kindly Uncle Teddy, who visited us in the summers and whose favorite I was, who took me on trips to nearby towns to gawk at the stores and buy ice cream cones. Uncle Teddy also took me walking in the woods where he urged me to take off my panties and caress his penis. Desperately uncomfortable with either being touched or touching, I'd gingerly do as he bid me until he would let me get away.

The only time I felt really safe was when our family was all at home sitting around the big, wooden dining room table with its kerosene lamp, my mother mending and the rest of us reading or doing homework. During the three years we lived there, my brothers and I remained outsiders at school. My mother told me that I shouldn't pay attention to the other kids when they mocked me. "You are much better than they are," she assured me. I wasn't sure in what way I was better, other than reading faster than anyone else in my class, but it was sometimes reassuring to remember that I was better when they ganged up on me. It didn't occur to either of us that this attitude was giving my schoolmates even more reason to scapegoat me.

In 1930 the Great Depression was beginning to stifle the country, and no more boarders came from New York. We left Mill River and moved to the town of Winsted in Connecticut, where my mother could find housework to support us. She was then in her forties, a pleasant-looking, matronly woman with a proud posture she was forever trying to get us kids to emulate. When she smiled she kept her mouth almost closed, teeth barely showing. It wasn't until later when a high school girlfriend told me rather brutally that I smiled "like a chicken without any teeth," that I realized for the first time how I was unconsciously copying my mother. I didn't even have her reason, which was that the gums of her cheap false teeth had turned an orange color and she was embarrassed to let them show.

Chapter 2   Christian Science

Returning from my Winsted school to the empty flat one day when I was about nine, I found a small, leather-bound black book on a stand next to the bed in which my mother and I slept. It was not a library book, but one my mother had actually bought: *Science and Health with Key to the Scriptures* by Mary Baker Eddy. I hadn't been successful in my attempts to read the *Bible* (having gotten bogged down in Genesis among the "begats") but I was curious about any book, so I started to read this one.

The first line in the preface sounded good. "To those leaning on the sustaining Infinite, the day is big with blessings." (We could certainly use a few blessings, I thought, though I had no idea how to go about leaning on the sustaining Infinite.) It continued "The wakeful shepherd beholds the first faint morning beams, ere cometh the full radiance of a risen day. So shone the pale star to the prophet-shepherds; yet it traversed the night, and came where, in cradled obscurity, lay the Bethlehem babe, the human herald of Christ, Truth, who . . ." and I got lost even sooner than I had in the *Bible*. It was difficult, old-fashioned language and I turned back to my library copy of Jack London's *Call of the Wild*. I didn't understand, of course, that my mother's book was teaching a new vision of truth, one that only people who were spiritually awake could see.

I hadn't been given any religious training, even though prayer was so much a part of my mother's life. She seemed to take it for granted that I would naturally know about God, even though no one had told me much about God or about anything else, for that matter.

I hadn't even realized that we were poor until I read a description of a poor family in the Winsted newspaper, and realized that our situation was just like theirs. Actually it was sort of a relief. If we were poor it made sense that we couldn't have new clothes, or the bikes we wanted for Christmas; and it explained why my oldest brother Charlie had to leave school at fifteen to help support us.

My mother would sometimes try to explain to me what Christian Science was about, and there were parts of it that made sense to me. I knew from the picture in the book that these were teachings by a stern-faced woman in old-fashioned dress whose name was Mary Baker Eddy. She taught that God is neither pink and blue nor egg-shaped, which was how I had imagined Him when I was little, looking down at me in a remote but kindly way, rather like Humpty-Dumpty in my picture book. Instead God was something impossible to picture like Infinite Love. Because Man was made in His image and likeness, each one of us is really the perfect, spiritual child of God, and He loves us all equally. We should claim all of His qualities for ourselves, like joy, loving-kindness, and the perception of Infinite Good. He did not create sickness or death, and therefore they are not real. There is only one Mind, one God, one Life, Truth and Love. It is necessary to turn completely away from what things seem to be like and rely only on the authority of the Bible, and on Eddy's book, *Science and Health with Key to the Scriptures*.

It sounded fine and with one part of my mind I accepted it, even including the teaching that bad things are not real but are illusions that we have made up and could see through, if we had enough understanding. It was up to us to "stand porter at the door of our thought" and not let in any negative ideas like sin or disease. The explanation about evil being like darkness in a room, that would disappear as soon as the light was turned on, made it all clear. I must have been holding the knowledge of missing fathers, poverty, and boys and old men who frightened and abused little girls sexually, in another part of my mind.

To me the Christian Science teachings were like a talisman, something to use when I felt bad, or when I wanted something that I couldn't have. I found comfort in the hymn, "He guardeth me, He guardeth me..." Sometimes I would address the many things that scared me by chanting the beginning of what was called the Scientific Statement of Being: "There is no life, truth, or reality in matter..."

In 1932, with the Depression getting worse, my mother and my two brothers decided that we would do better in California, and that we could get there in Charlie's canvas-topped touring car. We didn't have enough money to go all the way, but they were sure they could find work in the towns we passed. Since it was already fall, we would go the southern route. Everything we needed was packed in or attached to the car; the rest was left behind.

After a while we began to drive through towns in which everybody we saw was black. I'd never seen a black person before. Mostly, it seemed to me, they sat on their front porches and gazed at us with stony, angry faces. I was afraid, and I'm sure that my mother and brothers were too, though none of us said anything. How could strangers like us get jobs in a town where more than half the people were already out of work? We quickly learned to go straight to the mayor's office to see an overburdened, impatient white man, anxious to get one more family out of town, who would give us five dollars for gas and send us on our way.

We arrived in Louisville, Kentucky, broke and hopeless, so we turned to the Salvation Army for food and shelter. Her pride shattered by that point, my mother let them send us by train back to my father in New York City. He, too, was out of work and said he couldn't help us.

After a couple of days in a dismal public welfare facility in New York, Walter and I were taken to a charitable home for "better-class" indigent children called the Gould Foundation, named for the 19th century robber baron who had endowed it. It was a group of six self-contained buildings on a plot of suburban land in Pelham Bay in the Bronx, each housing twenty-four children and their caretakers. Our house contained boys and girls from six to twelve years old. I was one of the oldest, except for Walter, who was fourteen. (I guess they hadn't wanted to split us up.) I got to help the younger children ready themselves for bed and prepare for the morning. It was the first really solid, well-built and well-furnished place I had lived in since I was too young to remember. The food was good and plentiful, we were warmly dressed and the staff was diligent in taking care of us.

My mother got a live-in job cooking and cleaning at a private house not too far away, and came to visit us on Sunday afternoons. She and I would go for long walks in a nearby park, watching the leaves turn yellow and red and

26

brown and fall to the ground, as the weeks passed. I'd chatter on and on about what had happened at the Home since our last visit, trying not to feel her unhappiness, and almost relieved when the visit was over and I could go back to not having to feel bad for anyone.

One day, after I'd been there about six months, the housemother called me aside and brought out a brochure from a small, private girl's school in Vermont. The pictures showed a mountain campus, with huge old trees shading a series of handsome wooden buildings with stables in the background. On the front of the pamphlet was a photo of a young girl in riding clothes, patting a beautiful horse. I listened in a daze as she described the wonders of this school and told of my luck in being offered a scholarship there, through the kindliness of Mr. Gould.

The closest I'd ever gotten to riding a horse was a game I had played with the girl who was my sort-of friend in Massachusetts. We'd spent our lunch hours on the seesaw, pretending that we were riding horses. After my beloved books on dogs, I loved any book with horses in it. I'd never even thought of actually having a horse to ride— the idea was beyond my capacity to imagine. Things like that didn't happen to me.

Sure enough, it didn't. My mother greeted me tearfully at her next visit. "They want to send you away to Vermont! We'd never see each other! You don't want to go there, do you?" Her children were all she had in life. The idea of our being further separated must have terrified her, but I did want to go there. I wanted to be back in the country, among the trees and growing things. I wanted to continue to have warm clothes and nice surroundings and to know that my world was orderly and dependable. I wanted to be someplace where no one expected me to make them feel better, even though I couldn't. And I wanted to ride a horse.

"No," I lied. "No, I don't." It never occurred to me to say anything else. My mother would have been so hurt if I had said I wanted to go, and nothing was worse than that. She hugged me fervently, and the bright promise of the school in Vermont vanished.

Within a couple of weeks, Mama had found a place where we could live and she came to take me away. "I couldn't leave you here," she explained. "I don't even know you anymore! Besides, Christmas is coming, and we can be together with the boys." Charlie had found work feeding coal into a basement furnace that heated one of the big apartment houses. He had a warm room to sleep in, and the apartment manager had let him bring in Walter to help. Mama had rented a single room for the two of us. Now, she said, we were free to spend whatever time we could together.

In 1934, when I was thirteen, we set off for California again. It was still the depths of the Great Depression, and this time we did not expect to find work on the road. My mother and my brothers who, at sixteen and nineteen were almost grown men, had gathered together one hundred dollars to get us across the country. If the old black Dodge sedan that Charlie had managed to acquire didn't break down, we would make it all the way this time. Surely all things would be better in California.

We saw lots of other old cars with families and their belongings, heading west. We camped by ourselves and talked with none of them, feeling as always that we were different and better. Mother was philosophical about their

28

numbers. "Where there is room for so many other people, there will be room for us," she assured us. We made it to Los Angeles and I started Lincoln High School that fall, clad in the navy skirt and white blouse that were regulation, already taller than most of the boys. My mother found houses to clean; my brothers occasionally found day work. A couple of times we even managed to collect enough gas money to drive the twenty miles to the ocean to go swimming.

It seemed that the four of us were settled together again at last, but Charlie missed the excitement of New York City and his friends and the steady work he had found there. He was the first to leave. A few months later, Walter, now seventeen, took a job oiling the big engines on a ship bound for South America. From that point on my mother and I were alone. She had been the only grown-up to whom I really mattered since my earliest childhood. Now we had only each other.

Mama regularly attended the local Christian Science church on Sundays, and I usually went with her. Occasionally I resorted to Christian Science practices. In my fifteenth year, one of the popular older boys had lost his class ring in the big, crowded high school swimming pool. Everyone was searching for it. I chanted one of my mother's favorite quotations, "Nothing is lost in the Kingdom of God," and dove into the pool. As I touched bottom my outstretched fingers closed over the ring. No one else knew of my little miracle, though. I handed it to him so diffidently that he just muttered "Oh, thanks," before turning back to his friends.

The occasion on which I first left Christian Science happened later that year. My mother had given in to my pleadings and permitted me to skip church to go to a matinee of the popular movie *Camille,* starring Greta Garbo and John Gilbert. Even though I was dating quite a bit by that time, I had found nothing romantic about the very ordinary boys I went out with, or even about our occasional tentative kisses. I'd only experienced what felt like real emotions in my fantasies, and in the books about adventure and romance that I read constantly. This movie was the first time that the place within me where I felt excited and alive had been shared with other people, who were amazingly real on the movie screen. When I got home my mind was still filled with images of the tender scenes between the two lovers and the heartbreaking tragedy of the delicately beautiful Camille, dying gracefully of consumption at the end.

My mother was having an afternoon "kaffeclatch" with Mrs. Porter, one of her acquaintances from church. Mrs. Porter asked me where I'd been and I told her I'd been to see *Camille.* "Oh, my dear," she cried in distress. "You must never see such films, or even read about things like that! Disease and Death! You are opening your mind to Error. You must always remember that those are things of the flesh, and they are not real!" I gazed stonily at her, the fragile beauty of the dying Camille drifting behind my eyes. Mrs. Porter's rosy skin, like her dress, seemed too tightly stuffed. I looked at her red lips and sharp white teeth and thought of all the animals that had died in agony, to be mashed by those teeth to build the flesh that was packed so tightly against its restraints. She shook her head, picking up another piece of rich cake on her fork. "You must turn away from the works of man and see only Reality."

A decision was forming within me. If Christian Science said that these new feelings churning within me were unreal, Christian Science was wrong. Mrs. Porter and my mother were wrong. The choice seemed clear to me: either I accepted Christian Science and the dull, unimaginative, middle-aged lives before me, or I accepted the world and its sufferings that could lead me to a life of thrills and adventure. I retreated to the bedroom, resolved. Fiercely and dramatically I vowed to myself, "I choose Life!"

Actually I was emotionally numb, socially ignorant, badly educated, fearful, and often sullen. My childhood had left me with much unacknowledged anger and grief, and the feeling that wherever I was, it was only on sufferance, for I had no right to be there. I had little or no foundation for knowing how to live, except for the one thing that turned out to be the most important of all—the deeply buried conviction that somehow, somewhere, everything was all right.

When I was sixteen, my mother got us up at three o'clock in the morning to take a bus to the Easter Sunrise Service at the vast outdoor theatre, the Hollywood Bowl. Cold and sleepy, I felt remote from the whole proceedings. But then, as the first beams of sun touched the stage and the choir burst into the Hallelujah Chorus, joy such as I had never known erupted within me. It felt physical, a glorious energy that rushed through every cell of my body, as if I stood within a cone of warm, scintillating light. Within moments it subsided, and I was my sorry young self again, neither knowing nor believing any more than before. But I knew, again, that such an experience was possible.

When I was nineteen I met Frank Pickard. It soon became clear that he was romantically interested in me, which I thought was amazing and flattering. He was ten years older than I and a long time student (by correspondence) of the Rosicrucian mysteries. He was in such good physical shape that he could do one-armed push-ups. His clarity about matters of mind and body control was comforting, given my own confusion about life. After we had dated for a few months, never going beyond kissing and fondling, he began to talk of marriage. I had little sense of loving him, but marrying him seemed inevitable.

My mother was not happy when I told her that I was going to marry Frank: at the age of twenty-nine he had no financial base, no steady job, no particular prospects or career in mind; and he had no cultural background, as she defined the term. His father was a laborer, a window washer; his mother had deserted her husband and two oldest sons when Frank was twelve, taking several of the younger children with her. My mother cried out in vexation, "Is this what I raised you for, to marry the first man who asks you?" I answered sullenly, with far more truth than I knew at the time, "I guess so."

We married and had two children: first a girl, Laana, and then a boy, Ronn. I was given chloroform each time (apparently the customary thing to do then) and slept through both births. With my daughter I woke up muttering the words "continuation of consciousness," and remembering that my last thought before awakening was that it was a pity that I would forget all this. With my son I had an even odder experience. Afterwards I remembered that I had shared consciousness with him while together we awaited the moment of his birth. Then, with a wrench, (which was probably the birth itself) I felt the other consciousness disappear from mine.

Within a year after my son was born, I went back to telling myself stories, as I did all through my childhood and adolescence. (It wasn't till I was about thirteen that the tales I told myself about wonderful, faithful, protective dogs gave way to idealized romances.) The stories, seven years into my first marriage, over baby bottles and dinner preparations, were somewhat different. For the first time, they took place in modern dress; now the heroine was not a delicate little blonde, but had my own dark hair and eyes and tall stature. My hero was also tall, as well as brilliant, sensitive, and romantic, with a slight foreign accent. He saw beneath the housewife and mother to the dashing, adventurous woman I actually was, and loved me on sight.

After a few weeks of running this fantasy, I decided that I had better stop it and concentrate on being a better wife and mother, but it was too late. The next week, at a Science of Mind Church dance that my husband and I took turns attending, Ernst appeared. Handsome in a gaunt, lean-jawed way, knowledgeable about books and music and life, widely traveled, he attracted me immediately, and he was drawn to me. His deep-set, gray-blue eyes searched mine; his accent was an enchanting mixture of the Mexico where he'd been brought up and the German mother who had given birth to him in Africa. Ernst was my fantasy hero brought to life. For the first time ever, I was in love and nothing else mattered. After only a few months and with little hesitation, I left Frank to be with Ernst, taking the children with me.

I had never carried my fantasy beyond the exquisite moment of our being free to sink into each other's arms: it

33

had been a variation of the naïve, adolescent idea "and they got married and lived happily ever after." Even though I knew of Ernst's unstable past, now that we could be together, I assumed he would have such solid qualities as steadiness and loyalty.

The four years of our relationship brought me all the romantic heaven I had ever dreamed of, and more hell than I would have believed possible. We spent wonderful nights making love. We read together, and talked endlessly about our thoughts and feelings and the meaning of life. We brought his little daughter, Toni, who was Laana's age, to live with us, and tried to parent all three of the children. We both got jobs doing whatever we could, putting the children in free public nursery schools.

We drank quite a bit, hung out with friends, bought a little house in the Echo Park hills, started a small business and went bankrupt. In the middle of our second year, after my divorce from Frank became final, we even went to Las Vegas one weekend and got married. Marriage didn't make any difference though. Increasingly, I spent evenings and then whole nights alone with the kids, wondering where Ernst was and who he was with and how drunk he would be when he got home.

It was during this awful time that I discovered I wasn't really alone. After the children had gone to sleep, as it got later and later, my misery would grow until it seemed it would overwhelm me. Inarticulately, I would pray for help. Suddenly I could sense an intimate feminine presence surrounding me with such warmth and strength and gentleness that I could go peacefully to sleep in her comforting embrace.

After I could stand it no longer, Ernst and I parted for good. Frank remained in touch with me and our children for a few years and contributed a small amount to their living expenses. We still had a mutual interest in human consciousness, and when L.Ron Hubbard's book *Dianetics: the Modern Science of Mental Healing* came out in 1950, he and I both read it eagerly. It was such an extraordinary new way of looking at human difficulties.

As I understood it, Hubbard maintained that whenever shock blanked out the conscious mind in any way, a totally uncensored reactive mind came into play, and everything experienced during that shocked period was recorded in an "engram bank" in the brain. Later, when similar circumstances occurred, the person would act out any command his reactive mind had received during the time of the original incident, resulting in all the aberrations known to humankind. Through being brought to relive each such instance consciously and using their specific methods, a person's aberrations could be released and he (or she) would become happy and successful. It was not apparent at that time that Hubbard's ideas would become more sophisticated and more secretive. When his followers became the Church of Scientology years later, his ideas and methods would be seen as dangerous by a great many people.

Frank had taken some training in Dianetics. He came over one day and demonstrated his newly learned skill of bringing back childhood memories. Following his instructions, I was suddenly six years old, hiding beneath a kitchen table covered with a red and white checked cloth and hearing my father pound on the table and yell at my mother in German, which was as understandable as it had been when I was child of six. I didn't just remember it— I was living it, underneath that table. Frank was satisfied and I was startled, but since we were not very comfortable in each other's presence, we didn't try it again.

Instead, I focused on bringing stability into my life and into my children's lives. Jobs were much more plentiful by 1951, now that factories were gearing up for the Korean War. I found a job as a clerk at the huge Lockheed Aircraft Company that sprawled in the very heart of Burbank, a little town on the north end of San Fernando Valley. (I had read somewhere that Burbank was rated as having the second best public schools in California.)

My job was on the swing shift, from four o'clock in the afternoon until twelve midnight, and was only possible because my mother moved in with us and took care of the children in the evenings. After a year, I was upgraded to Personnel Assistant in the Industrial Relations Department for three pleasant, friendly, married men who were Industrial Relations Representatives. I was still responsible for filling out lots of forms, but I also got to handle phone calls and to interact with many different people, from the Industrial Relations manager to the workers on the production line. My new job was in the daytime, and I could be home with the children in the early mornings, and in the evenings and weekends. I told myself to be content.

Later that year the new manager of Lockheed's Industrial Relations Department decided to have every employee above the rank of secretary take an I.Q. test. My scores, which qualified me for MENSA, startled my bosses into considering what kind of career in management might be possible for me. But what could an aircraft plant do with a woman who had only a high school education, no aeronautical experience and no ambition? After a brief flurry of interest on both our parts, the whole thing was dropped. I was sure that my scores were a sham. I had not been able to sleep the night before the test, even though as far as I knew, there wasn't anything hanging on the results. Finally I'd gotten up and read my Christian Science textbook, *Science and Health with Key to the Scriptures* for a couple of hours. "God is Intelligence," it said, "and Man is made in the image and likeness of God." I'd finally fallen asleep at five o'clock in the morning, only to be roused an hour later by the alarm. I'd gone into the test with bleary eyes and a blurred mind, and some ordinarily inaccessible part of me answered those questions.

Despite the reassuring presence of my two children, my journals from this time reflect an almost desperate yearning for my life to be different. I wrote with wry contempt about myself and my plans, recognizing that I had little personal stability or social conscience. Unable to see any other way to break out of the life I was living, I returned to the idea of being a writer. For a while I rose at five-thirty every morning and wrote for a couple of hours before getting Laana and Ronn up and ready for school. For the second time I completed two thirds of a novel and threw it out. Clearly, I still had nothing worthwhile to say.

∞ ∞ ∞ ∞ ∞

I met Tony Pastor in 1956. Here was someone of whom my mother thoroughly approved. He had a steady occupation as a commercial artist and, although his parents emigrated from Hungary when he was only three years old, he had courteous, old-world manners. I hated the term "boyfriend", but what else did a woman call the man she dates, brings to parties, sleeps with, but isn't living with or

37

married to? Language hadn't caught up with the way people lived. With relief, I confined my interest in possible partners to him. Good, kind Tony, who brought my children presents and worried about the condition of my car, rubbed my aching back and made love to me once a week with such satisfying enthusiasm. With him I felt at ease, unconsciously aware that he would make no demands on me for more than I could give.

During those years, a yearning for some steady sense of structure pulled me back to Christian Science. I found I liked starting the day with a reading from the Christian Science textbook, with its frequent references to the authority of the Bible. I stopped feeling so fragmented, and I began to make some sense out of the Christian Science teachings. My undisciplined mind, bouncing madly from one idea to another, slowed down. I "treated" —read a section of Science and Health over and over again until I could accept the reality of what it said—for my son to have friends, as he tended to be rather unhappily alone a lot of the time. The next day he started to pal around with a neighbor boy. I "treated" to find the right car at the right price, and was offered one with no further effort on my part within a week. I treated for my daughter's adolescent acne to clear up and it did. Mostly I treated for serenity and a better disposition for myself, and my depression began to lift.

I felt sedate and quiet, dressing properly and going to church on Sundays and talking with the other ladies. Even though neither of my children nor Tony showed any interest, I decided that this was my destined road. I would study and become a Christian Science practitioner, a recognized and paid healer. I was still not happy, but at least I had a path that might lead somewhere.

The wife of one of Tony's friends was suffering from serious back trouble. Ty was a sturdy, vibrant, determinedly youthful woman in her forties. She had been hospitalized for a week in traction. She was in pitiful shape when we visited them, unable to stand upright and expecting an operation on her spine within days. Neither Ty nor her husband had any belief in spiritual healing and politely ignored me when I offered to treat for her. Nevertheless, the next morning I woke at six o'clock and read a section of the Christian Science textbook explaining that as a child of God she was perfect, that her illness had no reality. After a while I had a sense of something accomplished and forgot about it as I went through my workday.

A day or so later we went to visit them and were met at the door by Ty, standing triumphantly straight. She told me that her healing had occurred on the exact day and hour that I had treated for her (she had no knowledge that I had done so). Her pain had simply disappeared. "I don't understand it," she kept saying. "I don't understand it, and neither does my doctor." Not believing that my Christian Science work could possibly have had such a dramatic effect, I said nothing. Sure enough, when I confided in Tony later, he derided the idea, saying that it must have been a coincidence. I wondered, though. Exactly what *Science and Health* said would happen had happened, and at the precise time I had worked for her. Maybe I could become a practitioner.

Some weeks later, the children and I went to visit my mother in the beautiful, wealthy seaside town of

Laguna Beach.   At seventy-six, dependent on a small government old-age pension, she had found free rent with an equally elderly but well-off lady who wanted companionship. I knew she hadn't been feeling well, but I was shocked when I saw that her usual clear, rosy skin had turned sallow and her stomach was badly distended. My instinctive reaction was to get her to a doctor quickly, but she wouldn't hear of it. After more than twenty-five years in Christian Science, she couldn't give it up now. In a few weeks, even she admitted that she could not care for herself any longer. I asked her to come and stay with us. "It will only be a little while," she assured me, "Until I am better."

Both Laana and Ronn were happy to have her welcoming presence when they got home from school, even though Ronn had to give up his room and sleep on the living room couch. I did my best for her before and after work. Soon she was bed-ridden and getting weaker, but she remained determined not to seek medical help. I shopped, cooked, washed clothes, cleaned the house, and rose early to get the kids off to school and to help her prepare for her day alone, before I went to work.

To my dismay, I couldn't treat effectively for her recovery. I would sit down dutifully with *Science and Health*. I would try to follow the words, but neither quiet nor conviction would come. I sought out a doctor and described her condition. He said it sounded serious; I'd have been surprised if he had said anything else. As the weeks went by and she needed more and more assistance, I was torn between pity and exhaustion and resentment. It seemed that all my life I had felt guilty because there was something I was supposed to do for her that I was helpless to do. Now that she was dying, heavy guilt followed me through all my days. Even though I had begun to think that through Christian Science I was able to heal others, I could not heal her.

Eventually it was clear to both of us that I could not take care of her at home any more. She let the doctor come to see her, as doctors did then. He talked to her gently in German, assured her that the county hospital was like the great teaching hospitals in Europe, and she must let them take care of her. Once admitted, she lost ground from day to day even though the county hospital relieved the pressure on her lungs by removing the fluids that had built up. I didn't know what to say; I just combed her hair, held her hand, and brought her little treats to eat. In the last week she hardly spoke, but watched me on my daily visits with sad and puzzled eyes, clutching her copy of *Science and Health*. I didn't realize then how improbable it was that she felt discomfort but no pain, even though her intestinal cancer was long past being operable.

Choked with feelings I didn't understand, I was easily led when my brother Charlie suggested we go outside for a walk. While we were gone, she died—I had deserted her at the moment of her greatest need, and been useless, as always, to ease her pain. Shaken by what seemed like the unredeemed ugliness of her death and the fact that the teachings hadn't worked for her, I quit Christian Science a second time.

Years later, trying to deal with my still painfully unresolved feelings of guilt about her dying, I sat down to talk with her image. I told her how sorry I was that I had left her alone at the moment of her death. Instantly I heard the words, warm and gentle and forgiving, "But *I* wasn't alone. You were." I glimpsed her beloved family and childhood friends surrounding and welcoming her. Realizing for the first time just how alone and unhappy I had felt at the time, I began to forgive myself.

Chapter 3   Subud

Although Tony and I married in 1959, it wasn't until several years later that I learned why he had been willing to get married for the first time at forty-nine. He was convinced that a new kind of spirituality called Subud would change our lives, that practicing Subud would take us from being ordinary, troubled, rather unhappy and unsuccessful, to being the radiant, joyful and successful people we both believed we ought to be.

For me, the most important things about Tony were that we were comfortable together, he treated my children well and he believed, as I did, that our minds could transcend and shape our experience of the world (though neither of us lived as though we believed it). We had both experienced miraculous moments of joy and confidence that so far exceeded our ordinary experience as to belong to another reality. We were both sure that there must be some way of attaining such states permanently.

My mother had been a poor though well-bred German lady who was a Christian Scientist; his mother had been a poor though well-bred Hungarian lady who was a healer, and could read the future in a deck of cards. Tony and I had both accomplished what seemed to be spiritual healings, and we both had eagerly read books like Burke's *Cosmic Consciousness,* the life of the Indian saint,

Yogananda, and that of the American psychic, Edgar Cayce.

When Tony was in his late twenties, new to Los Angeles and just discharged from four years as a map-making specialist in the army, he stepped one day into a different realm. He was standing on the street before a large office building where he had an appointment with a potential employer, when suddenly and unaccountably the day turned brilliant and he turned brilliant with it. He felt an exhilarated certainty that all was well with himself and with the world, and that he could accomplish whatever he wanted.

Life became effortless: the editor hired him on the spot as a commercial artist to work on their movie ads; the new job proceeded with incredible ease; he was able to foresee what people would say to him, to understand exactly what each person wanted, and to always be in the right place at the right time. He moved differently, was stronger physically. Looking in the mirror, he saw that his rather ordinary face, with its light blue eyes and sandy hair, had taken on depth and character. For three weeks he awoke every morning filled with joy and the sweet surety of being in this blissful state.

Then one day he noticed that his new way of being didn't seem quite so clear. Helplessly, over the course of a couple of days, he felt it drain away. He had no knowledge of why it left, nor of why it had begun in the first place. All he knew was that life could be that way; *he* could be that way.

It was not until after he died forty years later (We had been divorced for almost thirty years.) that I learned there was more to his story, something he had never told me. Among his papers, Laana and I found notes describing how he had gone to a hypnotist, wanting to try another way of breaking loose from whatever was stopping him from being the artist he knew he could be. The hypnotist tried for an hour or two, but Tony could not be hypnotized. Finally, the hypnotist called in a medical doctor colleague to give Tony a dose of sodium pentothal to activate his subconscious. Nothing happened. He tried a higher dose but Tony just went to sleep, so they gave up. A few days later Tony had his epiphany.

Once his experience had completely faded, Tony spent six months with spiritual teachers, healers and psychics all over the country, looking for someone to help him access that wondrous state again. I'm not sure he ever admitted to himself that the experience might have been triggered by the hypnosis and the sodium pentothal— he wanted it to have happened naturally. He didn't realize how deep a letting go of his rational mind was necessary for such an experience to occur.

He returned to Los Angeles, convinced that there was a truth somewhere—a truth so momentous that nothing else in life was worth pursuing. He loved reading about people who said they had experienced this reality, and was always bringing me books or articles about seemingly miraculous happenings.

In the three years before we married we investigated quite a few spiritual groups. There was Nelson Decker, a youthful chiropractor who taught a version of positive thinking mixed with a smattering of American Indian rituals; an organization called Psynetics, which taught bodily healing with light, sound and/or herbs and oils; and Johrei, which taught the channeling of spiritual healing energy through the hands. (Johrei was brought to America from Japan, where they were reputed to have half a million members.) None of them maintained our interest, nor did their leaders impress us.

The people who were involved in the Subud movement seemed to be of another type entirely. Internationally known intellectuals and long-time students of the occult were studying and practicing Subud. There had been several books written about it; celebrities and others had reported astonishing healings and transformations.

The term *Subud* is a contraction of three Sanskrit words: *Susila, Budhi and Dharma*—which mean approximately "right living from within according to the will of God." By the mid 1960's half the countries in the world had Subud centers; there were twenty-seven centers in the United States alone.

Subud was founded by an Indonesian Moslem who became known to his followers as Pak Subuh. In his youth he had studied various spiritual teachings of the East, but decided that he was destined for an ordinary life as a business and family man. He was walking on the beach one day in his twenty-ninth year when a radiant light flared across the sky and entered his body. There began a sort of "inner working" on spiritual, mental, emotional and physical levels, strengthening and improving them all. He found that he could start the "inner working" at will, but he knew no way of teaching it to others. In his thirty-second year, he discovered that when he practiced in front of his wife, she went into the same state—he could transmit his experience. Pak Subah maintained that Subud was beyond any religion, yet it was imbued with the central Moslem belief in surrender to God, which is also a Christian teaching, "Not my will, Oh Lord, but Thine."

Tony and I perceived this as a real spiritual path, not just another kind of positive thinking. Instead of trying to create good in our lives, Subud taught that total surrender to the will of God would bring us to a higher good. The practice of Subud was called "latihan." A practitioner merely stood still, taking an attitude of surrender and of willingness to accept whatever happened mentally, emotionally or physically.

There were not many rules in Subud; everyone was expected to be able to access their own inner guidance after being "opened." Newcomers were required to go through a three-month probationary period to prove their commitment. We sat in the drab entrance hall of the center with other probationers for one evening each week for three months. Sometimes we were given a brief talk about Subud; sometimes we read one of their books. The latihan went on behind closed doors

We were told that the latihan would work in a way that was unique to each individual, in total harmony with his or her own nature and needs, free of anyone's authority or interpretation. We were warned that we might undergo "a purification" during our inner development: it could manifest as bodily symptoms like diarrhea, rashes, or various other physical problems, or as mental and emotional symptoms like depression or anxiety. We were assured that these symptoms would clear up, leaving us cleansed and ready for wonderful new experiences.

We were both excited when the three months were finally up. Two "helpers," a man and a woman, greeted us with a reserved friendliness. Both appeared to be in their fifties, he in a conservative dark suit, and she in a navy-colored dress. I immediately judged her jewelry to be rather ostentatious, a large pearl necklace and earrings.

Except for that one time when Pak Subuh discovered that he could initiate his wife, men and women never practiced together, so we were ushered into different rooms. The woman with the pearls read me a brief statement, advising me to regard the experience of initiation as sacred, to take an attitude of patience, sincerity and surrender to the will of God, and to accept whatever came. When she closed her eyes I did too, and stood waiting for what might happen. After about five minutes and without asking about my experience (which was fortunate, since I hadn't had any) she congratulated me, hugged me briefly and impersonally, and said I could now join the other women at the latihan.

Rather disappointed, I followed her into a large unfurnished meeting room where about thirty women were seated on benches around the perimeter, waiting for us. All were Caucasian with the exception of the few who were Indonesian. Some were hippie-type girls with long loose hair, dressed in shifts and granny gowns, while some were like my helper, in nylon stockings with beauty parlor grooming. None of them wore slacks—Pak Subuh had said that the true self came out during the latihan and the true self of a woman would naturally wear skirts. At a signal from the woman who had initiated me, everyone rose and stood in a circle. She said quietly, "begin," and closed her eyes. Probably I was supposed to close my eyes too, but I didn't.

Within moments an extraordinary change came over the group. One woman dropped to her knees and started

48

rhythmically beating on the floor; one sang a delicate, airy little song, a patter of sounds unlike any language I'd ever heard; another began a small, vaguely Javanese dance. Many stood in attitudes of prayer, or rocked back and forth, or made gestures with no recognizable significance. Some uttered odd throaty sounds, and several walked rapidly and aimlessly around the room. One woman started to cry. One young woman, who looked to be about seven months pregnant, suddenly keeled over and crashed to the floor.

From the men's room down the hall we could hear much loud yelling and other strange sounds. The uproar in both rooms grew to a crescendo during the first five or ten minutes. By the time the hubbub had subsided, most of the women were on their knees or lay sprawled on the floor. The men's group down the hall was as silent as ours was, except for a few gentle murmurings. After half an hour, the leader said "finish." Each woman got quietly to her feet (including the evidently unharmed pregnant woman) replaced her shoes and jewelry and left the room. Whatever experiences they had had in the room were left behind—outside in the hall many of them broke into casual chatter—and no one paid me any attention.

Later, I learned that violent activity and vocal sounds are phenomena of the early stages of latihan, when people are in a lot of turmoil. Older members do not experience these kinds of "purifications" unless there is a crisis in their personal life. Their usual movements and sounds are quite harmonious and gentle.

Tony and I spoke little on the way home. Apparently, nothing much had happened to either of us and we didn't want to become discouraged by talking about it. Nevertheless, he came with me twice each week for that first year. He never did confide in me what he was experiencing, nor did he want to know what had happened to me. He said discussing them might interfere with our individual experiences. That made sense to me, and I didn't notice how it mirrored our usual lack of communication.

The second time the group gathered for the latihan I closed my eyes and paid attention to what was happening to me. With no conscious intention, I found my body swaying, first erratically, then rhythmically, my hands making little gestures. I had a sense of my knees wanting to give way, but I found myself resistant. I hadn't prayed on my knees since I was a child, and such a posture felt phony and pretentious. Yet, each subsequent time I came to the latihan, my body swayed closer and closer to the floor without any conscious intention on my part. I knew I could stop the process, but I had no sense that I was making it happen. I experienced weeks of this slow melting during the latihan, until one night I found myself sinking to my knees and then further, until my forehead touched the floor and I experienced a sense of peace.

I had little imagery and few thoughts during the latihans and I made no sound. I was fascinated, though, by the mysterious movements of my body, the gestures my hands were making, and the oddly silent mental space I got into while this was happening. I always ended on my knees; sometimes I had the sensation of some jelly-like substance within my psyche becoming firmer.

Tony, meanwhile, was becoming more and more unconvinced of the value of Subud for him. Whatever he was experiencing wasn't enough; he wanted something much more compelling, something like the experience he had had during those dazzling three weeks years ago. After a year, he quit. Believing in the promise of Subud had allowed him to take on all the demands of marriage and children, yet Subud proved to be another dead end for him. As much as he was able, though, he stuck to his commitment to us and never mentioned what must have been his deep disappointment.

On the other hand, I felt a gradual softening in myself: I was less defensive and sometimes felt a degree of warmth toward people that was unusual for me. I experienced a slight rise of morale and even an occasional feeling of happiness. Nor did I resort to sarcasm or anger so easily when I felt unloved or disapproved of. And I was no longer so quick to take offense.

During the second year of Subud, I had become unable to attend latihan for a couple of weeks because of a familiar back spasm that almost immobilized me. When I returned, I stayed seated because of the pain and moved very little, though the empty and silent space in my mind occurred. Then, in the last five minutes of the half hour, I found myself making low, sharp, guttural sounds. "Eeh--aye--yah!" My face twisted into such a grimace that I was glad my hands were covering it, though I knew no one was looking. When the leader gave the signal, "finish," the sounds and empty mind stopped instantly, but I felt dazed. It was not until I was outside that I realized the pain in my back was gone. I didn't know what had happened, but something certainly had.

Often I'd come to the latihan frustrated, angry and unhappy with my life, and I would experience some other self of mine quietly watching. The resulting sense of warmth and happiness would last all evening. The peaceful

51

quiet that came to me in the Subud exercise, however, didn't extend to my ordinary life. By now, Tony was little involved with any of us: my fifteen-year-old daughter, my thirteen-year-old son, or me. Every evening he withdrew to his desk for two hours or more. To my astonishment I found that he was making intricate charts of the horse racing results of the day, though he never bet money on them. When I asked about the purpose of these hours of work, he said it was a form of mental training. I knew it was also his way of removing himself from any interaction with the rest of us, in the evenings after dinner. Our marriage had become less friendly.

The job I took after I left Lockheed Aircraft, as secretary to a physicist-inventor who built his own sonic devices, was not unpleasant but was basically clerical work and had no future. My brother Walter's wife, Marny, wrote that Walter was in a deep depression that seemed to be getting worse. One of the men I had worked with at Lockheed died suddenly. The sad and guilty feelings surrounding my mother's death became stronger.

The Cold War was in full force; the bright hope of collaboration among nations that had blossomed after the end of World War II into the United Nations seemed to have faded away. The Berlin Wall was being built; the Russians had long had the bomb. MAD (Mutually Assured Destruction) was in the newspapers and on the radio and TV every day.

I found myself becoming oppressed with thoughts of sickness and death, and with despair about the pain and brevity of human life. It didn't occur to me that such feelings might be part of a purification, because it was very clear how much unhappiness was in the world.

52

Nevertheless, I tried to keep dark thoughts out of my peaceful latihans. When these thoughts overwhelmed me one night, in the midst of a rising feeling of panic, I heard a quiet, impersonal voice: "Are you afraid of dying?" "No, I'm not," I answered without hesitation. "Then why are you fearful for others?" the voice responded. "Why should it be worse for them than for you?" I had the sense of having opened a telegram and found it to contain a birthday greeting. The anxiety and dread were gone in an instant. (Years later, a friend told me that his Indian guru had said, "Don't be afraid of death. It's not at all dangerous.)"

At times during the latihan a feeling of joy would arise out of nowhere. I kept hoping that these feelings would spread to the rest of my life, but it was only on rare occasions that they did. Once I came to the latihan feeling particularly depressed; I curled up on the floor as usual, and sent out a silent plea to God for help. In an instant it was as if the mists in my mind were swept away and I was in warm, golden sunlight on a mountaintop. I saw what a demeaning concept of God I had. I realized that the real God does not pity humans, because we are not pitiable! Wrapped up in my idea of God as full of pity, I had seen myself as helpless, pathetic, yearning above all for His compassion, His indulgence, His pity; I envisioned Him reaching down to me and dispensing unearned gifts.

The sudden exultant glimpse I had that session was of a different God. Not an ancient God, but a God who epitomized the qualities of youth—vigor, exuberance, power. Not in awful majesty, but in delight: a God who gave, not out of pity, but out of limitless abundance because it was His nature to give. A beseeching attitude toward Father-God had permeated my entire life. Now I could see Him, and me, differently. The joy of that thought pierced me. I stretched out on the floor, arms flung wide, absorbing this delight. Freedom! Freedom from self-pity!

Within days the whole episode seemed like a dream, the impulse of wonder and joy had vanished. My usual depressed habits of thought took over: I resented Tony; I was irritable at the kids. The daily news frightened and confused me. Politically, I found it impossible to tell the good guys from the bad guys, for there didn't seem to be enough difference between them. I couldn't figure out what was going on, either in the larger world or in my own internal world.

One evening at the Subud center, it was announced that several people had been accepted as "helpers." I went into the latihan thinking idly that if some of those people, whom I knew to be very ordinary, could be helpers, why not me? As soon as the latihan started I got my answer, swiftly and brutally. My life was laid out before me: it epitomized lack of character, lack of direction, lack of worth. What kind of a woman marries three times? What made me better than anyone else? The answer was—nothing, nothing at all.

I felt as if the glasses through which I had always seen myself had been askew, and were suddenly shaken into place. Incident after incident in my life paraded before me: I saw my feelings of superiority; my angers and petty wrangling with my family; my withholding of affection; my envy of people whom I thought had something better in their lives. I saw my constant need to be reassured; my looking for slights, intended or not; my feeling hurt with only a forlorn hope of being soothed. In that pitiless light my faults stood out with devastating clarity. Overwhelmed with this new and painful self-knowledge, I rushed home and woke Tony, demanding "How can you stand me?" He mumbled comforting words and fell back to sleep. I was not comforted. How had I become such an awful person?

For the next six weeks, every time I entered the latihan a movie of all the negative ways I had acted and felt and thought in my life played on my inner eye, and I would leave feeling shattered again. Finally I went to Earl Robinson, the solid middle-aged businessman who headed the center, and asked him what to do. He dismissed the whole thing as of no importance. He explained the necessity of watching whatever was happening in one's mind, while continuing to reach for the reality underlying all thoughts and emotions. That made sense to me, although I wasn't sure I could do it, nor was I quite sure I even understood what he meant. Eventually one evening the experiences stopped. I soon put them out of my mind.

The situation at home continued to deteriorate. Brought up by his stern father who was proud of having been an officer in the prestigious and highly disciplined Hungarian Hussars, Tony had formed rigid expectations of how a family should behave. Many of the things I did, and practically everything my teenage son did, annoyed him. Though things were usually better when my steady, cheerful daughter was at home, her friends and growing interests were taking her away more often. Also, she undoubtedly found our quarrelsome household uncomfortable.

I continued to attend latihan, but only received enough nourishment to keep me in the rounds of going to work, running the household, trying to keep our family life together, and waiting for the light, any kind of light. I had

had some astonishing and wonderful experiences, but I knew no way to bring them into my daily life. As a wise spiritual teacher I met years later said, "It's one thing to experience enlightenment; it is another thing entirely to live an enlightened life."

Slowly, almost imperceptibly, the latihans became less moving. There were some meaningful moments, but often it was just a time of quiet when my thoughts moved more slowly. My discontent with my life became stronger. I decided to try writing again, even though I was sure that I still didn't actually have anything to say. I thought that at least I could write the kind of formulaic short stories being printed in women's weekly pulp magazines. I was convinced that I could do it easily and a bit cynically, since I felt rather contemptuous of that kind of writing.

I wrote and sent to publishers half a dozen short stories. Though none was accepted, I received at least one encouraging reply. Then, a continuous twitch began under my right eye. I knew that I must be doing something that my inner self rejected, though Tony laughed at the idea. At the next latihan, I asked what the message was and I got an image of myself burning all the stories I had written. I went home and threw out six months of what I'd always thought of as trashy writing. The twitch under my eye stopped immediately.

On the morning of my fortieth birthday I woke up feeling depressed and bitter. My life was probably at least half over and what had I accomplished? Suddenly my mind centered and quieted. Almost in spite of myself, I had accomplished one worthwhile thing: I had brought up two thoroughly responsible young adults who respected education and were capable of living good and useful lives.

If I had had no college education, at least they would. Being as neurotically insecure as I was and frustrated in so many ways, perhaps I hadn't done such a bad job with my children. (It has pretty much turned out like that. Though they have followed their own paths and not mine, I am glad and grateful that they are good people, concerned with others and the world. We are in frequent and loving communication.)

That morning of my fortieth birthday, I knew that my job of raising my children was almost done. But now what was I to do? I clearly did not have the spiritual and moral qualities to be a Subud leader. Perhaps I could write about Subud and spread its teachings in that fashion. I knew, however, that an education with only a couple of night school college courses left me ill-prepared to write or teach much of anything. I decided to read more widely, to study writing and philosophy and religion on my own.

I found William James' *Varieties of Religious Experience* and discovered someone who had thought deeply about the subjects that fascinated me. I was enchanted, underlining and annotating my copy for weeks. Much that James wrote about spiritual experiences made absolute sense to me. I couldn't accept his dictum though, that you could tell if a spiritual experience was real if it changed your life. I was sure that the incredible moments I had experienced were real. Even though they didn't seem to have changed my life very much, they had at least given me a window on what was possible. I was eager to read more, to discover what other people were thinking about the way our minds and spirits worked. As I spent more time reading and studying, I went to Subud sessions less often.

∞ ∞ ∞ ∞ ∞

After a while I became physically ill. I was often dizzy and tired, and my performance at my secretarial job fell off badly. First was a period where I slept ten or eleven hours a night, then came another period when I stayed awake most of the night. The pains in my lower back were excruciating. I was sure that the source of my problems was not physical, but I couldn't think which way to turn.

I read an article about people with severe physical handicaps who managed to retain their good cheer and even dispositions. I figured that they must have realized how prone they were to resentment and depression, and had made conscious decisions not to go down that road. Surely my unstable emotional nature was crippling me just as their physical handicaps were crippling them, and this was every bit as good a reason not to let one of my downslides get started. I'd always told myself that I had no right to be happy when so many other people were in real pain, but now I decided to grant myself a dispensation: I would try keeping my mental guard up, and simply reject any impulse toward anxiety or depression. For the first time Mary Baker Eddy's words made real sense to me, "Stand porter at the door of your thought."

For the first couple of days it was hard to control my negative thoughts. Trying to "think a happy thought" was puerile and difficult to do on purpose, but I found that deliberately singing an upbeat popular song helped. At times I forced myself to smile even when it seemed stiff and unnatural. I felt rather embarrassed by this blatant pursuit of anything as banal as cheerfulness, but I decided that if I could attain and keep good humor it would not add to the tragedy in the world, and might, in some infinitesimal fashion, lift it a bit. To my amazement, after a few days the old mental habits started giving way, and I began to feel both emotionally and physically better. Within a week there were almost no depressing thoughts to reject. I began to sleep better and to get more exercise, and the back pains subsided. I functioned better at home and at work.

I hadn't wanted to close my mind to the reality of all the pain and terror that was going on in the world, or to forget the childhood experiences that I saw as the causes of my own personal unhappiness. After all, I'd made a choice when I was sixteen, in rejecting Christian Science, to accept what was "real." Now I began to wonder what possible good that had done. It certainly hadn't inspired me to go out and try to make things better in the world. This new attitude was not something that was brought on by surrender in the latihan, which produced a bliss and joy that came and went by its own timing, and couldn't be depended upon. This was a method to control my bouts of ill temper and depression. I could decide to be happy! I read Emile Coué on the effects of programming the subconscious mind. Coué had taught his patients to say, "Every day, and every way, I am getting better and better."

I began to use written suggestions to myself about sleeping better and generally being a more functional person. I tried it on my memory—and even my typing skills—and they began to improve. I worried a bit that I might be using God for my own purposes, but thought surely, if we had this ability, we were meant to use it. I wondered, could I autosuggest myself into having more faith in God or into having a higher purpose in life?

I decided that if I were creating my own difficulties through ignorance, then the best contribution I could make to peace and justice was to learn how that worked and how I could change things. If I could create what I desired with "mind-power," shouldn't I be creating faith, courage, love and wisdom? If my subconscious mind could bring into being whatever I concentrated on, wasn't the most important thing to raise the level of my thinking? But was it really true? Could I trust this idea?

I asked myself how the apparently unlimited possibilities of giving myself suggestions fit together with the Subud teaching of surrendering to inner guidance? I wondered if the relationship between the two lay in the fact that if I simply ask for a good, without detailing how it should come, the subconscious mind is quite capable of creating it in ways I never thought of. Perhaps if I were to ask for a closer relationship with God, my subconscious mind could produce such a relationship. I thought this conjunction might explain mysticism, and then realized that it in no way explained God.

Trying to figure all this out, I didn't even notice that I was starting the slide into depression again. One evening, after getting into another nasty quarrel with Tony, I felt completely dispirited and decided to go to a Subud meeting. During the latihan I gave up trying to direct my thinking and just surrendered, crying with all my being to Whoever or Whatever was out there, "What shall I do?"

A voice with total authority and assurance suddenly sounded in my head. "Go back to school," it said.

That was all, but I stopped, dazed. I remembered my sickness of heart years ago when I passed the students flocking into Los Angeles College as I drove to work after leaving my children in nursery school. I thought about the abortive attempt at night school I'd given up on years ago. The building blocks of a whole new life fell into place.

My first thought was to quit work immediately and enter a university, but I knew I couldn't ask Tony to support both the kids and me through college. I could continue working during the day, though, and begin to take night classes. So I did. I took as many beginning college classes as I could at the local State College. I also simply opted out of trying to resolve any unpleasantness at home, and sought solace in my studies.

Chapter 4   Getting Educated

In my first class at San Fernando Valley State College, I was startled to hear the young, shaggy-haired professor casually use the word "fuck." I'd never heard it used publically before, but if this was what was happening in college in 1962, I would live with it. I meant to get an "A" in every class, to prove to Tony and to myself that I had a right to be in college. The wave of post-war GIs was past, but the back-to-school movement of older adults had not yet started; at forty-two I was the oldest person in my classes and painfully aware of it. I didn't think of myself as better prepared to learn because I'd been reading and thinking and working and raising kids since I'd graduated from high school twenty-five years before. The feeling from my childhood—that I was only on sufferance wherever I was—resurfaced full force.

In my first year English class, we studied Thomas Mann's *The Magic Mountain*. I was infuriated by the book's ending, where the young protagonist, after learning so much about himself and about life, goes slogging off to get killed in the trenches of World War I. That was Mann's point, of course, but the pure senselessness of such a fate drove me to an impassioned protest. For once I was articulate in public, words and ideas flowed as I enthusiastically advanced my perspective. When I ended, the thirty or so other students just stared at me blankly.

Discussion was no longer possible as the ending bell had rung.

When I got in my car to go home, a harsh inner voice suddenly started to attack my hubris for thinking that my ideas were anything but trash. It scolded me about "your nerve for taking up the class's time, when most of them probably had a much better grasp of the material than you did!" It complained, "Don't you see that the other students were putting up with your ideas because they had to, and are undoubtedly now exchanging comments on your weirdness? How could you have thought you knew what you were talking about?" The vicious tongue-lashing went on for a good ten minutes, cunningly designed to exploit every low opinion I'd ever had of myself. I was left emotionally staggered and feeling as if I had been physically beaten.

The strident, unfamiliar voice was female. Her complaints were monstrously exaggerated versions of those I'd heard from my mother during my childhood and adolescence, ones I had unconsciously taken in and was using on my adult self. I'd gotten scolded: "You should be ashamed of joining those other children, teasing Mrs. Smith to give you candy!" or I was reprimanded: "You just walked right off while Mrs. James was talking. How can you be so rude?"

But the complaints had turned to indictments, the disapproval to burning contempt—coming from my own mind. Thoroughly cowed, I was quiet in classes after that, never feeling safe to speak up about ideas I had. The fact that the instructor gave my paper an "A+," and even called me at home and asked for a copy, didn't mean a thing to me. Once again I had encountered my "judge" within, a part of my consciousness that had surfaced in a more benign way in the Subud latihan, where I had been shown my ego-driven behavior. Now, I was at the mercy of my own self-hatred.

I plowed my way through the first two years of college at night, while running our household and holding a fulltime job during the day. I was secretary to Al Bodine, a physicist-inventor who had the remarkably far-seeing idea that a woman with children shouldn't work at an office forty hours a week. Rather than have his two female employees take sick leave on unexpected days, he gave both of us an afternoon off every week. Neither of us was gratuitously "sick" in the five years I worked for him.

Bodine was in his late forties, well-groomed and athletic-looking. I never met his family; I only saw the photo on his desk of an attractive, if a bit anemic- looking, blonde woman and two healthy adolescents. He was self-assured—a man who knew just what he wanted and went after it. He had hired me instantly, despite the rustiness of my shorthand, because he didn't have to spell for me the difficult words he dictated at our interview. He was always distantly friendly, and it never occurred to me to mind that he was "Mr. Bodine" and I was "Marion. "

At home one evening, I had a very strange experience. I had taken a few minutes off from my college-level anatomy textbook to try one of the exercises in a pop psychology book I had bought that day. It directed me to remember scenes from my childhood, which at that time was mostly a blank to me. I vaguely recollected one or two incidents and then dutifully returned to my anatomy book. Suddenly its beautifully delineated illustration of the human body became vivid and I saw subtle colors I'd never seen before. The veins, for instance, were faintly bluer than the arteries. Startled, I looked up and found that everything in the room was standing out in exquisite relief. There were minuscule red threads in the beige drapes and blue-green patterns in the rug that I'd never noticed before. Bemused, I wandered through the house, observing everything as if I had suddenly become an artist with years of training in seeing shapes and colors and juxtapositions.

In the kitchen were an assortment of seldom-used containers of spices and herbs. Usually, I couldn't recognize much more than the toasty smell of cinnamon or the eggnog-y smell of nutmeg, but now I knew the difference between the odors and tastes of turmeric and thyme, marjoram and paprika, and half a dozen others.

I went to tell Tony about the astonishing experience I was having, and his radio was turned on to some classical music. I was stunned. Usually musically semi-literate, I recognized this Tchaikovsky symphony immediately, knew which instrument was playing each note, and could anticipate which phrase came next. The music ended and the announcer's voice came on. I knew at once that he had played the role of the kindly uncle in a radio drama I used to listen to a dozen years before. I was so overwhelmed I didn't even to try to explain to Tony what was happening to me. Eventually I went to bed and in the morning all my senses had gone back to normal. I was left with the knowledge that abilities far beyond anything I ordinarily used were within me, though I hadn't any idea how to access them intentionally.

It was only much later in life that I understood some of what had happened to me that evening. In going back to scenes of my early childhood without any expectations, I had perhaps triggered a brief episode of the world the way young children experience it.

After two years of State College in the evenings I was able, with my savings and Tony's financial help, to quit work and transfer to UCLA full time in the daytime. During my years in college and university, my attempts at using positive thinking and autosuggestion were becoming less and less successful, as was my faith in any greater reality. I now knew how bad the troubles among the peoples of the world had been for millennia. I noted in my journal that faith was possible only if we cut off our reality-testing apparatus.

I wasn't sure what to do after graduation from UCLA. A Bachelor's Degree in Psychology didn't qualify me for any kind of professional work. A friend pointed out that going for a Master's Degree at a school of social work was much more realistic than trying to get a Ph.D. I could continue to study what human beings were all about and be ready to make a living in two years, instead of four.

When I brought the idea up to Tony, however, he said, "I don't want you to go to graduate school. I don't want any more of this nonsense of my having to do all the gardening and half the housework and you always busy with papers and study. I don't want to support you for two more years on the chance that you'll go back to work when you get your degree. I want us to have a normal married life, now!"

It became clear to me that caring about Tony and caring about what he wanted me to be, were two different things. I wanted to continue to grow and expand my knowledge, to be able to read and understand serious books and serious thinkers, to be able to converse intelligently

67

with people who had ideas. I wanted a profession. I wanted these things more than I wanted a home, or a husband, or even a secure financial future. Thirty years after leaving Christian Science at sixteen because I wanted a more authentic and exciting life, I was ready to leave Tony for much the same reason. When he saw how determined I was, he gave in.

The School of Social Work at UCLA was the only graduate school I applied to, and I was not surprised that I was accepted and even given a small scholarship. My one attempt to return to an official Subud latihan since starting college had assured me that there was nothing further in Subud for me, yet I still experienced guidance when I did the latihan on my own. It had told me clearly that I should pursue a Master's Degree in Clinical Social Work at UCLA.

Three weeks into my first year, I became an intern at a public health clinic where I was expected to do "therapy" with people who had come for help.   My supervisor was a woman fifteen years my junior whose approach baffled me. When I went to her office, hoping for instruction on what I should do with uneducated patients who were often in situations of real environmental distress, she said we should examine my feelings about them. My feelings were of sheer frustration, as I'm sure hers were also: we were both speaking earnestly and with good intentions, about entirely different psychological problems.

Since I hadn't the faintest idea what I was supposed to do with the men and women assigned to me, I just let them tell me about what was troubling them. It seemed to relieve them a bit, though it left me puzzled about what we were accomplishing. I remember one man shouting out his troubles and the director of the clinic coming to me later to tell me that such a level of noise was not permitted.

During my first year at the School of Social Work, we were taught three different approaches to helping people. One was behavior modification: how to set up a structure of rewards and non-rewards for desirable or undesirable behavior. Theoretically, if good behavior is rewarded and bad behavior is ignored, good behavior will result and bad behavior will cease. It seemed inhuman to me, as well as impossible to carry out in a county mental health clinic.

We were taught psychoanalytic psychotherapy: if people understood how their early childhood experiences had led to their adult minds and emotions, they would be better able to handle their lives now. Unfortunately, much of such conditioning was unconscious. Psychoanalysis aimed at making it conscious through talk about the patient's past, and through the patient's reactions to the analyst. (That was what my supervisor was attempting with me.) I knew this to be beyond my ability to sustain without years of study and practice. Besides, it wouldn't cure neurosis, Freud said, merely make it more bearable. It didn't seem worth all the work it would take to learn it, and my readings in psychoanalysis had left me with doubts about its value: it seemed to be focused on the consequences of breast feeding, toilet training, and psychosexual development in very early childhood. No one could explain to me how to use it in sessions with a man complaining of not being able to find a job, pay the rent, or stay out of jail.

I liked the third one we were taught, the humanistic or Carl Rogers' client-centered approach, the best. It maintained that real listening and unconditional positive regard are healing in themselves. Rogers took the position that the experience of receiving unconditional regard permits a kind of inner flowering and gives people the strength to solve their own problems. This approach, I felt, was actually doable. At least it allowed me to be supportive to the patients, though I wasn't sure that we could accomplish much in the short time we had. What bothered me most was that these three approaches were taught as separate disciplines with no relationship to each other. I thought that there must be commonalties among them since they all dealt with human beings, but no one mentioned any.

The next year I was assigned to the Fernald Reading Clinic, under the supervision of a friendly young woman who actually answered the questions I asked. I enjoyed that internship, even though our joint senior thesis showed that the work of the clinic with kids from poor neighborhood schools had not benefited them at all when they went back to their regular schools.

During my second year in graduate school, a number of students were complaining about being expected to do therapy without having experienced it themselves. We asked for an opportunity to be in group therapy with an experienced leader. The head of the school refused our request, saying that such experience was not necessary and, in fact, would be detrimental to our work as social workers. Apparently, there was supposed to be an impassible gulf between professionals and the people they were serving.

Eight of the other students and I decided to start a leaderless therapy group. It was a fascinating, painful, frustrating experience. We were all careful not to be seen

70

as attempting to take the lead, so we floundered around, poking at each other's vulnerabilities, without knowing how to bring about any resolution. I was acutely aware of being older than everybody else, though nobody addressed this issue. The closest we came was when one young woman, already reacting to me as if I were her mother, suggested that we do a mother-daughter scenario. "O.K," I replied cheerfully, "I'll play the daughter." Her indignant "No-o-o!" pretty much blew the rest of that session.

I could see the value in accessing our unexpressed feelings, even though I had utterly refused to do that sort of investigation with my first year supervisor. I was not very open in the group either. I was too ashamed of my dependence on others, my intrusiveness and hostility, and my wild anxieties. It was okay for them, they were *young*. But why was I was still like that? I felt middle-aged, bungling, and sure that I was resented or pitied by my younger cohorts.

At the School of Social Work graduation, we marched through the huge auditorium along with advanced degree candidates from many other schools at UCLA, all properly clad in caps and gowns. The ceremonies and the handing out of diplomas during the event made it feel almost like a real accomplishment to me.

I applied for the position of Psychiatric Social Worker at the Neuropsychiatric Institute of the UCLA Medical Center. I had been warned that they were steeped in psychoanalytic theory and all their staff had to adhere to it. Nevertheless, I had asked my latihan for guidance, and it said that the Neuropsychiatric Institute was the place for me. I waited almost a month before calling to get their decision. When I reached Marvin Brown, the head of the

Social Work Department, he said that he and his senior staff had just finished reviewing the applications, and they had decided to offer the job to me.

The month I started at NPI was the same month the director of the Institute, known for his rigid insistence on a psychoanalytic approach, had a heart attack and retired. (It took the entire four years I worked there for them to locate a new director, a man named Jolly, whose arrival was preceded by the rumor that he had killed an elephant by experimentally injecting it with LSD.) During the NPI's four years without a director, each department ran itself with very little oversight.

At the Out-Patient Clinic, where I was assigned, I worked with clients who were functional enough to be living on their own. (This was in California before totally nonfunctional people were turned loose on the streets.) I was expected to spend a few hours each day taking phone calls and assigning patients to specific interns or staff members. The rest of the time I saw individual clients, couples and families in therapy. In addition, several times a week I acted as a group co-therapist with one of the senior psychiatric interns. That left eight hours a week to take advantage of the rich learning experiences that were available. To my delight I was expected to attend the presentations at Grand Rounds as well as many other specialized lectures and seminars. Noted psychologists and psychiatrists from all over the world came to describe their ideas and approaches to the NPI staff.

I was expected to perform as well as to learn, though I was given no supervision when I was working with clients. The various forms of diagnosis I'd learned in the School of Social Work never stayed in my head. As far as I could see, people came in because they were either unhappy or weren't functioning very well, or both. I listened and tried to help them see what was going on and how best to handle it. There were undoubtedly better treatments I could have tried, but I didn't know what they were.

I decided that I had to experience being in therapy myself. None of the other social workers struck me as particularly able. The psychiatrists were all male, very distant and imposing; the psychiatric interns were all young men. Freda Morris, a new psychologist on staff, was a puckish, startlingly uninhibited woman who attracted me immediately. She wore no makeup and her light brown hair was casually short and straight, in an era when women wore make-up and had permanents. She took off her shoes and tucked her feet under her at meetings. She expressed flashes of unconventional wisdom, in her intermittent Oklahoma twang, often enough to make me respect her intelligence. She specialized in hypnosis and her Ph.D. dissertation had been in psychic phenomena.

I didn't know much about hypnosis at the time, though I knew how suggestible I was. I'd read about its early discovery in the work of Mesmer, who was convinced that it was actually the transmission of some kind of magnetic energy that was healing his patients. Still more interesting was the work of men like Elliotson in London and Esdaile in India, doctors who performed amputations and other surgeries with their patients under hypnosis, apparently feeling no pain. The invention of chloroform had supplanted hypnosis work in surgery, but the use of hypnosis to implant suggestions of health and well-being was well documented. I was eager to learn more about it.

Freda was thirteen years younger than I, a little shorter and a lot more athletic. She looked at me with wide, sleepy-looking blue eyes and accepted me as a psychotherapy patient. When we met later that week I found that I could go into a trance state easily, and that being hypnotized gave me permission to talk about myself with few inhibitions. I soon found out just how unconventional she was: at the end of our first meeting, she suggested that, in future meetings, we do hypnotherapy on each other, switching roles in each session.

My jaw literally dropped. This was unheard of. I knew enough about transference and counter transference —in which a patient reacts to a therapist in the same way as to her parents; and/or the therapist counters by doing the same thing to the patient—to know what our colleagues would think of such an idea. Besides, I had no training in hypnosis.

"Oh, I'm easy to hypnotize," Freda said airily. "And if we get into transference, it will just be more for us to work on. We won't give them a chance to disapprove; we won't tell anyone."

I was easily convinced. What a blast! To work closely and personally with this intriguing woman who was so insouciant about our imposing workplace. It didn't even occur to me how unprofessional this arrangement was. We met two hours a week for the next eighteen months, taking turns at being the therapist or the patient. After using guided physical relaxation or mental imagery to induce a hypnotic trance, we used every technique we knew: reliving childhood memories, analyzing dreams, investigating feelings and fantasies. Later, we learned more techniques for getting in touch with experiences that

74

were beneath our everyday awareness. We became close personal friends as well as each other's therapist and patient. And we did get into enormous transference with each other.

Along with respect and affection, we soon found ourselves full of rivalry and jealousy. Freda was always dashing ahead of me. She would be in a rage at me and I'd only realize hours later how angry I had been with her. She was the first to plunge into the haunting wish underlying much of deep psychotherapy: that the patient could be as important to the therapist as the therapist was to the patient. For a while she wanted to see me every day, talk during lunch, spend our evenings together. Divorced herself, she was jealous of the time I spent with Tony. For the first months I often felt like I was the grownup, parenting the child in her. But her open demands permitted me to admit my yearning to be important to her, and to recognize, finally, that I was.

We also got involved in each other's work life. Freda would get angry with me when she felt I was too passive. She would insist that I could accomplish something and grin proudly when I did—sure it was all her doing. I struggled to get her to "shape up" at meetings, was embarrassed by her easy anger and ready tears, and delighted when she suddenly showed her real abilities and gave a lecture with professional assurance.

After Freda and I had been working together for about six months, I attended a few sessions taught by Thelma Moss, another staff psychologist, on "Psycho-theatre." It was typical of NPI during that period that Thelma, who was also interested in psychic phenomena, was reputed to have a psychology lab on one of the upper floors with a sign outside the door, "Don't bother to knock. We know you are here."

A small, vigorous, blond woman, she had come to academic work almost as late as I had, after a fairly successful career as a stage actress. She told our group about method acting, in which an actor wanting to portray a certain emotion takes himself back to a scene in his own life when he had felt that emotion. "You do this by using your senses," she told us, "by remembering how things tasted and smelled as well as how they looked." To demonstrate, she asked if anyone could remember a smell.

One of the young psychiatric interns spoke of remembering the smell of grasses burning in Africa. Thelma called him to the front of the room and began telling him, in slow hypnotic tones, to direct his attention to exactly how the burning grass smelled and what sights and sounds were associated with it. In a short time, he paled and sweat burst out on his forehead. He described in harrowing detail a puberty ritual he had attended as a medical intern, involving circumcision of an adolescent boy.

Another student brought up the smell of chicken soup. In moments he was back in his grandmother's kitchen amid the preparations for the Sabbath, watching her neatly slice off a chicken's head. Perhaps stirred by the story just before his, he suddenly relived an atavistic male terror of her knife. We all laughed, but it was clear that the memory had shaken him.

"Okay," she said, "Let's try a smell that we can all work with: close your eyes and imagine that someone is putting a piece of chocolate in your mouth. Taste it as it begins to melt and run over your tongue. Really get the flavor as your teeth crunch down and break it to bits. Can you smell it, too, as it comes apart in your mouth?" I tried for the smell and flavor of chocolate, but got instead a vaguely familiar unpleasant flavor I couldn't identify. I felt uncomfortably stuck with it. All around me were self-conscious little laughs. "See how easy it is to go back on the thread of the senses?" she asked triumphantly.

I could hardly wait to get home to experiment further. Tony was working late these days, so I changed quickly and lay down on the living room sofa. "Chocolate," I thought, trying to remember the taste on my tongue, "Chocolate." Slowly my mouth began to work, as if I was attempting to spit out some bad tasting medicine. I let it happen, waiting for clarification. Then my whole lower face twisted and I began to gag. I was almost six years old again, in the shadow of the veranda around the old hotel where my mother and brothers and I were staying, on our trip back to New York. I had been left alone for a little while and was talked into going with some older boys whom I thought were my new friends. Opening my mouth in the expectation of being given sweet chocolate candy, I was sexually assaulted instead. I staggered to the bathroom and vomited again and again, my whole body sick and shaking, while some part of my mind watched in amazement. I had never forgotten that afternoon, but I hadn't known the memory was still woven into the muscles of my mouth and my gut.

I sat on the bathroom floor, leaning against the tub, hatred against those boys raging through me. Since I was six years old, I had lived with this ugliness in my subconscious mind. Determined to do what I could to be rid of the trauma, I lay down on the couch again.

"Chocolate," I thought, "Chocolate." This time, as the slimy taste came, wracking sobs of helpless anger and betrayal burst from me. I let them run their course, and when I finally quieted, I began again, "Chocolate . . ."

After two hours I was so exhausted I couldn't go any farther, though I didn't feel finished. I took a long bath, soaping my skin and brushing the inside of my mouth carefully, over and over. I pretended to be asleep when Tony got home, not willing to see or talk to any man. And still, part of me was fascinated with what was happening.

The next night I started the experience as before: "Chocolate." I saw the image of a bulging, out-thrust penis. Suddenly there was a knife in my hand and I struck at him. He staggered away screaming, crippled for life. I fell asleep with a smile. Each night after that, as I reran the scene, it would end differently. Once I castrated all three of them, one by one. Once I went on to plunge a knife into the hearts of all the men who had hurt me, starting with my father who had virtually abandoned me when I was three. Finally, after going through such savage imagery every evening for almost a week, I felt friendly fingers gently placing a piece of sweet chocolate in my mouth. I could actually taste it. A warm glow spread through my body and I knew the whole episode was finally over. Without conscious direction on my part, Thelma's simple cue of trying to re-experience the taste of chocolate had led me step by step to unearth and heal a deep childhood trauma.

Chapter 5   Gestalt

Freda and I went to weekend seminars at the Esalen Institute several times during 1969. Esalen was just beginning to come into prominence as a pioneering mind/body growth center. The physical location, on the wild, jagged coastline of the Monterey Peninsula south of San Francisco, is breathtakingly beautiful. Hanging on the pine-covered cliffs above the long expanse of the Pacific, within constant sound of the waves crashing below, Esalen's very location promised a new way of being. Despite my usual self-consciousness, the totally nude baths open to the sun and sea air didn't present a problem. My first husband Frank, my friend Jean and I had been members of a health-oriented nudist colony in the hills near Los Angeles thirty years earlier.

The residents, however, scared me. They felt alien to me but I wanted to be like them, as did most of us who were attending the seminars. They were so sure of themselves, so free of inhibitions, so casually affectionate with each other and yet so disdainful of us seminarians. I was thoroughly intimidated, as well as fascinated. In reality, they were having the same experiences we were, many times magnified. They lived there, participating in one workshop after another, experimenting with LSD and other hallucinogens, and with having multiple sexual partners. There was a rumor that a chart in the staff room had arrows indicating who was sleeping with whom that week.

I talked Tony into going to Esalen with me to a couples' workshop. Predictably, he treated the whole weekend as a social occasion and stayed cheerfully upbeat during all the confrontations. There were some astonishing moments, however. One woman had been in a mental institution and was certain that everyone was afraid of her because she was crazy. The leader had her go around acting her craziest and trying to scare the others. As she menaced each person, they instinctively pulled away from her. When she got to me, she went through the same weird, rageful behavior as she had toward the others, but it didn't occur to me to be afraid. When she got to the leader, a big, self-assured man, he took her in his arms and invited her to go completely crazy. She yelled and struggled against his unyielding restraint for long moments until she finally was still.

"Are you crazy?" he asked. Purged, she answered quietly, "No."

Thanks to my Esalen experiences, I was hooked on Gestalt therapy. Back at the university, I tracked down a local psychiatrist named Jim Simkins, who specialized in Gestalt. He had been one of the original group of six working with Fritz Perls as Perls created this new form of therapy.

When I arrived for my first appointment with him, Jim kept me waiting in his outer office for at least twenty minutes, while I grew more and more uncomfortable. My neatly crossed nylon-clad ankles and dark pumps began to look ridiculously prim to me. I uncrossed my feet and stretched my legs out, trying to relax. No, that felt too slouched, too vulnerable. I argued with myself, "Maybe I shouldn't be here. After all, no one at NPI takes this new Gestalt stuff very seriously."

Just before I made up my mind to bolt, the inner door opened and Jim Simkins stood there, not saying a word, just looking at me. I looked back, feeling instant disappointment. He was short, a bit overweight, his face so hidden behind a shaggy black beard and thick glasses that I couldn't make it out clearly. He wasn't even dressed professionally. Curly black hair burst out of the open throat of his sport shirt.

He nodded without returning my automatic smile. "Come in."

The office was large, airy and rather luxurious. I had a quick impression of several diplomas hung on one paneled wall. He gestured me to a seat alongside his desk. Still without a word he switched on a camera that showed an enlarged image of my own startled face looking back at me from a television screen affixed to the wall. Transfixed, I gazed up at it. What a strained, unhappy, unattractive face!

"What do you see?" he asked, without preliminaries.

I shuddered involuntarily, turning quickly away from the image to look at him. I chose what felt like an innocuous assessment. "The two sides look very different." My voice sounded quiet, controlled.

"Will you try saying 'I'm two-faced?'" he suggested calmly.

I glanced back at the face on the screen again. According to the books I'd read on Gestalt, I was supposed to try the idea on for size. I repeated the words as meaningfully as I could make them sound.

"I'm two-faced," I said, grateful that it didn't ring true. Surely being two-faced would be dreadful. "No, I am not, certainly not in the sense of deliberately dissembling."

He nodded without seeming interested. "What are you feeling now?"

That was easy. "Nervous." The thing was to be frank and open with him, make him respect me for that at least. On the screen I saw the strange face attempt a winsome smile.

"Why do you want to join my therapy group?"

"I want to understand myself better." The words felt more honest than the face looked. "I don't understand a lot of my reactions. I've been in hypnotherapy for a year now. I thought I'd like to try Gestalt." I caught a flash of amusement behind the glasses.

"Hypnotherapy?"

"With Dr. Freda Morris." I wanted to impress him with the "Dr.," and at the same time I felt a little fearful that he would know Freda, not take her seriously.

He shook his head and changed the subject. "Take your shoes off and stand up. That's good. Now slowly rock forward on your toes; stay there a moment. Now rock back on your heels. Keep it up for a while. See if you can find the balance point between your heels and your toes."

I did as I was told, when suddenly, unbelievably, I felt tremulous, my throat choked up and my eyes were full of tears.

Again there was a flash of interest. "What happened?"

I sat down abruptly, puzzled and shaken. "I don't know. What did happen?"

82

He shrugged. "I don't know. You're the only one who can know that." I didn't believe him. I'd probably betrayed my whole messed-up character to those indifferent eyes. But I knew that I wanted to join his group. I would have had to work with Freda for an hour to produce such a reaction.

He asked nothing about my background or problems. "We meet from eight to ten on Tuesday evenings; the fee is $30 a session." I nodded. He added, "Any questions?"

I was hesitant, off balance, not sure if the question was legitimate, but it seemed reasonable. "Would you explain just what Gestalt therapy is? I mean, what are its goals, and how does it differ from other therapies?"

"No." Again, he was brusque. "If you want to learn about Gestalt, there are at least half a dozen books. If you want to change, you can come and work." I nodded again, feeling thoroughly intimidated.

Before I left he asked suddenly, "What do you see when you look at me? What do you think I'm like?"

I was partially honest. "Not very friendly. Judgmental." I didn't add my other sudden thought, that he put on an act to scare people.

His manner seemed to ease a little, but I wasn't sure. "Okay. See you next Tuesday." Had he really smiled in farewell?

According to what I had read, Gestalt was a way of making the unconscious conscious by becoming fully aware of bodily, mental and emotional experience in the present moment. The methods used included dramatizing current experience through mental imagery, the acting out of various scenarios or dreams, confrontations and the deliberate exaggeration of reactions. The basic idea was that people suffer because they have lost touch with themselves, so any method that could break through denial and reach actual thoughts and feelings was used. "Lose your mind and come to your senses," Fritz Perls had famously said.

There were ten people in the group, six women and four men, mostly in their thirties or early forties. We were introduced only by first names. I never did find out much about anyone else's life outside of the sessions, for Jim didn't encourage social interaction among us. When each session began, he merely asked. "Who wants to work?" When someone volunteered, Jim would set up a situation to exaggerate the ideas and feelings expressed. Sometimes he used the other members of the group as foils.

"I can't take it anymore!" Carl, balding and a bit overweight, one of the two older men in the group, said abruptly one night, "My wife is impossible." There was a silence while Jim watched him carefully. Carl was breathing heavily, staring down at the carpet through lowered lids.

"Tell each person here, "My wife is a bitch," Jim directed him.

Carl hesitated a moment, then looked directly at Franklin. "My wife is a bitch!" Each word was clear, almost bitten off. Then to Roger, "My wife is a bitch!" And with mounting conviction, to pretty young Alice, "My wife is a bitch!" I was next. I waited, only slightly apprehensive. I liked Carl, found him intelligent and lively, with a masculine aggressiveness that was sometimes a little exciting.

His eyes narrowed suddenly. "All women are bitches!" He glanced back at Alice. "They start out by being sweet young girls and grow o—" he hesitated momentarily over "old" and finished "turn into bitches!" He turned and glared at me resentfully. My breath caught in my throat, and I felt my face go red.

Jim intervened. "Go on; tell the others that 'all women are bitches.'"

Carl left me and went on to Joel. "All women are bitches!" Joel grinned commiseratingly, breaking the unspoken rule that we were not to respond when someone was working unless we were really moved ourselves. "Right you are, brother," he said easily, "I've often thought so myself." The off-hand comment broke the mounting tension, and Carl's statements trailed off. When he had spoken to everyone he sat with eyes on the floor. "I guess I've got a lot of resentment against women," he said lamely.

We were all quiet, feeling unfinished. Jim asked, his annoyance plain, "How do you feel about Joel not taking you seriously?"

Carl shrugged. "Well, I didn't like it. But who can get mad at Joel?"

"I can!" Tension re-entered the room as Jim fixed Joel with a hard stare. "You don't take yourself seriously, that's your problem. You don't take anyone else seriously and they let you get away with it, that's their problem. But when you don't take what I'm doing seriously, that's stepping on my toes, and I'm damned if I'll let you get away with it!"

Big, good-natured Joel squirmed, looking suddenly young and vulnerable. His hands made uncertain gestures in the air. "I was only agreeing with him," he muttered.

Carl's unexpectedly personal attack against me had left me paralyzed, but my anger boiled up on Joel's behalf. He was the only man in the room who had gone out of his way to be friendly to me, the only man who felt at all supportive, the only one I felt almost safe with. I spoke to take the heat from him without even realizing that that was, at least in part, what I was doing.

"Well, if Carl doesn't want to work anymore, I do!" I had meant to sound firm and defiant. Instead I was shaking. Everyone turned to look at me. To my horror, I could feel tears starting behind my eyes.

Jim's eyes were speculative. I seldom volunteered to work. He sank back in his chair. "Go ahead," he said.

I forced myself to look at Carl. I wanted to yell at him, but my voice sounded weak and tremulous. "I resented the way you looked at me when you said all women turned into bitches when they got older!" I said.

Carl stiffened at my unusual turning on him. "If the shoe fits, wear it," he said briefly and brutally.

I stared at him, not knowing what to do next.

"You two willing to have a confrontation?" asked Jim, neutrally.

"You bet!" Carl grabbed up his chair and carried it directly in front of mine, glaring at me from two feet away. I forced myself to meet his eyes squarely.

"I said," he repeated loudly, "that all women are bitches!"

My hands jerked apart, and I felt a fleeting urge to claw at his sneering face. I forced my voice to steadiness.

"I resent your taking out your anger at your mother on me!" I could get to him through reason; make him admit the source of his anger.

He pounded his knee in frustration. "My mother isn't here! You are!"

I saw the way out and dived for it, knowing my clever words would protect me. "That's not true. You are acting as if your mother is here, and I'm not." I felt a little breath of acknowledgement going around the room, saw Carl wilt, confused.

Jim prompted me, "Tell him, if you really saw me, you'd love me."

I hesitated, finding that too scary to say, "You might like me and you might not."

Carl shrugged, defeated, "I guess you're right."

"Oh, shit," said Jim wearily, "Forget it. Let's go home." I knew he was displeased. I had managed to change into words the dangerously hot feelings just breaking the surface between Carl and me. But I felt headily triumphant. I had managed to protect myself in the only way I knew. I wasn't as completely at their mercy as I'd thought I was! As we went out, Joel threw a casual arm around my shoulders and gave me a brief hug. I felt grateful, and at the same time I knew he was acknowledging me as a fellow subverter of the very goals we were there to achieve.

Tuesday night became the focus of my entire week. I began to eat dinner more and more lightly as I recognized that it tended to sit in my stomach in a sodden lump and refuse to digest. The shakiness in my solar plexus on the drive over to Jim's office would not go away, even when I assured myself that I could just sit quietly this time, having worked the week before. Something still might happen that would put me in the hot seat.

The work of the other members fascinated me, though it troubled me sometimes that I watched as if I were at a movie. No not even that— I cried at movies. But here, when something particularly poignant would happen and others would lean forward with tears in their eyes, I felt sympathetic, but not part of it. As always, I felt like an outsider.

One night I got up the nerve to work on a dream I'd had about Tony, in which he decided to leave me. In the dream, the door was stuck, and no matter how hard he tried, it would not open. I felt relief, but then he circled over to an open window and was gone. Telling the dream in the group, I felt again my own bewildered resentment at his leaving.

"It's funny," I said, "I think about leaving him every once in a while, though of course I'll never do it. But I got really upset at his wanting to leave me."

Jim shook his head. "Will you people never learn? Everything and everybody in a dream is only another aspect of yourself. Go ahead, be Tony."

Speaking as Tony in my dream, I said, "I'm going to leave some day, it might as well be now." I was taken back at hearing my own words.

"Be the door," said Jim.

I felt a familiar sense of being stuck, unable to move. As the door, I was not only locked; all sorts of brambles were growing over me from the outside. "I can never be opened," I said grimly, "I have grown shut."

"Be the window."

I was the window, wide open. There was a soft, scented breeze outside, like the air in Hawaii. Somewhere in the distance I heard a girl's voice singing a carefree hiking song, "I love to go a-wandering, across the mountain trails. . . "

Almost dizzily I looked around, bringing the group back into focus. Jim was grinning at me. "So you'd never do it, hmm?"

Not again! Two divorces were bad enough; I couldn't even let myself consider another. "No!" I said, "I am not going to leave my husband!"

"Don't worry," Jim reassured me sardonically, "That overgrown door is as much a part of you as the open window." I didn't find that comforting. The door had felt so stuck, so heavy and solid and unable to move, overgrown with those thorny brambles. And the window had felt so free . . .

The next night Tony brought home some travel folders. "How about going on a tour to Spain this summer?" I looked at the folders: flamenco dancers, the Alhambra. "Colorful and exciting," the brochures said. Not exciting. I remembered the tour last year, careening through eight countries, watching the tourist attractions fly past from the big bus we were on with all those other dull middle-aged couples. I remembered how depressed I'd been after we returned home.

But there wasn't any place else I wanted to go that Tony would enjoy. I thought of the open window and a little impulse of excitement seized me, followed instantly by fear. I knew other women in their forties and fifties, without men, hungrily attending political meetings, dances, trying the singles scene, being shouldered aside by all the pretty young chicks who found older men *so* attractive. I shivered at the very idea of again entering that kind of competition.

"Let's not think about it yet," I said, sliding onto his lap. Dear Tony. He was such a good guy. His arms around me, warm and always available, felt so good.

∞ ∞ ∞ ∞ ∞

In Jim's group, everything that happened reached me through the screen of my own discomfort. I became more and more aware of being jittery and uncomfortable in social situations and most of all in Jim's group. One day he called attention to how I was sitting, apparently relaxed, but with one hand clinging to the edge of the chair. He told me to speak to my hand. I found myself sneering at it for its cowardice, but it insisted that it needed to hang on.

"When you get in touch with yourself," he commented, "It's always your top dog you are in touch with. You need to be in touch with the dizzy blonde in you."

I was silent, affronted. His notion that I must have a "dizzy blonde" in me felt condescending, but I didn't challenge him. Whatever I said, he would see through to the hapless, confused, demanding person within me and he would lead me into betraying that person for the whole group to see. I tried to tell myself that it didn't matter what they saw, what was important was what I could come to see about myself, but that didn't make me feel any better.

Finally I asked Jim for a private appointment. He didn't turn on the video, and seemed a bit gentler, more approachable. "I'm stuck," I told him, "I want to move, to

90

change, but it's as if I can't." I started to get agitated, hearing my voice break. "What's the matter with me?"

"I used to know a strong, powerful woman," he said carefully, "Who felt that she had no place in her life to use that power. So about once a month she would go out in the country and whip a tree to death."

I looked at him with horror. "How could she?" I'd always felt that trees were special, the most beautiful, nourishing fellow-beings on earth.

"She would take a whip," he continued inexorably, "and find a small sapling. She would whip it until the bark tore away, and the wood underneath cracked, and then she'd beat it into the ground."

"Oh, no!" I tried to laugh. "You are not suggesting that I do something like that? I couldn't possibly."

He shrugged. "I thought you came here to find out what you could do to help yourself."

"But what good could that possibly do?" I was playing stupid now, and I knew it. I was pretending I hadn't heard his description of the woman as powerful and out of touch with her power.

"Try it," he said.

I was beginning to feel a vague temptation. "Are you sure it will help?"

He turned to his desk, ripped off an office memo, and wrote on it, "Whipping trees helps." He signed it and handed it to me

I grinned uncertainly. On the top of the sheet was an impish little sketch of a man and woman engaged in copulation. If I refused, I would be admitting that the whole free and unconventional world I was trying so hard to enter was beyond me.

The next Saturday morning I went to a stable, and bought a cheap little whip. I drove through Griffith Park, searching for a place where no one could possibly see me, scarcely believing that I was actually going to do this thing. It was possibly illegal and beyond that, just plain sick. But I was letting a familiar numbness take me over. In this state I could do anything. In this state I could let a dentist work on my teeth, in this state I had passed my first wedding night. In this state I could whip a tree to death.

Standing before a slender little birch, I was revolted at the idea of hurting it. I argued with myself. There were lots of little trees there, competing for nourishment and sunshine. People cut down trees all the time. I needed this tree as medicine for my psychological health. Finally I took off my coat, braced myself, and reluctantly brought the firm little whip slashing down the side of the sapling.

A twig of leaves and a strip of bark tore loose, and a little thrill ran through me. I brought the whip up again and again and as it fell, a terrible rage seemed to come roaring up through my body from the ground. I slashed at the tree, seeing the bark strip away. In a kind of frenzy, I heard myself pant out curses and guttural, wordless sounds. Finally I hurled down the whip and stamped on the splintered sapling until it broke off completely. I crushed and pounded the stump until it was obliterated.

I stared at it, panting, a retching sensation growing in my throat. I staggered to a welcoming pine tree nearby, buried my head against its trunk and felt hard sobs shaking me. I didn't know why I was crying, anymore than I had known why I raged and wanted to kill the tree. The grief, like the anger, was without any content. Jim's talk of a powerful woman who had no place in her life to express that power was forgotten. I had contacted all that boiling rage and power and I knew that some terribly strong feelings had broken through, but I only felt shell-shocked.

By the next day my face was covered with a rash, as if I had contacted poison oak in the woods. When I told Jim that it had started the day after I'd followed his instructions and killed the little tree, I caught his knowing grin. Somehow I was showing the ugliness within me for all the world to see. I was only grateful that no one else could read the message.

A month later I drove myself to find out what would happen if I repeated the performance. Off in the woods, I struck at a little tree with the whip, but nothing happened within me. I was just standing there, pointlessly hitting a sapling. I stopped and touched it apologetically, then I went home. I never tried it again.

Nevertheless, life was incontestably getting more interesting. No longer did I sit at work molded into the pose of a good professional, always giving the answers that fitted expectations. I was beginning to stand up for myself more, and to feel more alive. The quality of my interactions with other people began to feel more real.

One day in the group Jim was trying to get some kind of authentic reaction from Joel. Finally he threw up his hands. "I don't think anyone could get a rise out of you!" he said, disgustedly.

"Oh, I don't know," I found myself saying without forethought. "I think I could."

"Go ahead," challenged Jim.

I turned to Joel, sitting beside me, and kissed him lingeringly full on the mouth and felt his very obvious reaction throughout his body. I was beginning to feel much surer of myself.

∞ ∞ ∞ ∞ ∞

At NPI, a small group of us, three psychiatric interns, a couple of staff psychologists, and one of the other social workers, decided that we wanted to form a staff Gestalt training group at NPI. We hired an outside psychiatrist who specialized in Gestalt to lead our group, but we didn't like him much. He tried to be tough like Fritz Perls or Jim Simkins, without being sensitive enough (or perhaps well trained enough) to know what he was doing.

I have only one clear memory of our work with him. The subject of fear of death had come up and I remarked that I wasn't afraid of death. "Oh, yeah," he sneered, "Well, put Death in that chair in front of you and talk to it." I turned to the empty chair, curious to see what I might find to say. Without noticing what my feet were doing, I hooked them underneath the rungs of the chair containing Death and pulled it towards me. Apparently I wasn't even unconsciously afraid, nor have I ever been able to find any traces of that particular fear in myself.

We didn't renew our agreement with him. Since I had more training in Gestalt than the others, they asked me to take over the leadership of the group. We liked working together, and several members are still my good friends.

It was during this period that the Social Work manager decided to have each of us on staff present our particular professional interest at our weekly staff meetings. Pleased by what I had learned about Gestalt, I volunteered first. I began the meeting by having all twenty-four of my colleagues pair off and then sit opposite each other and openly look each other over for a couple of minutes. They were amazed at their own reactions, for none of them had ever felt permitted to look openly and fully at one of their own colleagues.

They were so excited by this slight inroad on their inhibitions that they willingly participated in half a dozen other Gestalt processes I showed them. At the end I had a dozen people lift our boss in the air and rock him gently. "That was the first time," Marvin told me later, "that I actually felt supported by my staff." He continued to ask me to present for six more meetings. Partly as a result of those sessions, in the following year he offered me the position of Social Work Field Instructor.

Early that summer, before the new Social Work students arrived, we heard a lecture by a well-known psychiatrist from back East who had been invited to address the entire staff of the Institute. Enthusiastically, he described the use of a new mind-altering substance called LSD. "Have you ever looked at an ordinary desk, and been able to see the atoms whirling about in it?" he asked with wonder.

Freda and I decided to go off to some isolated land owned by a friend of hers to experiment. We went south on the freeway, then cut off on dusty side roads until we found the place. It was a little oasis: a creek overhung with trees, miles from any other people. I took the LSD tab the first day, while Freda remained on guard against an unlikely intrusion by strangers. All the visual display, with its gorgeous revolving colors, turned on for me. Wild, fantastic, creative thoughts surged through my mind. Then I looked at Freda, sunning her muscular young body in the nude. As I watched, her body became incredibly old and shriveled. I thought rather severely that nobody that ancient should display her body naked. It wasn't pleasing to the eye.

Then I looked at my own firm hand and saw that it too had become old and withered. I knew then that somehow, in not being fully in the world, I had cheated myself out of my youth and, in fact, my maturity. "Nobody," I vowed to myself, "is going to cheat me out of the experience of growing old!"

During the next months, however, I found that I was not willing to put up with the increasing appearance of age on my face. Though I was only fifty-one and my body was still firm and trim, the skin was beginning to sag alarmingly under my chin and around my eyes. I had lately had some rather extensive, and expensive, dental work done, replacing the removable bridges I'd worn since my thirties with neat fixed ones. My dentist had hypnotized me before doing some of the surgical work with me, and it hadn't hurt a bit, so I'd come to trust him.

He told me about other patients of his who had had facelifts with a particular doctor. "He is a miracle worker!" he enthused. "There are photographs in his office of his own father and mother actually looking young after he operated on them." It sounded like a fine idea to me. Tony and I lived very conservatively and Ronn and Laana had long been paying their own way, so I had enough money saved. Tony was supportive. When I returned to work six weeks after the operation, a number of people commented on how well I looked, and how much good such a lengthy vacation had obviously done me. No one seemed to suspect that I'd had a facelift, and I didn't mention it.

∞ ∞ ∞ ∞ ∞

I also decided that, instead of going on another boring European tour for a couple of weeks, I wanted to go to Maine to study Sensory Awareness with Charlotte Selver. Tony didn't want to do that, but he easily agreed with my change of plan, though he must have been disappointed.

Charlotte Selver was then close to seventy, a small, authoritarian woman with bright brown eyes, straight-cut brown hair and a rather shapeless body. She spoke with a strong accent of her native Germany, where she had learned the techniques of sensory awareness she was now teaching with growing success in America. Her own teacher, Elsa Gindler, had largely taught herself.

The story was that as a young physical therapist in Germany, Gindler had contracted deadly tuberculosis, in one lung. Her doctor commented that if it were possible to rest that lung and use only the other one for six months, she would recover. By tuning in to her body with infinite care, she had actually been able to shut down the diseased lung and permit it to heal. Building on that experience, she had discovered how people could learn to feel the most subtle movements and perceptions in their own bodies, simply by paying attention to them.

"Feel the flatness of your shoulder blades," Charlotte would encourage us. "How far is it between the tips? Can you feel them moving against your ribs as you turn your body?" She would have the class feeling the different textures of the flooring with bare feet, or lifting a partner's head with infinite patience to see how far it could easily go. Sometimes we listened carefully to the slowly diminishing tones of a small gong, or spent several minutes really tasting a segment of orange. After periods of this kind of work my chattering mind often quieted and a sense of focused calm came over me.

Not all of the two weeks at Monhegan Island, which I stretched to four, were so peaceful. In this new environment I found that my old feelings of rejection had not left, even though the dynamics were now much clearer. One afternoon, for instance, Charlotte castigated me for not taking the work seriously enough. In my room that night I felt increasingly depressed, until I suddenly saw quite clearly that I was deliberately making myself feel worse, just as I had done with my mother. I was hoping that Charlotte would see how bad I felt and be willing to be friendly again. Then I was able to laugh at myself.

That fall Tony began to be more resentful of my preoccupation with what was coming to be known as personal growth work. He refused to attend most social occasions with my new professional friends, and was uncomfortable when he did. For myself, I became all too aware of the rigidity of his thinking and behavior. My life was opening up, and he did not seem to be interested in making any changes in himself since he had given up trying to find transcendence.

"Grow old along with me," Tony had quoted to me years before, "the best is yet to be." I had recoiled at his words. I had a lot of new things to do before I was ready to grow old, and Tony now seemed determined to remain exactly as he was for the rest of his life. One day I was complaining to him again about his lack of interest or participation in my new life. He said coldly, "Well, if you don't like it, why don't you just leave?"

And I did, though not without private reluctance and tears. I stayed for several weeks with my friend

Serena, a psychologist from the Gestalt group at work, before I rented an apartment of my own. I let Tony buy my share of the house, since he wanted it and I didn't. It took five years after our divorce for Tony to forgive me. After that we remained on friendly terms for the rest of his life. I never stopped being fond of him. At times when I was particularly lonely, I would wonder whether I should go back to him. When I listened within, however, I always got a clear "no." So I didn't.

Chapter 6   Arica

During my fourth year at the Neuropsychiatric Institute, I finally admitted to myself that, though my colleagues and I functioned better, we were not much happier or more loving than our clients were. Certainly I was not. In addition to my Subud experiences, I'd managed to get a Bachelor's degree, a Masters in Social Work, and a profession. I'd explored hypnotism and done many different kinds of inner investigations with Freda. I'd discovered what I was really feeling, over and over again, with Gestalt. I was unquestionably doing better in my life, but I was not happy, or getting anywhere near the transcendent spaces I'd touched briefly earlier in my life. I tried returning to Subud, but got the message, "There is nothing here for you." I took it calmly: it was what I expected.

I investigated other teachings, sometimes with Freda. Ida Rolf was just becoming known through her workshops at Esalen, so Freda and I went to a Rolfing weekend. As explained to us, Rolfing (later called Structural Integration) aimed to align and integrate the body so that it could function more fully. For that to happen, Ida said, the fascia between the muscles had to be freed by physical manipulation. We were disappointed that she did not demonstrate her new method, but only described it. She told us that the work took ten individual sessions and was extremely painful, though the results were worth it. Since I wasn't aware of how constricted my body was nor how that might contribute to my psychological constrictions, I wasn't much interested in Rolfing; and Ida's manner tended to be dictatorial in my mother's German fashion.

I tried a few sessions of meditation under the tutelage of a monk newly arrived from Japan. When I quieted my thoughts by counting my breaths as he instructed, my mind went into a neutral space that seemed neither positive nor negative, but simply blank. As I complained to a friend, "I just sat there in my body, with nothing going on at all." It didn't seem very interesting to me and the monk didn't speak English well enough for me to ask him questions, so I quit this too.

I attended workshops in Gestalt therapy given by several other teachers, wanting to learn how their styles differed from that of Jim Simkins. Most Gestalt therapists, I found, were kinder than Jim. (When Jim and I met at a psychology conference some ten years later, we both said almost simultaneously, "But you have grown so much softer!")

During my fourth year at NPI, I saw an ad about a weekend workshop in Arica, claiming that its teachings lead easily to higher states of consciousness. Arica was described as a physical, mental, emotional and spiritual training, the creation of a Chilean man named Oscar Ichazo, who had spent years studying at monasteries and ashrams around the world. I learned later that a well-known workshop leader and writer, Claudio Naranjo who was also Chilean, had met Oscar on a trip back to South America. Naranjo had been so excited by Oscar's teachings that he made a circuit of the growth centers springing up in the United States, rounded up about fifty of their members, and went with them to the small town of Arica in Chile, to study with Oscar for nine months. Afterwards, a dozen of those same students went to New York City to teach what they had learned. They gathered their first class by placing a full-page ad in the *New York Times*: "'Satori,' for three months and three thousand dollars!" (Satori, as I understood it, is a Hindu word for an authentic experience of the Eternal.) They were offering weekend workshops in New York to demonstrate his teachings.

The first weekend Arica workshop I attended was at Elysium, a growth center near Los Angeles. I had never been there but had heard that they practiced nudism. I didn't have anyone I could bring to a place like that (Freda had left NPI and gone off on her own adventures) so I registered by mail and drove to the secluded "ranch" in the foothills.

It looked like it had been a real ranch at one time, with its low-lying big wooden house. It also had a swimming pool, and several of the outlying buildings were used for workshops. There was shrubbery and colorful bougainvillea everywhere. Nervous as always among strangers, I entered the small, pleasant meeting room and hardly glanced at the others attendees. I took the only unoccupied cushion on the floor and found myself seated between two tall, personable older men. To my pleasant surprise, I became aware as the day went on that they were both flirting with me.

George Seaton was a thin, good-looking fellow with an English accent and an Oxford background. He was a divorced, dropped-out engineer who had been experimenting with different kinds of psychotherapy, bodywork and meditation. The other was a big, sturdy, balding man who was a vacationing professor of English at NYU. He turned out to be gay, which didn't stop him from making overtures to me. On a daylong hike several days later, he told me that he wasn't having much success with young men any more. Several of his friends had partnered successfully with boyish-looking women as they got older, and pairing up with me seemed like a possibility to him. It certainly didn't to me. And I hadn't been told that I looked boyish since I was ten years old!

When the exercises called for partners, they both turned to me, but George was the one I responded to. The whole group reached some instant highs by chanting together and doing interactional processes. Then we did physical exercises out in the sunshine, shedding our clothes bit by bit; during the afternoon we entered the warm baths. George and I kissed tentatively, without otherwise touching each other. He assured me that we were playing the "man-woman game." I was both puzzled and excited. The idea of being sexual at the beginning of a relationship was new to me. A decade before, I had watched the "flower children" from a rather astonished distance.

The three or four leaders were casual and friendly to everyone, and seemed very peaceful and at-home with themselves and with each other. Toward evening they told us of going to the seaside town of Arica in Chile and studying for nine months with Oscar Ichazo. They had learned how to reach higher states of consciousness easily. They explained that we could learn it too, by investing three months of our time and three thousand dollars. It sounded attractive although entirely impractical. I had come out of my divorce from Tony with slightly less than nine thousand dollars.

I saw George again at a second Arica workshop a month later. We gravitated toward each other immediately. That night he spread our sleeping bags in an empty room and made love to me. I was shaking. It was the first time I'd slept with anyone other than Tony in fifteen years. But George was both assertive and gentle, and though I didn't feel much response to him, it was all very exciting to me. I went peacefully to sleep that night, and woke the next morning with the certain knowledge that I was going to take the Arica training with him that summer.

The next weekend George came to my house. I had a couple of tabs of LSD a friend had given me. I'd only tried LSD once before with Freda, and George didn't have much experience with drugs either, so we had a big breakfast beforehand. For a long time nothing happened, but eventually the changes in colors and shapes and feelings started for both of us. George told me he could see my essence and asked if I could see his. At first I saw only his shining curly dark hair with a touch of gray, his aquiline nose and merry, testing, dark eyes. Then suddenly I actually saw *him*, not in relation to me, but as a totally separate human being in his own right. I was dumbfounded and fascinated.

I asked my boss at NPI for an unpaid leave for the summer months from my job as a Social Work Field Instructor, saying that I wanted to take some specialized training in San Francisco. He said that people who took extended leave made him nervous because they tended not to come back. I assured him that I would. It wasn't that I lied, or actually believed I would return. I simply did not think about the end of the summer. My future, beyond the Arica training, didn't exist.

I hadn't felt such a wild, spontaneous upsurge of joy since my mother and I attended Easter sunrise services at the Hollywood Bowl when I was sixteen. Then, the exuberance was unbelievable but lasted only a few minutes. This time it lasted for weeks. I discovered that it is actually possible to feel as if there is champagne bubbling in one's bloodstream. I decided that my inner guidance was telling me that something wonderful was going to happen. (Much later I realized that feelings of joy are in response to what is happening now; they aren't about the future.)

George and I drove to San Francisco. Caring little where we lived as long as it was cheap and in the city, we rented an ill-furnished apartment on the fifth floor of an old brick apartment house on Fillmore Avenue, between the black and the international sections of the city. We walked around in the brilliant early summer weather, feeling the sea breezes and leftover dampness of the fog. I was excited and joyful, and also scared: I was aware that George was eyeing every pretty young woman who passed.

In the morning, we took a streetcar to the Arica headquarters on the second floor of a big, old office building at the corner of Second and Market Streets downtown. There were fresh flowers all around, and a huge image of the octagonal blue, gold and mauve Arica symbol covered one wall. Four or five young people, easy to identify as staff by their cheerful and insouciant manner and general air of well being, were taking signatures and sending people for interviews. Others, men with long hair and Indian shirts or girls with even-longer hair and bright-colored gypsy dresses, were members of the class just beginning. There was no sign of the varied group that had taken the workshop at Elysium. My anxiety skyrocketed.

On the second day the class officially started. We met in a big, newly painted room with many windows looking out on other downtown buildings and rooftops. There were seventy-six of us and when we spread out to begin the prescribed physical exercises, we got in each other's way. I was dressed too warmly, expecting a cold San Francisco summer. The sea of strange, youthful faces all around me—whispering together, greeting each other with glad cries and long, warm, loving hugs—continued to alarm me.

I went out during the lunch period to buy a couple of lightweight blouses for the sunny eighty-five degree day. As my bus passed Fourth St., I heard a band of young people with shaven heads and orange robes rattling tambourines and chanting, "Hare Krishna, Hare Krishna." The bus driver, sweating in his crumpled blue uniform, snorted to me, "Crazy kids! They belong in a booby hatch." I murmured an agreement.

Twenty minutes later, in the big, second floor hall that the Arica staff had rented for the summer, I sat cross-legged on a round cushion called a zafu, chanting "Hare Krishna! Hare Krishna!" A couple of the staff rattled tambourines. Our so-far-unseen leader, Oscar Ichazo, was quoted as saying, "If you can learn to meditate in downtown San Francisco you can meditate anywhere"

It was clear that I wasn't with George in the sense of being a couple, even though we were living together. We were both in an unknown world, where the past was not relevant and we were signed up to learn new ways of being.

107

We had agreed to have no expectations of each other. Neither of us was ever entirely sure we wouldn't have been better off with someone else, but neither of us wanted to be alone. And, in fact, we spent our nights and most of our weekends together that summer.

It didn't occur to me to bring any of the psychology I'd learned to bear on this novel situation. I had left behind family, friends, home, and work—my entire hard-won adult identity. I was alone in San Francisco with a man who lived with me and made love to me, but often seemed to resent me. We lived in a bare apartment without a familiar object in it; we were doing activities whose purpose I could seldom discern with a group of people who felt alien to me. The Arica leaders were serene and dedicated, without apparent difficulties of any kind—and unreachable. I realized later that they were doing exercises in their minds that allowed them to be so completely objective. Those exercises were what we had come to learn.

The leaders seemed to derive great satisfaction from their interactions with each other. During the breaks they would sit or lie on pillows on the floor with their arms around each other: men or women, it didn't seem to matter. They were always caressing each other, grinning knowingly and whispering lovingly. Most of the students began to imitate their ways, even those who hadn't been familiar with such behavior before. Many, I learned, were from Esalen and this had become a way of life to them. It certainly wasn't for me.

Chanting was a big part of the course, as were strenuous physical exercises, even more strenuous psychological exercises, and many forms of meditation. We met from ten in the morning to eight o'clock in the evening on weekdays, and were instructed to be in "objective silence" on Saturdays. Objective silence meant that one did not say anything to anyone except for such necessary requests as, "Please pass the salt." I found it to be wonderfully restful. George couldn't stand it. After several attempts at a silent day together, I reluctantly agreed to ignore the rule in order to keep peace between us—and also to keep him from going off to find a more cooperative companion.

On Sunday mornings, we would climb a steep hill in Golden Gate Park, carrying as heavy a rock as we could manage and murmuring the Jesus Prayer, "Lord Jesus Christ, have mercy on me, a sinner." Not considering myself to be either a Christian or a sinner, it didn't make much sense to me, but not many of our activities did. It was, however, nice to be outdoors in a beautiful park.

I've lost my list of the almost ninety exercises we did, though some of them are unforgettable. One of our assignments was called Kiné rhythms. We sat on zafus; legs crossed and leaned sideways a bit to make it more difficult, as we chanted a complicated series of Hindu phrases. In rhythm with the chanting, we moved a small stone in a specific pattern in front of us, nine times without a pause. The idea was to do it as slowly and under as much control as possible. One of the leaders performed the whole thing in spectacularly slow motion to demonstrate. I never got close to matching him; even finishing the whole process nine times without a break was a triumph for me.

Another task I remember was to sit across from another student, silently repeating the words of a Buddhist mantra while my partner made insulting comments about me and my general appearance. Since most of the students were the age of my children, they could come up with a lot of comments that stung. Eventually I learned that focusing on my mantra, and letting their words flow past, allowed me to remain calm in the face of their thrusts. And I quite enjoyed insulting some of them back, though I chose more innocuous comments for those who seemed fragile.

We received almost no explanation of what the different exercises were expected to accomplish, or assistance when they didn't have much effect. Late in the summer, we did an exercise called Trespasso. Day after day we sat for fifteen minutes gazing at the left eye of the person in line across from us; a chime rang to tell us when to move on to the next person. We were supposed to make a psychic connection with the soul of the person, or maybe even see a past incarnation. I saw very little other than many different left eyes.

George and I tried LSD again a couple of times, and we smoked a lot of marijuana. The LSD led to the usual extraordinary visual effects and a wonderful, though passing, conviction that everything Arica taught was absolute truth. The second time, the LSD renewed the startling realization that not just George, but everyone else was a person all in himself with an entire life that did not include me. It seemed that I'd not been aware of that perception of people before. My change in perspective was so great that for a couple of days I went about wondering how other people saw each other: as undifferentiated from themselves or as separate and whole human beings? It seemed to me that there was no way of checking that out, because unless you had clearly gone from one to the other (as I had) it was impossible to know which view you were taking.

Our pot smoking eased my transition from monogamy, with a straight-arrow husband, to more colorful and enjoyable sex with my current widely-experienced partner. Sometimes, we would work together on assignments. Once, when we were supposed to be tracking down feelings of shame, a memory I'd vaguely remembered but never felt fully, came back with searing pain. I was eight years old and had matter-of-factly accepted the job of pushing a sack containing our neighbor's newborn kittens under water. (After all, I knew my big brothers drowned ours, though I'd never gotten to watch.) I experienced my mother's voice again, her horror when she found out what I'd done. "How could a little girl do something like that? How could you possibly have been so cruel? Have you no conscience, no morals, no concern for the poor little kittens? Shame! Shame!" I had never let myself feel my devastation at her reaction. George held me gently until I quit sobbing and shaking, then he made me a cup of tea.

One evening midway through the course, after we had smoked a lot of pot, I began to hear an audible hallucination. A strange, high-pitched, nastily querulous female voice sounded clearly in my head. It berated me, accusing me of all the things I was actually doing: leaving my husband, my home and my professional life, shacking up with a man I hardly knew, taking this crazy and costly course with a bunch of people half my age, having no sensible plans for the future. I'd never consciously thought that perhaps these were bad things to do; they were just what I was doing. The voice which I had heard only once, ten years before, when I'd been so outspoken about the book we were reading in class, kept on and on, savagely accusing me of my "sins." This time, since I had no intention of stopping anything I was doing, I simply turned her off by no longer smoking pot.

Some wonderful experiences also surfaced during the Arica course. Once, during a guided meditation on breathing, while trying to follow their instructions, I suddenly ecstatically felt my breath happening of itself, moving throughout my body; each element of my belly, diaphragm, and lungs was as clear as if I actually existed as each organ, in its turn. When a voice in my mind whispered "You're doing it wrong," the experience stopped abruptly.

Another evening, we were sitting in circles of nine as the leader led us through a visualization that started with where we were and eventually reached the outermost reaches of the Universe. Each part of the exercise began with a long series of "Oms." At the end, I was suddenly lifted out of myself, tremulous, filled with ardent love for all beings. When it was over, I found myself joyously exchanging hugs with the people around me.

Sitting opposite Oscar Ichazo during our only individual interview, I was amazed to see something that looked like a half-inch wide strip of light outlining his body. It was bright yellow, as clear and distinct as a neon tube. He was telling me that my face revealed to him that I needed to clear up my relationships with both my mother and my father. I agreed submissively, too astonished both by the strip of light (which didn't look like any aura I'd ever heard of) and his prescience about my parents, to ask any questions. I never asked questions of the leaders: I was too embarrassed by my unwarranted ignorance of these matters.

Early in the course, as my resistance to the whole Arica experience was crystallizing, I had a dream. A group of us were milling around in our meeting room. There was a weird contraption in the middle: a bunch of harnesses swung from the arms of a central axis as if to attach oxen to a grindstone. There were people shackled into most of the harnesses, going round and round. Some of the leaders were lounging around the sides of the room on big, colorful pillows, laughing together. A couple of them were encouraging us to let ourselves be fitted into the harnesses. In the dream I was resistant to this obvious subjection and yet reluctantly permitted myself to be shackled. The instant the bonds fastened around me, I was completely and deliciously free. Nothing constrained me at all. I was welcome to walk over and join the leaders, or to go flying out the window if I chose. My dream had produced an extraordinary metaphor for the training as it was meant to be.

It was our work on parents, however, that led to an experience I still treasure. We were instructed to sit for half an hour, starting at midnight in a room lit only by three candles placed in a triangle before us, and to do three nights of this for each parent. With each outbreath we were to say, "I send you my good will." At the end of the three nights devoted to my mother, I found myself overflowing with love and compassion for her, imaging her in my arms, gladly exchanging forgiveness.

It was more difficult to send good will to my father, who had deserted us so callously when I was three. My first teeth-gritted statement was, "I send you my good will wherever you are in Hell!" Over the next three nights, as my mood softened, I expected to feel love and compassion

113

for him, too. Instead, after completing the work, I felt myself surrounded and embraced by the purest, strongest, most beautiful sense of being totally loved that I have ever known. It seemed to permeate both me and the atmosphere around me, as if I were being held in a cocoon of love and safety. Miraculously, it was still there when I awoke the next morning. The sense of being completely surrounded by love continued for a few days before it slowly diminished, leaving me convinced that, even though we were parting, I was in love with George. Though I didn't then make the connection between my feelings for my father and my feelings for George, I knew that separating after our three months of Arica was somehow foreordained.

The grand finale of the course was called "the Desert." In Chile the students had been sent out into the real desert for three days in solitude, with only what they could carry for food, water and shelter. Since this wasn't practical in the middle of San Francisco, our instructions were to gather supplies and retreat alone into a room where we were to chant and do breathing exercises and meditation.

On the day before we were to start, I was in a little local Italian grocery store buying trail-mix and other things to see me through. Suddenly, totally unexpectedly, I felt my will power as if it were a living force— a liquid draining out of my body— leaving my chest, my pelvis and my legs and going out through my feet. I was left in a strange state of emptiness, as if a distinct part of me had gone. I continued following instructions like an automaton, not exactly frightened but numbly puzzled.

This strange state continued all during the three days and nights of the Desert. I stayed obediently in my impersonal, poorly furnished room, with its dun-colored walls and tattered shades drawn. I chanted, did the exercises, ate and slept mechanically, feeling more and more bereft. Nothing happened; I experienced no contact with anything. Finally the agony of disappointed expectations, of getting nothing out of so much struggle and effort, was too much. On the last evening, I suddenly realized that I could keep on agonizing or I could stop worrying about the whole thing. So I gave up completely and went peacefully to sleep.

The next morning the expected knock on the door came, when one of the leaders visited me to end the Desert. A tall, clean-cut young man I hardly knew entered. We sat facing each other and I told him calmly and frankly that the whole thing had been a bust. He responded only, "Look into my eyes and tell me what you see." I looked into his dark, level gaze and heard myself say, "Power." He nodded silently and left. Later I learned that whatever we saw in the eyes of the person who came to break our Desert was considered to be a projection of our own state at that moment. Apparently, by finally surrendering, I had reached a state of peace and power but didn't recognize it.

The next morning, the leaders told us that they had received a million dollars in grant money and would hire any of us who wanted to become a trainer and spread this knowledge. Some of my experiences during the summer had been so unusual and compelling that, even though the idea of quitting my secure position at NPI scared me, I accepted. Young people were going to India in droves, seeking adventure and transcendence. San Francisco in the summer of 1972 was my India.

I went back to Los Angeles to close down my apartment and to quit my job at NPI, and then I returned to San Francisco. A lot of the class had also accepted, though most of them didn't have jobs to quit. We were paid a perfectly adequate living wage of $1000 a month for doing little but additional exercises, since we didn't have any students. George and I split up as we had planned; he moved in with one of the other women students. I moved to Mill Valley, across the Golden Gate Bridge in Marin County, with six other Aricans (none of whom I knew). It was a beautiful big old house among towering redwood trees, but I took little pleasure in it. My housemates were all young and as totally enwrapped in their own experiences as I was in mine. I couldn't relate to any of them. I had permitted my never-too-strong image of myself as a competent, respected professional woman to be completely destroyed and all that I seemed to be left with was a scared child in a middle-aged woman's body.

I am not sure that what I tasted for brief moments during my three months in the San Francisco Arica class was Satori; I had experienced enough dramatic shifts in consciousness to be enthralled, and I had had moments that might have been Satori, glimpses of another way of being. Whatever they were, those experiences seemed totally unrelated to my current life. The heights I had touched during the summer vanished. The further training I engaged in, intended to break us through to more self-honesty and group cohesion, resulted in my feeling more isolated and at sea. During that summer we had done many arcane and dramatic exercises intended to undermine our ego structures. The idea was that we would learn to act objectively, rather than from our customary mental and

116

emotional reactions. The "ego reduction," intention of the training, however, became ego destruction for me and probably for many others.

Only a few times during this period did I experience something truly remarkable. As I drove across the bridge one morning to my job on the reception desk, while chanting the mantra, "I am empty," my head disappeared. It was an extraordinary experience. Without warning, there seemed to be nothing physically existent above the level of my shoulders. My thoughts were carrying on in pure space. It occurred to me that anyone could simply put a hand through the place where my head had been and would encounter no obstacle. (I admit that it did not occur to me to try.) Along with my head had disappeared all reactions to, or considerations about, the world around me. I parked the car and slowly walked a couple of blocks to the Arica offices, rather amazed but not frightened. As I went up in the elevator I found myself becoming more normal, but not quite. When I took a phone call from one of the leaders, he began yelling at me: apparently I wasn't making any sense.

I didn't tell anyone about that experience for months because it didn't fit anything I'd ever heard of. As far as I could tell, it had no aftereffects other than adding to my personal knowledge that states of consciousness so totally "other" that they were beyond imagining were possible for human beings. (Some years later I was fascinated to discover Douglas Harding's little book *On Having No Head*, describing almost the same experience as I had had. He had made an entire teaching out of his.)

A month later I drove to Yosemite for the weekend with a young man who was also in the training. (He was the only person of the six who had planned to take the trip with

117

me who hadn't changed his mind.) It was late October on a weekend between rainstorms, and the beautiful park was almost empty of tourists. I went off by myself and wandered near the bottom of Yosemite Falls. I sat there for more than an hour, feeling lost and miserable amid all the beauty and grandeur, and flung questions at the rocks and trees, "What's it all about? What shall I do now?"

Suddenly I felt the physical sensation of having my consciousness move abruptly from the left side of my head to the right side, putting me in a clear space of peace and joy. After a startled moment of relief, it occurred to me that I could probably go back. I experimented with moving my consciousness to the left side of my head, and misery immediately engulfed me. Hastily I leapt back to the right side and was once again serene and joyful. The beauty of the falls, the vivid colors of the flowers and trees and rocks—all came back to life. I breathed the scented air gratefully and rejoiced in the warmth of the sun. This blissful mood continued for the remaining two days of the trip. It finally eroded as we drove out of the valley, when I was swamped by the unhappy mood of my young companion. He had had no such experience.

There was a lot of politicizing and dissension between our San Francisco Arica staff and the new leaders who had come from New York. Several weeks after that extraordinary summer, a story was passed around that Oscar was overheard mourning aloud that his teachings were intended to reduce the ego, but most of his closest followers had only achieved bigger ones. Having some pretty negative feelings myself about most of the teachers, I could believe it.

In one extraordinary session, they demanded that each of us stand in front of the rest of the group and swear that we would put no other concern above Arica. One man refused indignantly and walked out. I thought about having the courage to do the same and decided that if they were silly enough to ask for such an oath, I was under no obligation to be honest with them. I made the statement without meaning it, simply wanting to find out what happened next. Shortly afterwards, the leaders announced that three-quarters of us would-be trainers were to be laid off. It was a relief to have an excuse to part with the insanity that my Arica experience had become.

Chapter 7   The Fischer/Hoffman Process

Shortly after I left Arica, I met Freda strolling down a
street in San Francisco. Over lunch I told her that I
needed to find a place to live. She said she knew of a
recently divorced woman judge who wanted the
companionship of mature women in her big house across
the bay in Oakland. I went to see the judge immediately
and found my new home. She and I agreed that we would
accept only women over forty as housemates. It worked
out amazingly well: each of the women knew how to run a
household and willingly took turns cooking and cleaning.
We called the house "Textaxi," from the letters its phone
number spelled out.

I missed the excitement and promise of the Arica
summer, though, and stayed open to other possibilities.
Freda's new partner, a psychiatrist named Lee Sanella, told
me about two women who had a practice called "Massage
to Music." He said that his session with them had led to the
only authentic past-life experience he had ever had, so I
went to see them. Their method was a deep massage that
felt as if it went across the muscles rather than with them,
while evocative classical music played on the tape recorder.

I became a woman in the last century, taking my
young son across the ocean from England to join my
husband in India. The ship foundered; I was flung into the
ocean and I could see the huge ship's hulk sinking. I clung

to the leg of an upended table with one arm, while clutching my son with the other. I didn't have the strength to continue hanging onto both the floating table and the child. A terrible decision, for we would both drown if I let go of the table, and I couldn't be sure that my child was still alive. Then I was alone and dead, floating in the endless sea. I sobbed, heartbroken, for ten minutes.

Perhaps it was a past life, but I saw my melancholy imagery as a metaphor for my current life: the ship of Arica had floundered, George was dead to me, and I was alone without a solid connection to either my ordinary functional personality, or to the part of me that had experienced radiant epiphanies during my summer of Arica training.

A few weeks later, another disenchanted Arica student called to tell me of a group called SAT (Seekers after Truth) led by Claudio Naranjo, which was described as "Arica with heart." Claudio was the teacher who had brought the contingent of fifty young seekers to Chile to study with Oscar Ichazo. Rumors hinted that Oscar had drummed him out of the group, when Claudio came back from his experience of the Desert saying that he had found enlightenment and no longer needed Oscar as a teacher. I joined Seekers after Truth immediately. Claudio's teachings were like Arica work, but had both heart and a strong admixture of the Gestalt psychology that he had taught before joining Arica.

Claudio was lean and intense and engaging, and he had the affection and trust of the young people who followed him. He had been in the United States long enough to be seen as an entirely normal (albeit enlightened) person. It was his intention to teach people how to connect with others, and how to learn and grow together, which is what had happened in the first SAT group. Many of them remained close friends, deeply involved with each other's lives years after ending their work with SAT. By the time I joined, however, the classes were much larger and less intimate, but still much more human and accessible than the Arica training had been.

I was living in a pleasant home with compatible adult women, none of whom had been in SAT or Arica. In 1973, the almost $1000 a month I was getting in unemployment was enough to live on comfortably in a communal house like ours. I wasn't interested in getting a job, and none of the bored clerks at the Unemployment Bureau where I reported each week seemed to care whether I was looking for a job or not.

Claudio told us that we could continue to work with him over the coming summer, or we could sign up for a different three-month course he highly recommended. This other course was structured so that it was amazingly effective in helping participants separate emotionally from their parents. I was immediately interested, as none of the previous psychological work I had done had focused on my relationships with my parents.

I remembered a time when, just out of high school in 1939, I'd gone as my friend Jean's guest to her junior college night class in psychology. The instructor posed the question, "What would happen to children if they could be brought up with no contact with adults?" I had grown excited and was whispering so urgently to Jean that the teacher noticed and invited me to give an answer, even though I wasn't a member of the class.

"They wouldn't have any emotional problems at all!" I blurted out. The instructor laughed and told me I was wrong. He cited an experiment, reputedly done by a curious monarch in the seventeenth century, who had had a group of orphaned babies cared for physically, but without any human interaction or speaking. His goal was to find out what language they would use naturally. The experiment was not completed, for all the babies died.

I admitted that the teacher was probably right, that some kind of parenting was necessary for children to become adults. But I was convinced that I was right, too. At seventeen, I had known that children learn many of their destructive ideas and harmful values from their parents. I decided to pay the $400 fee and take the Fischer/Hoffman Process, in the hope that it would "cure" me of my father's and mother's bad influences.

The class was held in a classroom on the University of California Berkeley campus. Forty people showed up that first night, and I was relieved to see many ordinary looking adults among the young hippies who usually crowded classes in this kind of nontraditional work. At 7:10 pm, Bob Hoffman strode up to the lectern, a middle-aged man in a carefully tailored gray suit, a little fleshy but solid. His darkish blonde hair had been cut by an expert; he had a high-colored, slightly pudgy face and a self-confidant manner. He moved like a boxer, a bit forward on his toes, as if he were ready to take on anyone who might confront him. He announced that we would wait for another couple from Palo Alto, some 40 miles away. Indignation joined my doubts and hesitations. Why should forty of us wait for two?

I learned later that the husband of the couple we were waiting for was a psychiatrist and Bob was eager to have him and his wife in our class. I no longer thought of myself as a professional in mental health, so it didn't occur to me that Bob, with no degrees of his own, might also be glad to have me in the class. We waited restlessly for forty-five minutes until a well dressed couple in their forties, flushed with haste and embarrassment, arrived and our session began.

"Good evening, neurotics!" Bob boomed out cheerfully, waiting a beat till we got the impact of his greeting. "Anyone who is still in (negative) love with either of his parents is a neurotic!" He went on to say, "The Fischer/Hoffman Process will be a bittersweet experience, a period of hell during which you will hate me as well as your parents! But you will find peace and joy and love by the end." He assured us that, until we learned to love ourselves, it was wishful thinking that we could love others. "The fourth part of your 'Quadrinity' of body, intellect, and spirit is an emotional child who has never matured past puberty," he said. "You are therefore at war with yourself, and in pain. We will re-educate your child so it can mature to its actual age, which will stop the war and end your pain."

During the Fischer/Hoffman Process we would go through several stages: We would "prosecute" both Mother and Father for the crimes they committed in raising us to be both unloving and neurotic. When our anger against them was released, we would then defend them because we would see how they, too, had been programmed by their parents. Ultimately we would achieve complete forgiveness of our parents, bringing an end to the war between our intellectual adult and our emotional child. "By the closing session," he promised, "we would love our parents, have compassion for them, and be able to

125

genuinely love ourselves". His cocksure manner grated, but his ideas rang so true that I couldn't understand why most people didn't see things his way. It would be years before much of what he said about the "child within" was taken for granted in mainstream psychological circles.

"You learned your negativities from your parents," he pounded home, "because they modeled them for you, or because they deliberately taught you to behave a certain way, or because you rebelled against them and did the opposite of what they wanted." He held up his hands, linking the index fingers and pulling them back and forth to demonstrate the bind we were in. "When you try to love your parents, your anger at what they have done to you won't let you. And yet, when you are righteously angry with them, your positive feelings toward them won't let you be truly angry either. You need to feel your anger completely; then, and only then, will you be able to become truly loving."

As he went on, I grew more excited: I was being given permission to explore how resentful I felt at both my mother and father. Bob was promising me a way to see and to break free from all the negative effects they had had on me. The episodes of loving them so deeply during the Arica work seemed now to exist on another planet. And, for the first time, a therapy made complete sense to me.

A small, dark haired woman interrupted him, her voice high and angry. "If I'm expected to love the father who used to amuse himself by beating the crap out of my mother and me, I won't take this Process!" Without answering her directly, he was suddenly gentle and understanding. He talked about how self destructive it is to live all our lives with such feelings of rage. She quieted, and said that she would wait to see what happened. He spoke of the overriding need every child has for a parent's love and acceptance, in the hope of which we adopt their ways of acting. He talked about how deprived of love we were, when our true nature is to love and be loved. I put aside my immediate thoughts about my relationship with my own children to focus on past interactions with my parents.

We all diligently took notes for the homework we were expected to produce in three days. It started with "Describe your ideal man or woman," followed by "Consider two trees, one whose seed has fallen on rich earth, with plenty of water and is sheltered from the winds to become flourishing and beautiful. The other barely survives on the shallow ledge of a mountainside, lashed by winds, with little nourishment, and is stunted and barely clinging to life. Which tree are you?" and concluded with, "How much do you want to be done with the negativities in your life?"

In answer to the last question I wrote, "Even though I say 'more than anything in the world,' I am full of doubts. A large part of the story of my life is a lack of conviction and commitment. I will try to ignore the doubts and do this with my full will. I am sick of my recurring depressions. I want to give up criticizing myself and other people all the time, but I wonder if it is possible."

We were told to list as many of our parents' negative traits, moods and silent and overt admonitions as we could remember. I came up with dozens. I had known for a long time how bitterly I resented my mother's and father's negative influences on me. Now I had permission to blame them for all the things that were wrong with me.

127

When I arrived at the next class, I was handed Bob's taped half-hour response to the pages I had sent him. It was fascinating to hear him speak directly to me on the tape, responding to the paragraphs I had written: "Good, you understand that perfectly. Look how many of your mother's traits are ones of self-doubt and distrust of everything around her. Do you see the connection between that and your own doubts? How could you trust yourself, or me?" He read back phrases from my description of an ideal woman as "a quiet, sustained joy . . . with faith in herself and in the order of things . . . with the gift of intimacy . . . and a sense of her own power and worth," and asked, "Isn't it too bad that at fifty-two you have not learned how to be that person?" I felt tears start in my eyes, and heard his next words with sudden hope: "But you will be, darling. You'll see."

After we put away our tape recorders the second session began, with more insistence on total dedication and commitment. He talked more about the goals of the work—to find out who and what we really were. To be able to give for the pleasure of giving, not just because we hoped to get our own needs fulfilled. We had all shown in our notes, he said, what kind of negative programming we had. Some of us were "goody-goodies," who were parroting him, some were "hostiles," who were angry with him, and some were "zombies," showing no feelings at all.

He talked about the uses of anger and told us that we would learn how to recycle its explosive force into constructive energy: "When you really see what you are angry about, and give yourself permission to experience your righteous anger fully, it will burn itself out." That sounded good to me, for I was very aware of the incomprehensible rages that sometimes erupted in me.

He took us on a guided visualization to a beautiful, peaceful natural scene. I am not good at visualizing, but I got the impression of soft green grass and overarching trees with a beautiful river nearby. I could feel the warmth of the sun and the caress of the soft, flower-scented breezes. When he evoked the presence of a guide, I got an image of a youthful male figure, tall, lean and graceful. His wide-set eyes looked at me lovingly, with serene good humor. Where did he come from? At other times in my life when I had experienced a strong presence of guidance and support, it had always felt feminine, although there had never been any image. "Jeremy" conveyed his name to me, and reassured me that he would be with me whenever I needed him. He seemed astonishingly real.

We were given a sixteen-page list of possible negative traits we had witnessed and admonitions we'd been given by our parents, either overtly or covertly. First we were to check off those that our mothers had displayed, and then we were to review the list a second time for characteristics that our fathers had displayed. I recognized dozens for my mother: dependency and unending anger at men, generalized hostility, the world is a dangerous place, nobody loves me, I'm not loveable, withholding, anxiety, unhappy, depressed, self-important, insensitive, superiority/inferiority, domineering, envious, self-conscious, and self-involved—her traits went on and on.

We were directed to write out the scenes in which our parents had displayed their negative traits and taught them to us. It wasn't an easy task; I hadn't ever thought of each scene's being a teaching for what I had become. We began to investigate our childhoods systematically, often through the use of imagery. What were holidays like, we were asked, and how about school? What messages did we get about sex? Until I relived those moments in detail, I could not imagine how strong were my girlish feelings as a child who did not get the love and approval she needed.

We were asked to write descriptions of dozens of these scenes as if they were happening right now, and to give them as much reality as possible. As I did so, I began to recognize how my needs had been ignored, my tender feelings trampled on, and my belief in myself destroyed. I could see how often I was frightened, hurt and angry.

As I explored my childhood, I found that blatantly traumatic happenings were not the whole story. Daily learning in hundreds of connected incidents drove those early lessons home, deeply and bitterly. It was only when I considered what I had learned, in seemingly unimportant events, that I could see the long term destructive consequences.

When my father chatted with my aunt at dinner and ignored my mother, I learned that men can't be trusted to be loyal. When my mother told me that I was better than the children who shunned me during our three-year stay in Massachusetts, I learned to feel superior as a way of protecting myself. These kinds of seemingly innocuous lessons had become ingrained attitudes in me that had lasted my lifetime.

Our recognitions were encouraged to surface without restriction, and without the need to invalidate the experience by considering our mothers' or fathers' sides of it. Bob pointed out that we could not really feel the painful emotions of childhood in our hearts, while at the same time holding in our heads that our parents loved us to the best of their ability. Attempting to do so could create a sort of internal paralysis.

Like many others in the class, I had forgotten much of what happened in my childhood and how it had affected me. Only as I wrote about the scenes and relived them did I begin to realize how complex the learning of childhood is. I hardly remembered my father, whom I scarcely knew after I was three, and not at all after I was six. I had never had conscious fantasies of him, but I remembered how desolately I had cried at eight years old, when I realized that Santa Claus wasn't real and would never come to our house.

I remembered myself at seven, sneaking up on my mother with a bunch of spring flowers I had picked for her, and how she had scolded me for startling her, saying that her nerves were so bad. Nervousness and wariness were thus modeled for me. I remembered a story she had told me about a time before I was born, when she and my father had to run away from an oil well fire that had broken out near their house. She had carried both my brothers, while my father carried his latest invention. I learned that fathers were callous and uncaring, and women had to take on the burdens of family. I also heard, and took into myself, her bitterness, self-pity and resentment as she told the tale.

As I wrote many such scenes, I began to feel righteous anger at my parents for having taught me so many lessons that led to my lifelong unhappiness. Then we were introduced to the "Bitch Sessions;" which were held in a place where it was okay to make lots of noise. We were instructed to imagine our mothers on a large pillow on the floor and to beat them with a plastic bat for all the

negativities they had taught us. I flunked "Mother Bitch."
All I could do was lean against the wall and cry. Bob
rushed up and pretended to inject a syringe full of anger
into my arm, but nothing happened except that I wished he
would go away. I didn't even get mad at him; I had gone
numb.

The next day, the dozen of us who had failed this
crucial step met in a large secluded private home. One of
the assistant teachers asked craftily, "How many of you felt
responsible for taking care of your mother when you were a
child?" Every one of us raised a hand. The sudden
realization that any overt anger against our mothers had
been forbidden to us as children freed us to get angry. One
after another broke into rage. I remember feeling that my
mother was a pair of glasses through which I saw the world
and smashing them to bits. Afterwards I felt amazingly
free and powerful.

When we got to father, I had no trouble getting
angry. Without hesitation, I tossed away the bat and
attacked the pillow with an imaginary knife. Gone was any
memory of the atmosphere of love I had lived in for three
days after doing the "sending good will to father" ritual at
the Arica training. I felt pure rage take over my body and I
killed him bloodily.

After we had "bitched" enough, and gone through
our anger to a true sense of power, the Process abruptly
changed direction. An imaginary deathbed scene was
created for our mothers and fathers. Our dying parents
whispered their last words of sorrow for how they had
treated us, the details of which were fresh in our minds
from our recent work, and they pleaded for forgiveness. By

then it was easy for us to take the next step into compassion, forgiveness and love for them.

In later sessions, through the guided imagery that Bob called "Mind Revelations," we experienced further dramatic and positive interactions with our mothers and fathers, and also with images of our own inner trinity of Emotional Child, Intellectual Adult and Spiritual Self.

Our next assignment was to write about how our parents had learned the negativities they had passed down to us from their parents, and also to write about the positive things that they had done and taught us. Knowing little about my mother's childhood and nothing about my father's, it was nevertheless clear to me that they had learned their behaviors from their parents, and that neither of them was to blame for my unhappiness, any more than I was.

I wrote that my mother was a good woman, who had stuck with her children and worked hard to support us. She had made sure that I went through high school. She had a sympathetic and hospitable side, loving and happy, with a capacity to enjoy life with almost childlike enthusiasm. I remembered the wonderful Christmases she managed to arrange; saving up for months to be sure my brothers and I had a few toys and some new clothes. When I was a little girl in Massachusetts, we celebrated in German style, the children never seeing the decorated tree until after a special Christmas Eve dinner, when the doors to the otherwise unused parlor would be opened to its candle-lit beauty. It was harder to find good things to say about my father, because we had parted so early. I wrote that he was sometimes loving before I was three, and that the vibrations he gave out were strong and vital and male.

Bob taught us a mental process he called "Recycling," which was remarkably effective for me. It involved my imagining the letters spelling out the negative trait I was experiencing as hanging on a clothesline in front of me. For instance, the letters of angry traits were often jagged and red; the letters of fearful traits were gray and tattered. Jeremy would appear, placing the letters in a big bag and proceeding to disintegrate them with powerful rays from his fingertips, until only tiny, sparkling seeds were left. Jeremy would sprinkle the seeds on the earth and beautiful flowers would sprout, spelling out the opposite of the negative trait I had wanted to change. Again and again I found that this worked for me; my mood would change and I would experience the new feeling the flowers spelled out.

In the two remaining weeks, I did guided image scenes of loving acceptance between my Intellectual Adult and Emotional Child, who had become real internal figures by this time, and my Spiritual Self, with Jeremy overseeing the whole process.

I found the "Final Therapy" session to be particularly dramatic and emotional, and I responded to the evocative music accompanying each step. We had been instructed to come dressed in white. As we entered, we were given a white flower by a smiling, white-clad assistant teacher. Bob wore a white suit. Our inner children grew to imagined adults, year by year. A trait-by-trait disintegration of our every negative trait and acceptance of its positive opposite was staged, and finally there were scenes of love and acceptance between our parents and ourselves.

At the end, when we were told to open our eyes and look around, many of us were dissolved in joyous tears. We hugged each other happily and gratefully, and toasted each other with champagne. A small part of me hung back, though, wondering if the positive effects of the Process would stay with me as I moved on into my "real life."

Chapter 8   Textaxi

Over the next few weeks, I became convinced that the Fischer/Hoffman Process had worked. I was able to drop my resentments toward my father and my mother for the ways they had treated me. I was happier than I had ever been. I felt strong, loving and open, with a sense of direction new to me.

I was sure that human beings could learn to function in a better way when the elements of their negative programming were dismantled. I decided that everybody was partially right: Freud, about the powerful influence of early childhood; Behavior Modification, in that behavior could be intentionally modified; and even Mary Baker Eddy, for her insistence on the unreality of what we thought to be immutable about ourselves. I began to see how different psychospiritual ideas fit together.

I also became aware of personal traits that I hadn't let myself acknowledge before, even though they had been laid out clearly a dozen years ago in Subud. Now that I could recognize them as learned in childhood, I knew that they were not my fault. I saw and accepted my negative feelings about my body and about men. I recognized the extent and viciousness of my self-criticism. It seemed that I could live in a new way. I wrote in my journal that I wanted to sing and dance, and be able to teach what I had learned to as many people as possible.

Two months later I took the training course to prepare students to be Fischer/Hoffman Process teachers. I was disappointed though. Bob Hoffman was both less loving and accepting than I had thought he was, and less knowledgeable. When one of the other would-be teachers asked him what to do about her loneliness, he suggested that she get together with other women and go to the movies.

Nevertheless, I was never again able to believe that my "negativities" were anything other than reactions learned in childhood. When I felt myself sliding back into anxiety or depression, I was able to come back to center by using the imagery we had learned in the Process.

I returned to being a mental health professional. I began to see psychotherapy clients, particularly those who had taken the Process but were still having problems. One of the psychiatrists who had been in my Process class, asked me to join him in teaching a group of his private patients. I was having a good time with the other women in our house, meeting interesting men and women who came to dinner, and enjoying those we invited to stay a while.

I began a beautiful sexual friendship with a man named Bill, an old friend of Freda's, who was now living in our community house. (Alas, we'd given up our only-women-over-forty rule.) Like my former loves, Ernst and George, Bill was engaging, warm, sexual, educated and intelligent—and unable to be monogamous and uninterested in learning. Since I thought that I could now love in a non-possessive way, this didn't bother me. When a new woman moved in and she and Bill began an ardent affair, however, I suddenly found myself in the hell of jealousy. I reasoned about it; I did imagery; I worked with hypnosis and body work; I talked with friends; meditated and visited spiritual teachers: all to no avail. Now that I had lost his sole attention, I felt myself to be in love with Bill, even though I was sure that I was again living out my pattern of yearning for my lost father.

My moods careened from the agony of watching him turn to other women, to the intense pleasure of having him back with me. I did my best to keep in mind that it was my own view of things that was making me miserable, and he was just being himself. I did notice that if the price of having Bill's love was being stuck with him for the rest of my life, I wouldn't be willing to pay it.

By mid-January I was determined to get past the jealousy that had taken over my life. What I wanted was the feeling of my authentic self that had been there for a short time during the Process and immediately after, but I couldn't seem to get it back. I knew that I was creating my present situation, but I couldn't figure out how to change it. I told myself over and over that there had to be a way to drop all these nonsensical feelings and find what was— real.

I went to see Marny, my brother's Walter's widow and my own beloved friend. Marny was living in Bishop, a little town east of the Sierras. After a few days in her presence, in the clean high desert air and away from the emotional hothouse Textaxi had become for me, my agitation calmed. Alone in the hills, I found a renewed connection to myself, and awareness of the strong presence of my guide, Jeremy. He told me to stop asking what I should do, and ask instead what God wanted me to do. I returned to San Francisco much comforted, though also feeling curiously remote: I was unsure what God wanted me to do.

Freda had discovered the pleasure of injecting Ketamine, a children's anesthetic, which when given to adults at one-tenth strength, allows access to non-ordinary states of consciousness. She and Lee came to share it with me a few days after I returned from the Sierras. Besides being a medical doctor, Lee had a deep interest in psychic phenomena and spiritual matters, and had written a book called *Kundalini: Psychosis or Transcendence?*

Shortly after Lee injected Ketamine into my arm, I became part of a design of elaborately changing colors, mostly purple and green, a strange, non-human form of existence. I knew Freda and Lee were there, but I had no sense of myself. There was no particular meaning to the experience; it was completely unworldly. As I started to come back, it seemed incomprehensible to me that human beings could have such experiences and still go through the emotional gyrations that we do. For days afterwards, I felt no anxiety or depression, but also no happiness or love, nor any cosmic awareness. I was back in the neutral place I had found so disappointing at the beginning of my meditation experiences.

Since the Ketamine hadn't had a salutary effect, Lee brought over a cylinder of high-concentrate oxygen, and instructed me on how to breathe it through a mask. He explained that I could simply take the mask off if the experience grew too intense. After a few false starts, I was suddenly on the edge of a lake, in the greatest terror I have ever felt. I was absolutely sure that if I took one step into that lake, I would be psychotic for the rest of my life. Vaguely I remembered having heard that if you went into

140

absolute fear you could transcend it, but I didn't have the courage—the danger felt too great. I ripped off the mask and ended the experiment. This kind of activity wasn't taking me in any direction I was willing to go.

I wondered what career to pursue. I didn't think I had the necessary self-assurance for teaching the Process, especially since I knew that I was only helping clients to construct one of many possible worlds. People, however, were willing to accept and trust me as a therapist. As soon as I turned my attention to someone else with the intention of helping them, I became a different person: present, wise and helpful. It seemed obvious to me that this was why people who have serious problems in their own lives can be effective therapists, teachers and leaders. Without being aware of it, they simply switch to another, better, identity.

My relationship with Bill gradually changed, and I began to see him as not only sweet and lovable, but also self-centered, self-protective and occasionally covertly hostile. I was still attracted to him, though it was no longer so painful. More and more, I was aware of my own lack of initiative and drive, of not being motivated to do anything. I was reminded of the old beggar in the Swedenborg movie, *The Seventh Seal.* "I always wanted to do the Lord's will," he murmured as he died, "But He never told me what it was."

I was so free of responsibilities that it was scary. I had enough money, a comfortable place to live, friendly people nearby, good health, and competency in several disciplines. So what shall I do with myself? "How can I serve you?" I asked my Spiritual Self again and again. My head would go still and I would feel quiet and centered, but no answer came. (It didn't occur to me that being quiet and centered might be the beginning of an answer.) I continued to mourn the mediocrity of my life and thoughts. I felt that I had never been truly creative. It seemed that everything I did was copied from someone else who had thought of it first. I had to get myself in hand, so I reread my Process summary and started to recycle my depressing thoughts, and in a short time I felt better.

I kept puzzling about all this, motivated partly by reading Joseph Chilton Pearce's fascinating, *Crack in the Cosmic Egg*. But I couldn't accept his argument that since we create it all, we also create the Higher Beings with whom we are in contact, so that their only reality is what we have given them. I didn't believe I had made up Jeremy or the other guides who had come to me so fortuitously during my life.

My housemates and I continued to go to lectures and workshops, and to meet with various teachers and psychics. We went to Ken Keyes' "Living Love" seminars, which I thought were a quick, superficial version of the Process. We went to Betty Bethard's lectures on an Americanized version of tantric sex, and were amused when she embarrassed her much younger husband by asking him to help her demonstrate how it worked.

We cooked celebratory dinners at the slightest excuse, talked for hours in various combinations, and sometimes were hostile and analyzed each other's neuroses. We gave parties, ate pizza, and went rock-climbing together. We talked of buying land in the country and starting a "real" commune, but I couldn't see myself being part of another communal living arrangement as a single woman.

I went with Freda and Lee to one of Robert Monroe's weekends at Esalen on "Out of Body Experiences." I never got out of mine, though all weekend consisted of alternately sleeping two hours and listening to weird taped sounds for two hours. Another time, the three of us went to a haunted house to see if we could contact its ghost. He, or she, was supposed to be hostile, but I woke during the night feeling a presence that was deeply sad.

Now that it had become less painful, I had weekly Rolfing sessions. I got readings by two well-known psychics, Helen Palmer, who had taught herself to be psychic, and Ann Armstrong, who had become psychic when her husband hypnotized her to try to cure her migraine headaches. Like most psychics, Ann Armstrong demonstrated her abilities by telling me things about my life that she could not have known. When she told me I was a "kinesthetic telepath" who absorbed other people's emotions into myself as though they were my own, I knew it to be true. Just the previous week, I'd entered an elevator and inexplicably found myself feeling a sudden gust of rage. As we left the elevator a man whom I hadn't even noticed standing behind me began cursing his companion in a low, furious voice. It was much later when I realized that we are all "kinesthetic telepaths" to a degree and can unknowingly absorb the feelings of those around us.

When I meditated regularly, I felt more peaceful. For weeks I experienced times of a still mind and quiet happiness, alternating with depression and anxiety. I yearned to be centered, balanced, and self-possessed, as well as open, warm, loving and, of course, attractive to men. I also wanted to be competent and deeply engaged in professional work that I loved. Again and again I came to

143

the conviction that human beings create all that happens to us, though often I could not apply that knowledge to my own life.

I had several sessions with a rebel Scientology practitioner named Rod, who had left the organization. He used a version of the original Scientology device, the e-meter which was a pair of small tin cans that you clutched in each hand with wires leading to a reading instrument. The reading instrument registered moisture in the palms to indicate your emotional response to whatever you were talking about. It was a simple form of biofeedback: he'd say "there" to let you know that you should stay with the current topic, because it had created an emotional reaction.

Once, as I was investigating loneliness, an extraordinary scene that felt like a clear memory of another life unfolded. I was a young woman in peasant dress kneeling by a stream, sobbing helplessly because the nobleman who had fathered my six-month old baby had given it to a passing gypsy tribe. Nothing more happened in the scene, until Rod suggested that I follow the baby.

Suddenly I became the child, now six years old, totally alienated and alone in the gypsy camp—dirty, hungry, unable to hold my own with the gypsy kids, and afraid of the adults who mistreated me. Then I was about eleven, scheming to run away, but scared of the unknown world outside the camp. Before I could leave, I was raped by a couple of the men in the tribe. Feeling ruined, I no longer dreamt of another life.

At fifteen, I fought back and got into a wild battle with one of the gypsy girls who had hit me. I was brutally subdued by the others and the tribe moved on, leaving me behind. I could see and feel the tattered blanket I was lying

144

on, and the stiff yellow-brown autumn leaves rustling against my face in the cold wind. "What happened then?" asked Rod. "I died," I answered bleakly. "And what happened then?" asked Rod once more. At this unexpected question the scene changed. An angelic, radiantly glowing figure of a woman stood before me. As I rose and ran into her welcoming arms, I knew that she was my mother from the beginning scene.

There in his office, tears of joy streamed down my face. I felt again the engulfing sense of love and safety I had had after sending good will to my father during the Arica work. Whether fantasy or memory of another life, the scene I relived in Rod's office that day comforted me for years. Whenever I contacted that loving space, it stayed, not just in memory, but on the edges of my consciousness.

The next weekend I drove down the Pacific coast to Esalen, to attend a workshop in Sensory Awareness with Charlotte Selver and Charles Brooks. It had been more than two years since I had taken the month-long workshop on Monhegan Island in Maine with them; it was before I'd ended my marriage, quit my job and become a sort of middle-aged hippie. Esalen was beautiful, but, as usual, I was aware of being there by myself, and of being older than the other participants.

During one of the classes I was told to do a simple exchange, standing and breathing quietly while a partner placed a hand before and behind my midriff. The gentlest touch completely disrupted my stance and my self-connection. "Anyone can throw me off balance," I recognized in dismay. "I still have no center of my own."

The next weekend Leonard, an intellectual lawyer friend from Los Angeles, arrived for a visit. He wanted to know what was happening in Berkeley, so I called Freda and asked her and Lee to come over and give Leonard a Ketamine trip. After Lee gave him the injection, Leonard lay quietly on a sofa for hours, hardly speaking or moving. When he finally returned to normal consciousness a different man looked out of his eyes, gentle and infinitely loving. His mood lasted the rest of the evening, and for years afterwards he spoke of the experience as if it had been a brief visit to heaven.

One day when I asked my guides (Jeremy had been joined by a feminine guide whose name was Mercy) what I should be doing, it seemed as if they were pouring love into me. I felt relaxed and expanded as if a hard core of resistance in my stomach were softening. No matter how often I did it, the results of asking for guidance continued to amaze me—although I would fall back into my ordinary way of being within hours.

Sometimes answers came in surprising ways. We had let a quarrelsome and demanding young woman move into Textaxi. For the first time I had a housemate I disliked and who obviously disliked me. At supper one night with a few of our friends, she attacked me openly. Everyone, including Bill and Freda who had been my friends for years, stayed elaborately neutral. Then they all hurried off to their separate interests, leaving me alone in the house.

I felt betrayed. At four a.m., agitated and unable to sleep, I jumped into my car and drove northward, sobbing and cursing as I went. I wound up in the redwoods a couple of hundred miles away, where I rented a little cabin and stewed all day. Toward evening I sat by a nearby

146

stream, becoming more and more depressed and feeling completely alone. Briefly, I sent out an inner call for help but there was no reply; even my guides had deserted me. I walked miserably back to the cabin.

As I opened the door, without warning and without any perceptible change in my thinking, a great gust of laughter rose from my belly and took me over. It was not hysterical laughter, but true, rich amusement. An image of the whole episode as a TV soap opera came to me. I continued to laugh until I fell asleep, still chuckling. That mood was still with me when I work up in the morning.

When I was home a couple of days later, I felt peaceful and amused still, but knew that I had to leave Textaxi. It had been a haven for several years, but it was time for me to move on. I had just enough money in my dwindling bank account for a month at a Selver and Brooks workshop on Monhegan Island. I drove my dependable old gray Volvo across the country with a box of celery, carrots and cabbage beside me, so I wouldn't snack on fattening foods.

At the Maine coast I left the Volvo in a big covered garage and took the short ferry ride over the sun-glistened sea to Monhegan. The island is full of green trees and is a place where you are always within sight of the restless ocean. Nothing seemed to have changed. There were no cars other than official ones permitted, and the individual house generators still roared to life every half hour or so. Charlotte told us to let the noise pass through us, and after a while I was able to do so.

I was glad to have my little room up under the eaves on the top floor of the big weather-beaten old hotel. I'd had enough socializing and I appreciated my seclusion. I avoided the tiny, touristy village and enjoyed the quiet paths circling the island. In class, the gentle encouragement to awareness of my senses opened me to new experiences of myself and others. Careful observation of the tensions in my arms and back brought on an experience of pure anger. Attention to the muscles in my face showed a perpetual faint snarl around my mouth. With further exploration, the expression spread to the rest of my face and I could sense fear.

There were many personal moments of ease of movement. At one time I felt a rush of tenderness for a student whose head I was holding between my hands; at yet another time, I felt pure exhilaration. Sights and scents grew brighter. A woman artist gave us lessons in drawing from within ourselves. We began with twenty minutes of meditation; then we made large, spontaneous movements in the air with our hands and arms, until gradually we brought a piece of charcoal to paper to make sketches of startling freedom and veracity. As we boarded the launch to return to the mainland at the end of the retreat, one of the men hugged me and exuberantly told me I looked twenty years younger. His girlfriend hushed him in embarrassment, and then added thoughtfully, "but ten years, for sure."

∞ ∞ ∞ ∞ ∞

I retrieved my Volvo and drove to New Orleans to meet my beautiful and opulent friend, Serena Stier, from the Neuropsychiatric Institute at UCLA. She was an official at the American Psychology Association Conference which was being held simultaneously with the Humanistic Psychology Conference I planned to attend. As an officer, she had free quarters in one of the magnificent old hotels and had generously invited me to share her rooms. She also took me to professional events in the evenings, where rich New Orleans food and wine were spread out. After all the careful inner work among the simplicities of Monhegan, her matter-of-fact friendliness and the luxuries we enjoyed at her largess were another world.

The sensory awareness work, however, had a more important kind of reality to it, and I had decided to go to New York City that fall to take Charlotte's classes there. I was sure that I would be able to get a job as some kind of a social worker. I still had my California credentials. Three days before the end of the conferences I woke with the single word "California" ringing clearly in my mind. Somewhat startled, I laughed and assured myself, "No, no, I'm going to New York."

When I awoke the next morning the performance was repeated, still more insistently. "California!" said the voice clearly and firmly. On the third morning, waking to it again, I gave up. "O.K., California it is," I agreed. I had no idea who or what was making the demand, only that it seemed to be much more certain of where I should be going at this point in my life than I did.

As I drove back across the country, I decided to visit Marny in Bishop, a couple of hundred miles from Los Angeles. For over twenty-five years, we had been each others' ports in the various storms in our lives. When I arrived, she urged me to stay for a while in the beautiful high desert of the Inyo-Mono Valley; she found me a little rental trailer within a mile of hers, on the edge of the Indian reservation. After meeting the friendly old Scandinavian couple whose house was nearby, I rented their trailer and settled down to quiet living.

It was a joy to be there in the high desert, with Marny living so close. Although the Inyo-Mono Valley itself was no longer lush and green, as it had been in the years before it was robbed of its water to feed the colossus of Los Angeles, the air was crisp and clean and country-scented. There were lots of trees and wonderfully craggy rocks, surrounded by the magnificent Sierra Nevada Mountains. At 4000 feet, it was too high to be desert-hot in the summer.

Route 395 went right through Bishop, and was the only highway from the south to the ski resorts and hiking trails of Mammoth Lakes. Both Marny and I lived a couple of miles away from town though, so the traffic didn't bother us. Mammoth Lakes was forty miles away, past the still waters of the moonscape-like Mono Lake. Above it was June Lake, jewel-like in the midst of its setting of summer-green or winter-white.

That fall I learned where to gather pine nuts and how to dry them, played scrabble with my landlady and her husband, went to meditation groups and met Marny's spiritually-oriented friends. I made careful notes about my hours of introspection, and recorded dozens of elaborate dreams and my findings from working with them. I would describe the dream into a tape recorder when I woke during the night, type it out the next day, and then, Gestalt-fashion, speak as if I were each person or important object in the dream. For example, "As the mountain, I feel solid but remote and uninvolved in all these goings-on." More than once, I dreamed my old anxiety nightmare of struggling to get someplace through an ever shifting landscape but never succeeding. Seeing my own patterns so clearly acted out in my dreams fascinated me, even though they often reinforced the unsatisfactory things I already knew about myself. Now that I had unscheduled time to understand them, surely it would be possible to change them.

And then there was Warren. He was a big, fat, good-looking Piute-Shoshone Indian who seemed to love me with an unwavering love from the day we met. He had been to City College in Los Angeles and had worked in LA as a draftsman for several years. When he was diagnosed as diabetic, he returned to live on the reservation with his mother. He was assistant manager at the Indian Health Clinic near my trailer. Like everyone else I met, he was Marny's friend before he was mine. She and I went to a small exhibition of his paintings, which I thought pleasant but unexceptional. I was pleased to be there though, because I hadn't met any of the local Indians and it seemed like an interesting thing to do.

At Marny's urging, I went on a drive to Mammoth with him that Saturday, and found myself talking more freely than I had in years. I was completely comfortable in his presence and enjoyed the day hugely. Some months later, after we had become a couple, a woman I knew slightly from my professional life in Los Angeles, aware that Indians and white folks did not mix in Bishop, asked me simply, "Why?" In response, I asked her if she had ever heard of "unconditional positive regard," which is what I always felt from him.

Warren and I had no social life together, other than with Marny. He did not interact much with other Indians, and the whites and Indians in Bishop did not interact socially. Marny wasn't interested in social activities, so she and I went to meditation groups or to meet spiritual teachers. Warren wasn't good at physical activities and

Marny was no athlete, so I hiked and square-danced with others.

From the first time he kissed me gently on the cheek and I instinctively turned my mouth to meet his, making love with Warren was sweet and intimate in a way entirely new to me. With all his weight and lack of virility because of the diabetes, he took such joy in pleasing me in any way he could that I found myself responding gladly. Being with someone so uncomplicated, who had nothing on his mind other than what was happening in the moment, was new and incredibly nourishing.

After a while I could see a different side to Warren, too. There was the gentle, deeply loving human being who could easily make a strong emotional connection with me, and then there was the uncertain man/child who simply slipped into whatever role was expected of him. Whatever idea or experience I brought up, Warren would respond by agreeing with me and enlarging on what I'd said, often by describing a similar experience he said he'd had. Sometimes it felt as if he was enacting one of the characters from the book *Rabbit Boss,* a recent, deeply sympathetic novel about the members of an Indian tribe. "He had to learn to be like the White Man, only thus could he get hold of their Power."

There was something in him, though, that was strong and sure and very real: his loving smile, his deft hands soothing away my headache. His very being was genuine in a way that was unmistakable. When I reminded him that I was at least ten years older, he told me matter-of-factly that it didn't matter since he would certainly die before I did. For a while, I thought of settling down in the valley and making a life with him. I began to see clients and started an ongoing personal growth group, using the various physical, emotional and spiritual processes I had learned.

But one day Marny announced that she had received guidance during meditation that she was to move to Hawaii for the coming few years. I sadly accepted her leaving, and even rented the little house she had moved into half a year before. After she was gone, I continued seeing clients and writing and being with Warren, but I soon recognized that the heart had gone out of Bishop for me. Much as I'd always known I loved her, I hadn't quite realized that it was Marny who had made Bishop work for me. She was the one who kept coming up with new and interesting things to do and talk about. She was the one who truly mattered to me. My fondness for Warren wasn't enough to keep me there. Within a couple of months I was bored and chaffing to get back to life outside the valley.

Warren was briefly distressed when I told him, but then his usual resignation to whatever was happening kicked in. He said simply, "I knew that you would leave after Marny did." We talked of his coming to San Francisco to visit me as soon as I was settled, and of my making return visits to the valley to see him. He gave me a beautiful big turquoise ring and bracelet as a going away present. A few years later, in India, the turquoise was stolen from the ring. I had it replaced with the stone from the bracelet and I still keep it carefully, though it no longer fits me.

Chapter 9   A Course In Miracles

I had taken two women individually through the Fischer/Hoffman Process during the months before I left Bishop.   Seeing the positive changes in them revived my conviction that the Process was the most powerful form of therapy I knew.   I asked a friend in San Francisco to track down Bob Hoffman and Ernest Pecci and to set up appointments for me with each of them.   Dr. Pecci had purchased the Fischer/Hoffman Clinic from Bob when Bob was diagnosed with cancer; Pecci had paid Bob to be a consultant while he recuperated in Mexico.   But Bob was furious because Pecci wasn't willing to be told, long distance, how to run the Process.   Friends told me that Bob had said, "Just because he's a psychiatrist, he thinks he can run my Process better than I can."   Pecci had said, "After all, I'm the psychiatrist."   So Bob was starting a new institute.   My friend told me Pecci's secretary had asked that I write for an appointment, but Bob had invited me to lunch.   That made the decision simple: I accepted Bob's invitation and forgot about Dr. Pecci.

When I arrived in San Francisco, I learned that my brother Charlie had been rushed to a hospital with internal bleeding and was about to be operated on.   I was scared for him and wanted to drive down to Los Angeles immediately, but I felt strongly that I must see Bob first. Bob was his usual ebullient and hospitable self. Over an abundant lunch he told me about his plans for taking the Process to new heights. He was sure that Pecci had corrupted their previous staff so he wanted to start with a fresh slate, and he asked me to be his assistant. "We'll do it together," he enthused. I was hesitant; I hadn't expected it to be just the two of us. I didn't like him much, nor was I comfortable with gay men.

I told him about my brother Charlie's being hospitalized. He said he would look psychically and see what was happening. After a moment of silence he assured me, "He'll be okay. I can see him walking out of the hospital." Another silence, "Oh, he'll have to go back in a week for something minor they have to fix. But it won't be a big deal." I drove to Los Angeles that afternoon. Charlie improved rapidly after the operation, and did walk out of the hospital. And, a week later, he had to go back for a minor correction of the surgery. Bob had proved again that he was far more than the huckster I found so abrasive. As soon as Charlie was out of danger, I returned to San Francisco and started work for Bob. The next fifteen months were so busy that I had no time to write down my thoughts about what was happening in my life.

After the Fischer/Hoffman Clinic had been in operation for some months, Bob decided that he needed to write a book to publicize the Process. He hired Dennis Brisken, a bright, eager young ghostwriter who knew almost nothing about psychotherapy, and who had never produced a book before.

Bob's story of the beginning of the Process was that he had been friends with a psychiatrist named Siegfried

156

Fischer. Fischer didn't believe in life after death, so Bob had suggested that since Fischer was older and would probably die first, he should come back and admit that he had been wrong. Six months after Fischer died; Bob woke one night to find Fischer standing at the end of his bed, saying that he knew now how therapy should be done. Bob said, "Fine, go tell a psychiatrist. I'm a tailor." Fischer demurred, and claimed that his contact with Bob was so strong that he wanted to give the Process to him. "Well," said Bob, "I've got some personal problems. Why don't you take me through it?" For the next five hours, Fischer took him through a simplified version of the Process. At the end, Bob knew that his life had been changed, but he didn't see how he could teach such a course. "Don't worry," Fischer said, "the doors will open."

Bob was already giving private classes in psychic abilities. He began to take his students through an early version of the Process, and found that they made tremendous progress in handling their personal problems. The psychiatrist Ernest Pecci heard about Bob's work and sent him a couple of his most recalcitrant patients, who improved remarkably. Pecci began to have dinner with Bob once a week to discuss what was happening in the classes. After a year, they formed a partnership and opened the clinic where I had taken the Process. But Bob still insisted that all he knew about psychotherapy was what Fischer had given him that night, plus the advice that Fischer continued to give.

Bob decided that I should attend the meetings when he and Dennis reviewed the material Dennis had written, and that I should work with Dennis in preparing upcoming chapters. At times I thought, wryly, that my primary job was keeping these two tempestuous, argumentative men from killing each other. Frequently, I had to interpret one's point of view for the other.

In the end, the book we produced gave the theory and explained the methods of the Process, using quotes from a number of our clients. Dennis, also a photographer, celebrated by giving both Bob and me framed copies of a photo he had taken, of three white birds flying upwards. Bob spoke generously of our work in the Acknowledgements, and took us out to dinner at a fancy downtown hotel. The book was titled *Getting Divorced from Mother and Dad: the discoveries of the Fischer/Hoffman Process.* Later, when he was angry with us, Bob changed the title to *No One is to Blame,* and dropped our names from the Acknowledgements. Dennis threatened to sue Bob and his name was put back. I didn't think of doing that, so my name was dropped permanently.

Bob's publicity skills and personal charisma were enormous. Within a year we were handling classes of twenty-five to thirty people and had a staff of five teachers, plus half a dozen teachers-in-training. As a leader, however, he was often frustrating and infuriating. When I made a list of forty-five problems I was handling as the Assistant Director of the Fischer/Hoffman Institute, a third of them were related to getting Bob to change his attitudes and behavior, and to stop invalidating everyone else on staff.

The other problems were about working with the staff and trainees and keeping in touch with ongoing cases; with revising and simplifying the Process; and with integrating the new processes Bob came up with, when it became clear that some clients were having trouble with the processes we were using. We were also working on a new brochure, better methods of training teachers and more organized schedules of the steps of the Process. The later was necessary because Bob would take the transcribed lectures he had given during the previous course and redo the entire Process, so that instruction sheets for each class had to be rewritten.

But still, we could see most of our clients changing as they dealt with negative feelings about their parents and we watched them go from dependency to strength, from anger to forgiveness. At each Closure ritual the joy was palpable. We started staging a "Family and Friends" evening the week before graduation. Hearing our clients publicly describe the remarkable changes they had undergone during the Process was a rush every time.

∞ ∞ ∞ ∞ ∞

In the summer of 1976, Lee invited Freda and me to "something new." We heard Helen Schucman and Bill Thetford talk about the material she had channeled, *A Course in Miracles,* on their first visit to the West Coast. These two people were different from anyone else I'd met who claimed to have some special dispensation of spiritual knowledge. They were conservatively-dressed, educated and articulate Americans, who spoke calmly about the extraordinary events in which they had participated. Furthermore, they spoke about her revelation with a kind of diffidence that was the opposite of proselytizing.

It was Helen who had actually received the material, and she seemed to be keeping her distance from the entire project, even to be faintly embarrassed by describing it publicly. She was a small woman in her sixties, intelligent and charming, with a slight New York

159

edge to her humor. She said she had asked those who were using her as a channel why they had chosen her, as she had never been entirely convinced of the authenticity of the whole experience. "Because you will do it," they said. Bill Thetford looked to be fifteen years younger than her, and gave the impression of a thoughtful and kindly uncle. In their presentation he talked less than she did.

Two small points stand out in my memory of the evening. One was Helen's offhand comment that she had learned Pitman shorthand in her youth and had continued to use it all her professional life—a remarkable and useful skill in taking down material that would eventually come to nearly 500,000 words. The second was when a woman in the audience said she wanted to buy a set of the books, but didn't have any money with her. The "with her" didn't carry to Helen, who immediately responded that they would give the woman a free copy rather than deprive her of an opportunity to study the Course. It was the authenticity of these people that impressed me.

Helen had been brought up as an isolated only child, largely ignored by her father and mother and cared for by servants. Her parents were Jewish, her father a non-believer, her mother a restless seeker who considered herself to be a Theosophist. As Helen grew up, her governess took her to Catholic services and their cook took her to Baptist services. Despite their efforts, she never felt any connection with God and, as an adult, considered herself an atheist.

Bill's parents had been Christian Scientists, but they quit the church when his ten-year-old sister died, despite having received both Christian Science and mainstream medical treatment. In graduate school he had worked as a teaching and research assistant to Carl Rogers with his Client-Centered Therapy. Bill continued his professional life at several major universities and was the director of the psychology department of a respected Eastern psychiatric hospital, when Helen, also a psychologist, joined the staff.

According to their story, the work atmosphere at the psychology department was poisonous with rancor and competitiveness, and they agreed that they had to find a way to improve it. Soon afterwards, Helen came to Bill and told him that she was afraid she was going crazy because she was hearing a voice in her head. To alleviate her fears, he suggested that she write down what she heard and bring it to him the next morning.

These are the first words she brought to him: "This is a course in miracles. It is a required course. Only the time you take it is voluntary. Free will does not mean that you can establish the curriculum. It means only that you can elect what you want to take at a given time. The course does not aim at teaching the meaning of love, for that is beyond what can be taught. It does aim, however, at removing the blocks to the awareness of love's presence, which is your natural inheritance. The opposite of love is fear, but what is all-encompassing can have no opposite. The course can therefore be summed up very simply in this way: nothing real can be threatened. Nothing unreal exists. Herein lies the peace of God."

Helen said that she frequently reacted to the voice with agitation and sometimes downright panic; yet it continued for years. During that period, she filled over a hundred notebooks with shorthand and Bill typed every word. The voice never seemed disturbed when her attention was needed elsewhere. It picked up again in the middle of a sentence if she had to answer the telephone, or was otherwise interrupted.

The entire Course consisted of a Text, a Workbook, and a small Manual for Teachers. Each part had been dictated, and months elapsed between parts. Initially, Helen and Bill didn't know what to do with the material. Fearing that it would earn them the derision of their fellow academics, they kept it locked in a file cabinet for five years before they told anyone about it. When they were convinced that it should be published, the only changes made in the material were to add paragraph and chapter breaks, as the original dictation gave none.

In my Ph.D. dissertation ten years later, I wrote, "The Course offers a view of the universe and the situation of human beings therein which is profoundly different from that of either orthodox Christianity or humanistic psychology. Its central thesis is that this world in which we live and work and have our being is nothing but a dream, in which all of the purposes on which most people have expended their lives and energies—romantic love, money, power, business or professional accomplishments—have no meaning. The world is only a stage for learning that we made a mistake in thinking we could choose to separate from our Christ-self. That mistake, and therefore the world as we experience it, can be changed in the moment that we fully recognize the truth of our situation. It also teaches that every step in the direction of this truth will lead to dramatic improvement in the illusions that we experience. As these dreams become happier they become thinner, and easier to pass through to reality.

"Would-be students of the Course are sometimes troubled by the Course's derogatory attitude toward the ego, the body, and special relationships, ⌒ although the course makes it abundantly clear that (if placed under the guidance of the Holy Spirit) all of these things can become vehicles for the return to God and our Christ-self. To the members of a society which is based on the value of the individual, and has only lately discovered the importance of the body (from the standpoint of optimum health and the enjoyment of kinesthetic and sensory awareness) and is forever enamored with special relationships, these ideas can bring dismay. Another problem some students find in the Course lies not in the spiritualization of their present lives, which is usually highly salutary, but in the acceptance of its ultimate goal—transcendence of the ego-self and union with the one changeless, eternal reality."

When I heard Helen and Bill speak, I felt that Christian Science had come back into my life in a new guise, and I was fascinated. I bought a set of the books, intending to study the Textbook and follow the lessons each day. I didn't always do that, but I found myself returning to the Textbook when I drifted away. It seemed to be saying the same things that Christian Science did, but much more comprehensibly. I often turned to it for support, as I had turned to Christian Science when I needed it.

∞ ∞ ∞ ∞ ∞

I also began to explore bodywork, which I saw as an effective way to access material below the surface of my consciousness. I wanted to reach the core of my own inability to find a solid person within me, in spite of all the work I had done. I'd read in spiritual literature, "Before you can become no-self, you have to be a self." I was convinced that, somewhere within me, there was a Self.

163

Wilhelm Reich, one of Freud's early associates, broke with him because he thought that Freud's work ignored the importance of the body. Reich came to believe that the universe was permeated by a primal life force he called "orgone." It was drawn on by all living beings, but was often blocked by a kind of character armor that childhood experiences had created in the muscular structure. For example, despair was often fixed in a permanently down-turned mouth, compulsivity in a stiff upper lip. Rage might be held in an outthrust jaw, or in the hunched muscles of the shoulders. This armoring made it impossible to come to full orgasm, which Reich believed to be the proof of good health. The idea that our muscular structure could become like a shield that did not permit free access to our emotions seemed sound. Maybe, I thought, this kind of work was the missing part needed to complete the Process.

I worked for a while with a Reichian and Rolfing practitioner named Giovanna. Giovanna also taught me Autogenic Relaxation, a series of steps in which you first instruct your arms and legs to be "warm and heavy," then your belly to be "warm and soft," then your feet and hands to be "warm," and finally, your forehead to be "cool." Each step has to be fully experienced before going on to the next. Autogenic Relaxation is based on the finding that a person being deeply hypnotized has this sequence of experiences. It is a wonderfully effective way to relax the body that I still use occasionally. I also had ten sessions of painful Rolfing from Giovanna, along with the Reichian work.

In one Rolfing session her husband, also a Rolfer, took over because of the rigidity of my muscular structure.

He was twice as big and strong as she was. He released something along my breastbone and, when it jerked lose, my whole body shuddered and uncontrollable sobs came with no emotional content at all—and it really hurt.

I began working with Lee Sanella's friend, Hal Streitfeld, whose practice included Gestalt psychotherapy as well as Reichian work. Hal took me deeper, to the tumultuous emotions that lay beneath the surface of my public self. In our very first session, his gentle touch on the back of my head and at the base of my throat evoked a storm of tears. In other sessions, I felt my shoulders and back as a block of concrete, frozen in position. Once when my longing for my father surfaced, he translated it into "my Father who art in Heaven" and we both cried.

I did not feel honest to myself, or with anybody else. Why was I pretending that people would feel happy and free once they had taken the Process, when it hadn't been true for me or for Bob? One day Bob's longtime lover, Harold, left him. Ebullient cocksure Bob, who railed at us if we weren't happy after taking the Process, proceeded to fall apart. He lost weight and went around looking like a shell-shocked war victim. He broke into tears at the slightest insensitive remark. He was totally distraught and incapacitated. Suddenly the Process and the Center were no longer important to him. "You'll have to handle things," he told me piteously. "I can't."

When Harold returned, Bob was happy again. Love and joy shone from him. He was totally transformed; his arrogance had turned to humility, his abrasiveness to gentleness. Bob and Harold went off to Hawaii on a "honeymoon." I wrote in my journal: "Life is infinitely beautiful. I am grateful for each moment. Each human being is a miracle. I love the world. I appreciate everybody, every moment, and all life. " It all felt true, so I didn't notice how I had absorbed Bob's feelings.

I continued to do bodywork with Hal and went through enormous emotional reactions. I was finally beginning to experience myself as I actually was, although I was dismayed that it had taken me fifty-six years to do so. But I was excited at the promise and the possibility of finally becoming real. During the next few weeks of 1977, I rocketed back and forth between my new sense of solidity and peace, and my familiar depression and despair. Sometimes I fell into rages, cursing God over the pointlessness of all the suffering and tragedy in human life.

I was grateful for the realness I was experiencing, both in my personal self and in my "higher consciousness." It felt as if I had reached the first true sense of peace and connectedness I had ever known in my life. I was happier than ever before for days on end. The combination of the Course in Miracles and the Reichian work with Hal was beginning to make a profound improvement in my life experience.

After publication of *Getting Divorced from Mother and Dad*, Bob took off on a book tour for a month, leaving me in charge of the Center. We had about fifty people taking the Process, some of whom were also learning to teach it. The month without Bob went by with much less friction at the Center. He returned and took over as director again, but things had changed between us. While we were writing the book, I had studied the steps of the Process carefully and figured out how each one worked. I was sure that I understood it thoroughly by this time.

Bob's unequivocal pronouncement that he was always right, and that therefore arguing with him was not only pointless but showed ill-will, was becoming more and more difficult for me to accept. It was even more troublesome when he rode roughshod over the clients, although he could also be warmly encouraging to them.

After each Process was completed, we would have a magnificent party for the graduates at Bob's luxurious home. Staff was expected to bring dishes of food, and to clean up afterwards. One of the teachers calculated that we were making about seventeen cents for each hour we put into the Process. Nevertheless, Bob's zest and enthusiasm created such a stimulating atmosphere, and the Process was so clearly the best therapy around, that most of us stayed.

Once a couple of severe-looking men from the American Medical Association arrived and challenged us, but I had a valid LCSW license and Bob had cannily gotten himself certified as a minister. After the men left and before the AMA could investigate further, Bob held a formal ceremony and made all his teachers "ministers of the Church of the Quadrinity."

"Quadrinity" meant "body, emotional child, intellectual adult and spiritual self" to Bob. The staff found the word embarrassing since it had no linguistic excuse for itself, but Bob was adamant. According to him, Fischer had given him the word. Actually, whenever anyone challenged his ideas about anything, Bob would cut off the discussion with "Fischer says..." When the son of the late Siegfried Fischer threatened to sue if Bob continued to use his father's name, Bob renamed the course "The Quadrinity Process," although he continued to insist that Fischer was guiding him.

Bob met Werner Erhart and scheduled us to take the "est" training. est is an acronym for Erhart Seminar Trainings and it is also the Latin verb, "to be." Bob was available for only part of the first morning of the seminar, so Werner's people set up a private session for eight of our staff to bring us up to speed. It led to another extraordinary experience for me.

After an explanation of their point of view, the woman leader began a hypnotic repetition of the question— "Who am I?" She asked it loudly and quietly, emotionally and in detached tones, assertively and gently. I had a bad cold that day, and I found myself more and more focused on the discomfort in my nose. As my hypnotic trance deepened, I began to experience the movement of fluids in my sinuses, then the inflamed tissues, and finally the actual structure of the nerve cells. All awareness of me as a person disappeared, and I was filled with the most extraordinary level of exuberant joy. As the leader brought us back to the room, a thought surfaced clearly: "Wow! If fully experiencing a cold is like this, dying must be absolutely wonderful!"

My reaction was unique; others in our group had very different experiences. One of them said in puzzled tones, "Who am I? Why I'm Miriam. Who else would I be?" This was the period during which Werner Erhard challenged the people in his classes to "try to explain to anyone else what happened over the weekend!" I couldn't have explained to anyone what had happened to me.

As described on the Internet today, the est training was intended to shake up a person's conception of themselves and their world, so that they could experience what they were actually feeling and thinking and doing. As far as I could see, our exposure to the training didn't have much effect on any of us; perhaps we were too involved in our own work.

I got a new Process client during this period: slim, golden Gilda from Rio de Janeiro, who had requested me as her teacher. I was attracted to her immediately, but had to tell her that I had time for only one student and I'd already accepted someone else. Gilda just nodded agreeably. My intended student dropped out the day before the Process started, which didn't seem to surprise Gilda at all.

I liked Gilda from the start; she had so much "élan" and intelligence, such energy and enthusiasm. However, her stories of Umbanda in Brazil—a combination of Catholic Christianity and an indigenous belief in many gods and spirits—and of her sister's being a medium who was sometimes taken over by an old male spirit, filled me with fascination and vague alarm. A mutual friend who had known her in Brazil told me how strange and powerful their rituals were. He suggested that Gilda may have unintentionally brought with her some malevolent forces that would try to keep her under control. When we did the Process visualization to access Gilda's guide, he turned out to be odd and mysterious, rather than caring and reassuring. I knew that Bob's psychic powers were much stronger than mine, so I asked him to redo her session. The guide he reluctantly helped her access was all we could have wished for.

One evening soon after that, while meditating alone at home, I suddenly had a distinct sense of something evil and powerful, and almost visible, in one corner of the room. To my amazement, my initial reaction of fright immediately changed to boiling rage. I screamed at it to go

169

do its trip somewhere else; there was no place for it here. It dissolved as quickly as it had appeared, leaving me both shaken and triumphant—and also cured of my childhood fears of the supernatural.

Now I had to ask myself why I acted powerful only when I felt justified in being openly furious with someone. How can I surrender to God, if I only feel truly alive when I act out aggression? And furthermore, how could I distinguish "surrender" from "denying my feelings?" Surrendering felt like acting out my tendency to sit back and let someone else take the lead. I had always been "at the effect" as the est training called it, of someone or something else. I concluded that maybe I needed to see myself as being "at cause" for a while, and forget about surrendering.

After this experience, my anger at Bob mostly dissolved. I knew that he was a genius and a spellbinder, and I thought he was right about what we were doing and needed to do. He was an astute businessman, as well as a totally self-absorbed manipulator. He was who he was, and my goal in this work was the same as it had always been: to spread the truths of the Process.

∞ ∞ ∞ ∞ ∞

I took a weekend workshop with Margaret Conway, a Psychosynthesis teacher about my age. Psychosynthesis was the teachings of an Italian psychiatrist, Roberto Assagioli. His was one of the first truly knowledgeable and sophisticated attempts to meld psychological work with spiritual understanding. According to Psychosynthesis, we not only have a conscious and a subconscious, but a super conscious as well, analogous to the Emotional Child, the Adult Intellect and the Spiritual Self of the Process.

170

Psychosynthesis took the position that although we often experience different selves, the personal self and the true self are not separate. Both are the Self, manifesting differently. Psychosynthesis was based on Dr. Assagioli's thorough knowledge of psychoanalysis, existentialism and the newer humanistic approaches, as well as on spiritual traditions. His methods of growth-work included much imagery, and accepted that parts of the Self are so divided from each other that they need to learn to communicate.

In one of the great puzzles of the New Age movement, this deeply authentic and wise approach to elevating human experience was taken over, in America, by a powerful and charismatic male leader who managed to turn it into a full-blown cult. When people spoke publically about the shame they felt because they had become mesmerized by him, the whole association went down. Assagioli's profound explanation of human experience, though, has continued to permeate many other approaches.

Margaret Conway and I took an instant liking to each other and arranged to meet outside the workshop. She'd been a nurse and a suburban housewife married to a successful doctor. Their four children were half grown when he walked out. After raising their children, she had gone to Italy to work for a year with Assagioli. She had also been a volunteer with Werner Erhard's est. As Margaret and I became friends, I learned about the recent death of her oldest son, Danny. At twenty he had rolled his Volkswagen bus and become a paraplegic. When he was able to get around in a wheelchair, she took him everywhere. She said, with an odd sort of pride, that he was probably the only person in a wheelchair to have been thrown out of a bar in Las Vegas for disorderly conduct. A few months previously, when his father took him whitewater rafting and their raft overturned, Danny drowned.

She thought that taking an LSD trip would connect her with his spirit in a meaningful way, and make his loss more bearable. We went to a cabin owned by a friend of hers along a little creek in the Sierras. Margaret took her tablet that day. She sat quietly looking at the water most of the time, and later told me that she had made a contact with Danny that comforted her deeply. The next day she was able to be with me peacefully while I took my tablet. After the shape and color display faded, I began to be absolutely certain that everything I had come to believe about life was entirely true. Just as the thought was sinking in, I remembered that I was on LSD and therefore couldn't trust my mind.

I enrolled with a friend in a course taught on a houseboat by a man named Paul Solomon. Solomon did psychic readings somewhat like those of Edgar Cayce. He told us that the difference between victim and master is whether we take responsibility for our own experiences. He pointed out that if a man can make you angry, he is in control. "We are enrolled in a mystery school," he said, "and we are all apprentice Gods. The more challenges you meet, the more will be sent to you. Our lessons are custom-designed for us." He taught us a way of resolving a difficult relationship by looking at both our own needs and the other person's and writing it all down, while asking for the lessons we were each meant to learn.

He talked of being able to reach alternate states of consciousness by strongly intending to get there. He advised making imagined places of peace and power so real in our minds that they became real in experience. He gave us wonderful methods of prayer and meditation, exercises for each part of the day, and powerful visualizations. I did the practices, saw that they worked, and was amazed to remember how long I had known most of this without using it. I took elaborate notes on all that he taught us, and forgot most of it within weeks.

I continued to feel that there was something I had to do before I could go forward, at times actually writhing in the agony of not knowing what was missing. Then my mind would clear and I'd recognize: it was love that was missing. People followed the popular Indian guru, Muktananda, because he said, "love yourself in me," thereby giving people permission to love and to bypass the ubiquitous fear of being rejected. I came to the conclusion that the incredible feelings of safety and love that I'd felt while sending good will to my father in Arica training were possible because the ritual gave me a way to drop my hatred for him, so that I could feel the love that had been there all along.

Meditation each morning, incorporating one of the daily statements from the Course in Miracles, often took me into a space of happiness and peace. Sometimes however, I was afraid that I was recreating the Course as truth for myself, just as Bob was making the Process real by the intensity of his belief. Looked at this way, it was difficult for me to believe in either the Course or in the Process.

Staff members at the renamed Quadrinity Center resented Bob for his bullying and closed-mindedness. We couldn't accept his conviction that the Process was a total cure. The new ideas he came up with, and insisted that we use, were becoming progressively more bizarre. When he decided to dramatize the "walking on egg shells" feeling that our clients often expressed about their parents, we gave each participant a hardboiled egg to crack during a Bitch Session. This idea was abandoned when our secretary decided one day to cook the eggs in the office coffee maker. As the clients smashed them between their fingers, the half-cooked eggs splattered all over them. The clients accepted it as what was supposed to happen, but the scene was too much for the attending teachers, and we laughed so hard that we cried.

It was about this same time that Bob decided that all students must physically vomit out their parents. We had to give clients salt water and show them how to induce vomiting by sticking two fingers down their throats. We hated it, but when Bob had an idea no one could gainsay him, and the clients seemed to feel purged.

∞ ∞ ∞ ∞ ∞

Freda and Lee and I often told our dreams to each other in the mornings. I couldn't control what was happening in my dreams, but I often knew that I was dreaming. One night I found myself flying, exhilarated and partly in control. At breakfast the next morning, as I told Freda and Lee about my dream, they just sat and stared at me. They had gone to sleep the previous night in the room next to mine after programming each other hypnotically to have a flying dream, and neither of them had succeeded, but I did.

When I asked for a dream that would advise me on my spiritual progress, I dreamt that I was driving a car and had suddenly left my body. My consciousness expanded

174

into the sky and became infinitely large, a magnificent sensation. When I realized that I wasn't in the car and couldn't keep it from crashing, I tried to wake myself up by biting my tongue, which sent me instantly back into the car. Then I remembered that I'd left a baby in the trunk and, if I hadn't returned, the car might have crashed and nobody would have known she was there. Lee thought it strange at my age to be having a dream advising that I mustn't take off into higher consciousness because I needed to take care of my inner child. It didn't seem strange to me; I was very aware that I still had little sense of having a self, my criteria for taking the next step.

I took a course in the Enneagram from Claudio Naranjo and Kathleen Speeth. Although Gurdjeiff is credited with bringing the ancient system of nine different character types from the East to the West, and Oscar Ichazo gets credit for bringing it to the United States, Claudio is the man who turned it into a psychological tool, and it is his name that is referenced in the many books on the Enneagram now available. For Oscar, the terms for the nine variations of personality, also called fixations, were all derogatory: Number 1 was "Resent" for resentment; #2 was "Flat" for self-flattery; #3 was "Go" to represent the American business man; #4 was "Melon" for melancholia; #5 was "Stinge" for someone who is stingy with himself; #6 was "Cow" for coward; #7 was "Lust" for someone who wanted everything; #8 was "Venge" for one who desired vengeance on the world; and #9 was "In" for indolence. For each fixation there was a "Holy Idea" that would lead to freedom from the thrall of the ego. For a 9, it was Holy Love, for a 6 it was Holy Faith, and so on.

Claudio also saw the various machinations of the ego as something to go beyond, but he thought that the fixations were simply to be experienced and not judged. He (and later Helen Palmer) renamed them to reflect a kinder, gentler view: Number 1 was "Perfectionist;"# 2 was "Giver;" #3, "Performer;" #4, "Tragic Romantic;" #5, "Observer;" #6, "Devil's Advocate;" #7, "Epicure;" #8, "Boss;" and #9, "Mediator." Other names have been used since then but the basic nine categories remain the same.

Claudio's method of acquainting us with our own type was to gather a small group of people with the same Enneagram number and have them discuss their experiences of themselves in front of the class. It was easy to see how much alike we were in our approaches to life, no matter how different each of us seemed to be. One man in the group, Bob Ochs, was a Jesuit priest on leave who took the Enneagram back to the Jesuits who have used it extensively.

I found this method of learning more about oneself interesting but not helpful, as I never had liked putting people in a box by diagnosing them. Oscar Ichazo of Arica had "diagnosed" me as a 4, a Melon, from a photograph; Helen Palmer and others thought I was a 9, the Mediator; other knowledgeable friends were sure I was a 1, the Perfectionist. It also troubled me that although people with various Enneagram numbers are as easy to recognize as are those with various astrological signs, no one has been able to find a relationship between Enneagram types and astrological signs. Within their own view of the world, each seems to work fine for some people.

I was intrigued by an exercise that Bob developed called the "Light Trip." We would ask the person to keep dropping below whatever inner experience they were having at the moment to "the next level down." After dropping and deepening through levels of pain, grief and anger, they would inevitably come to an experience of light and goodness within themselves, often quite dramatically. It was enormously convincing to our students to know that they had a Spiritual Self, especially those who hadn't thought they did.

I had taken both clients and staff through the Light Trip, but I hadn't experienced it myself. When I told this to Bob, he insisted on being my guide. As he repeated, "And what is on the next level down?" I went into a trance state and described image after image. The feelings didn't turn positive, however; there was no Light. After almost an hour I found myself on a ledge overlooking a vast drop into a valley far below. "I want to jump," I said and Bob said "Go ahead."

I floated down toward a green meadow on a valley floor, with a tiny white square in the middle. As I came closer I saw that it was a blanket with a baby lying on it. I looked into its wise dreaming eyes, and saw that they were like the eyes of the sky baby in the film, *2001*. Then I disappeared completely, as did the baby. For one blazing instant I was aware only of an enormously vital scintillating energy. As I came back, I knew with absolute certainty that there was no evil of any kind in existence, and that all things— though there are no "things"— were pure.

Chapter 10   Muktananda

My experience on the Light Trip convinced me that my worries about not having any real goals were nonsense. My goals were the same as they had always been: to awaken from this painful dream, and to help other people awaken. Working with A Course in Miracles on a daily basis continued to change things for me. I could believe that Bob was my friend who had accepted the role of enemy to help me grow spiritually, and that he was doing me a great kindness when he confronted me with the flaws in my ego-self.

I began to act more lovingly toward Bob and the rest of the staff, and the atmosphere at the Center improved. After a while, however, it seemed as if the more I followed the Course's instructions to stop thinking and to surrender to its teachings, the less clearly I was able to think and act on a daily basis. I found that I needed to understand what actually happened in the Process, to be able to translate it into terms that others could understand.

The Course in Miracles says, "There are no joys in the world." I did not see how this could possibly be true: I'd known a lot of joys. (It didn't occur to me that my joy was in me and not in the world.) And wouldn't the promised "unchanging light and bliss" be a bit dull? It said, "It was all a tiny mistake from the beginning." I found it discouraging to consider that all human effort and evolution was the result of a "tiny mistake." When I continued the daily exercises, however, I felt stronger and less reactive, which made me more disconcerted by the detachment I was experiencing.

I decided that Hal Streitfaeld's focus on eliciting emotional reactions was stirring up too much emotion in me, while the Course led to too little, so I quit working with both methods. I had some sessions with a Feldenkrais practitioner named Shlomo, under whose skillful hands I briefly experienced a whole new sense of bodily trust. Moishe Feldenkreis, originally a physicist, believed that people stopped learning how to use their bodies long before they could use them well, so the resulting arrested physical development caused unnecessary limitations on their physical, mental and emotional capacities. If they followed his instructions and guidance in freeing their bodies, people could find new freedom on all levels. However, Shlomo went back to New York, and I didn't know anyone else with his level of skill.

I had heard of Baba Muktananda in 1975. He was an Indian guru in the United States who was attracting the attention of my friends and colleagues. A small group of us met with him in the living room of the upstairs apartment where he was staying. As we waited for him, a couple of girls played Indian instruments and chanted in Hindi. After two hours, without changing either their rhythm or their wistful tone, they began chanting in English, "Muk-ta-nan-da, where are you? Muk-ta-nan-da, where are you?"

Eventually Baba Muktananda arrived. He was a hearty, brown-skinned man wearing a robe and a baseball cap, whose lovely dark eyes reminded me of my brother Walter. In a few moments he was followed by Ram Dass, a well-known American spiritual teacher, who flung himself on his knees before Muktananda and was received with smiles and reassuring pats.

The friend who had taken me to Muktananda had told me that, after several meetings with him, she had decided he was not the teacher for her. As she drove off, the engine of her old Volkswagen bus exploded directly under the window of his apartment. She was thrown into the street, and regained consciousness to find Muktananda and others gathered around her. "Does this mean," she asked groggily, "that I'm supposed to follow you?" She did follow him—to India and on his worldwide tours. Though I was intrigued, the idea of following a guru felt alien to me.

With other friends, I went to a workshop by Jinendra Jain, who had been Muktananda's student and interpreter for ten years. Jinendra taught the path of Kashmir Shiavism, which was the official name of Muktananda's teachings. I found him to be a quiet, intelligent and thoughtful human being. While listening to Jinendra, my mind seemed to turn on again. I was relieved to hear that in his way of perceiving, the world was real even though it had been created out of consciousness. To him, "illusionary" meant having no permanent reality.

I read an article by Dr. Frances Clark, making the same point. He said that the steps to transcendence were two: 1) identifying with our experience and owning it, and 2) dis-identifying with it and letting it go. That is a concise summary of what we were trying to teach, step by step, in the Process, and it is the basis of most of the psychospiritual teachings I know.

Jinendra said something else that I've always loved. At lunch one day someone brought up the subject of "grace." I asked Jinendra whether he believed, as is taught in some versions of Christianity, that grace is given only to those chosen by God. "Absolutely," he said, and then added quickly in his lilting English. "But God is always anxious to choose everyone!"

Within weeks I was feeling depressed again. It was clear that the promises of the Process didn't work for everyone. Bob insisted that, after completing the Process, one could be alone without being lonely, but he himself had fallen apart when his lover Harold had left him. And as hard as I tried to get beyond it, I was lonely at times. It seemed that it was mostly those who had someone in their lives to love, and to be loved by, who did the best after the Process

Something had to change, but I didn't want to disconnect myself from the Process entirely. We needed a training manual, so I offered to take three months off to write one. Bob was delighted. During this time I had a dream: I was frantically trying to break out of a prison cell although the door was wide open. When I finally saw the open door and jumped out, I found myself drifting through a void—seemingly forever. Suddenly I was in a beautiful green valley with joyous friendly people welcoming me, and I knew that there was no need for a special companion; everyone loved everybody else.

Now that I was leaving, I could be fond of Bob again. As I watched him battle with the staff, I felt separate and adult. Bob insisted that the problem was that the staff inexplicably continued to resist him. I could acknowledge my own life-long resistance, a subtle inner "no" to almost everything. I took myself through all the Fischer/Hoffman processes on resistance. I bitched against my mother and father for teaching me resistance, forgave both them and myself, and recycled all aspects of my resistance. I ended up deciding that a person would have to be a complete idiot not to resist Bob's domination. I withdrew from the Center and stayed home, preparing the teacher training manual.

Life became infinitely simpler. I began to think about getting a Ph.D. There were so many things I wanted to know. In meditation, I could reach a space of empty mind with nothing else happening, which sometimes felt like a source of peace. I went to hear Sydney Banks from Alaska, who said that he had been walking along the beach when he was overwhelmed by a stunningly brilliant experience of God which had remained with him. Listening to him and being in his presence, I was convinced that he spoke the truth and that such a state was possible for an ordinary human being, without denying the world.

Friends were going to India to visit Muktananda's ashram, and I was tempted. I was ready to do something drastically different and that sounded just exotic enough. I'd done a weekend workshop at Muktananda's ashram in Oakland and often went there to meditate, but I had never felt that he was my guru in any sense. On the other hand, after six weeks in India, I might feel differently. The roundtrip fare was nine hundred dollars, and I could just about manage that.

When I opened the Sunday paper, I found a full-page ad proclaiming, "80 Days around the World, for $800!" It offered any stopping off place you chose, as long as you were back in eighty days. That sounded more like it: I could visit many places, not just India. I went over to

Gilda's apartment to tell her of my plans. She picked up the phone and began making international calls. Within a short time, she had arranged for me to stay with friends in Paris, and to get low- cost university housing in Kyoto, Japan. In the following weeks, Ron Kane, another Process teacher, introduced me to a friend of his who wanted to do a Fischer/Hoffman Process workshop with me in Germany, and who knew someone I could stay with. Freda's husband Lee gave me the address of a remarkable psychic outside London, and told me of a good inexpensive hotel. Blessed Marny invited me to stop with her in Kauai on my way back. Another friend was happy to stay in my apartment until I returned. The whole thing fell into place so rapidly that I ignored the tensions beginning in my solar plexus.

London in July was cold and wet and interesting in a dreary big-city way. Glad to have a reason to go elsewhere, I took a train into the countryside to visit Lee's psychic, who told me that my lost family stood around me, loving me and wishing me well. Unfortunately, all of the names he came up with were unknown to me, so I couldn't take anything he said too seriously. I wished I could believe him; it would have been nice to know I had loving companions in this new venture.

Paris was a definite improvement. Gilda's friends owned a small apartment as well as a tiny room on the floor above, where I stayed for a week. My hostesses were a delightful pair, friendly and welcoming. One evening they drove me around in their small car, even though they seldom took it out of its garage. They chattered continuously to each other in French, except when they pointed out the sights to me in very good English. I walked until I was exhausted each day, not wanting to miss anything. My only disappointment was that the Lourdes Museum was closed for repairs.

In Hamburg, Ron Kane's friend, Jerry Kogan, and I met with about fifteen people who wanted to learn about the Process. I was happy to discover that I could understand their German, and that they could understand my English, even though we hardly spoke each other's languages. They would speak in German and I would reply in English, just as I had done with my mother. It was a good evening. Afterwards Jerry escorted me to Ron's friend's house, where I immediately fell out of my role as teacher and into that of self-conscious guest.

The next morning my hostess served breakfast, an incredible spread of breads, cakes, cheese, preserves, sliced meats and sour herring. She loaned me a huge striped umbrella to go forth in the rain to find the jewelry store where my mother had been assistant manager. I found that it had been rebuilt since the war, with the circular staircase that mother had told me about at the rear. I imagined that the staircase led up to the closet where she used to climb on a stool, convinced that her fashionably laced up shoes somehow would hurt less up there.

My next destination was Bombay, as it was then called. I went directly to the train station and bought a ticket for Geneshpuri, the site of Muktananda's ashram. There were masses of people rushing about, most of them with dark Indian faces: women in saris and men in western pants and short-sleeved shirts. Here and there I saw a turban, a few light-skinned Europeans, and hordes of small, ragged, begging children. Confused by my short hair and slacks, one little girl kept tugging at my pants leg, "Mister, Mister, please!" Her huge, sorrowful eyes pleaded with me, but I'd been told that once you gave anything to a beggar child, you would be assaulted by dozens of others. I turned reluctantly away and climbed the wrought iron stairway, painfully aware of her following me, still calling, "Mister, Mister!" The image of those pleading eyes stayed with me for years.

I climbed hurriedly onto my train, forgetting that there were separate cars for men and women. I didn't notice until we were underway that the car was crowded with Indian men, who weren't fooled about my sex. After commenting to each other in Hindi, they gave me a seat to myself in a corner, and offered to lift my baggage up to the shelf above our heads. Hugely embarrassed, I sat and gazed stoically out the open window as we rattled the fifty miles to Geneshpuri.

There were half a dozen buses waiting when I arrived; a spruce young Indian in a clean white shirt pointed out the correct bus for me to take. He looked so well dressed that I took it as a kindly-meant gesture, and only after we had taken off did it occur to me that travelers' tips were his income.

On the bus, packed with both men and women in well-worn native dress, the courtesy shown me on the train vanished. No one offered me a seat, and I stood as we careened down the narrow dirt road. I was the only white person aboard, but they'd seen my ilk going to the ashram before and ignored me. Standing at the front of the bus, I discovered that the driver was playing an Indian version of "chicken." The dirt road was barely wide enough for two vehicles to pass each other, and ox-drawn wagons or cars dilapidated beyond description often blocked our lane. The driver would gear up and speed past them before we met someone coming in the opposite direction. I found myself clinging to the wooden seat back and squeezing my eyes shut at crucial moments.

The bus let me off in front of the Sri Gurudev Ashram. We had been passing only countryside and one-story native buildings for hours, so it was startling to come upon the four-story building, freshly painted mint green.

The formal entrance to the ashram was a round doorway made of highly decorated glass, with narrow glass panels on each side, all outlined in white and green. A balcony above it was covered by a flat roof, trimmed with dark green and elaborately embellished with painted white curlicues. Just to the right was the colorful working entrance, with "Gurudev Siddha Peeth" above it in gold paint. Behind the wall, with its intricately painted Hindu symbology, was a lush garden. The windows in the front of the building were arched and recessed; on one side was a great ornamented dome that towered several floors above the rest of the building.

Muktananda's favorite saying, "Love yourself in me," was repeated on English signs throughout the ashram. Like other schools of Indian philosophy, Muktananda taught that ignorance is the cause of human bondage and knowledge is the only means of human liberation. "Ignorance" means non-recognition of our True Nature, which is God, the Ultimate Reality. In Western psychology, this "ignorance" is known as the ego: our sense of individuality as well as our separation from the one Self. This separation can only be understood intellectually until it is actually experienced. According to Muktananda, the way to attain spiritual experience was through the grace of a Siddha Guru, a fully self-realized being. The giving of such grace was called shaktipat, and Muktananda delivered it by a touch on the shoulders with a wand of peacock feathers. (Years later, Western eyes saw Muktananda's giving of shaktipat to adolescent girls quite differently and he was accused of sexual abuse. He retired from public life and died soon afterwards.)

I arrived in the office at the same time as an English woman of about my age. A businesslike young American assigned us to different rooms and different work details, and gave us general information on the layout of the ashram. He assigned me the easy job of painting flower decorations, and her the more strenuous job of sweeping the pathways; we each dutifully fulfilled our assignment for the next six weeks.

I was given a cot in a small dormitory with five other European or American women. Muktananda's Indian followers, who comprised half of the several hundred people in residence, were housed separately. They slept communally in large dormitories, one for men and one for women. In the Indian dormitories, there were people moving about or carrying on conversations in normal tones all night long, which would have driven Westerners crazy. During the daytime talk was discouraged; we were to meditate during meditation hours.

The temperature was pleasantly warm, though the sun could be replaced by rain at any time as it was monsoon season, so everyone walked about with an umbrella. Many of the women, including Europeans, wore saris. The rest of us wore simple cotton dresses. Word came down that we were to wear slips under our dresses— evidently someone had gotten a glimpse of a woman's body through her transparent wet dress.

It took a while for me to get the hang of things, and I was lucky to have guidance from several people I knew from Berkeley. The day's first meditation, in the big hall, was at six a.m. Only chai (sweetened spiced tea) was offered before then, but there was a "café" where I could buy coffee and sweet rolls to see me through until the first meal of the day at noon. (There was always a café at Muktananda's ashrams. "Shakti loves sugar," our diabetic guru was reputed to have said.)

Lunch and dinner were frequently the same: something like squash, rice and dal (lentils), along with chapattis, a sort of bread. We sat cross-legged on the floor in long rows, each with our own large tin plate. The servers would stop before each person, bow, and offer food from a huge metal bucket. You could take as much as you wanted but you had to eat whatever you took, so adults with children had to finish whatever their child had not eaten. (There was hardly a grain of rice thrown away at the end of each meal.) When we were finished we took our dishes outside, rinsed them under faucets, and placed them carefully in piles. There were no towels. Our hands dried quickly in the tepid air, even when it was raining.

There were often feast days when a rich follower donated money for a more elaborate meal. Sometimes a feast day meal would run to a dozen different dishes, all unknown to most Westerners, who were sometimes surprised when what looked like dessert turned out to be spicy hot. Someone once donated an entire week of feast day foods for everyone. On the fourth day we heard that Muktananda went roaring through the kitchen, demanding that it stop. "Everyone is going to the toilet all the time!" he complained.

189

I learned that a glass of lassi, a wonderfully refreshing drink made of yogurt and sweet lime juice, and half of a large papaya from one of the little shops across the street made a far more agreeable supper than whatever was being served in the ashram dining hall. More agreeable, but perhaps not very wise. Two weeks before I left I came down with something nasty that resulted in my leaving the ashram seventeen pounds lighter than when I arrived. Feeling very sick the day before I left, I asked the Indian nurse who gave me pills if I should postpone my plane trip. "Why?" she asked, puzzled, while behind her rose an image of the sick and starving multitudes of India. Why, indeed, for a little digestive upset that was curable? I retreated, ashamed.

Baba Muktananda was in evidence at every turn, either in person or in a hundred large pictures. All the temples and other buildings, however, were dedicated to his teacher, Nitchananda. At the beginning of each meditation, Muktananda went behind his throne-like seat and made obeisance to Nitchananda. I could appreciate the reverence in which each of them was held, and could almost believe that they were both great beings.

One of my roommates told me that, before she even knew who he was, she was meditating when a small image of Muktananda appeared to her, circled through the air and then entered directly into her heart. It was much the same story that Marny had told me regarding her guru, Kirpal Singh: she had dreamed of him for months before she saw a picture of him. Nothing like that happened to me. I could let my mind go silent during the chanting, which was the main form of meditation, but it never lifted me out of myself to feel a part of something larger. I did not attain

190

either the faith or the joy I had hoped for, though I felt quiet and focused during most of the days.

One of the main feast days was Muktananda's birthday. After he circled the ashram grounds on a beautifully bedecked elephant, we all gathered in the courtyard to hear him speak. Before he began, he demonstrated his amazing dexterity and speed in removing and rewinding his white turban, to enthusiastic applause. When he wasn't being official, he liked all sorts of different hats; his favorites were American baseball caps.

At the end of our stay, each of us got to have an interview with Baba Muktananda, a great honor. Clad in a sari I'd bought especially for the occasion, I was excited to be making a personal connection with the guru. As soon as I was seated on the pillow before him, he thrust a large, chewy piece of a specially blessed sweetmeat called "prasad" into my mouth, and made a brief statement. His translator explained that he had said I should take care of myself and that he wished me well. Finally, Muktananda struck me lightly on the shoulder with his peacock feathers. When the assistant ushered me out to make way for the next person, I was still unable to speak because my mouth was full.

On the plane to Delhi some sort of tension left me. For the first time since I had arrived in India, I felt blissfully happy. I wasn't sure if this was the result of my visit to Geneshpuri, the fact that I was leaving the otherness of the ashram behind, or that the bacterial illness I'd suffered for the past two weeks was beginning to clear up. In Delhi I checked into a clean and cheap YWCA hotel I'd heard about, and set out the next morning to see the sights of the city. Within a couple of blocks I'd had to say "no"

191

three times to hopeful young Indian men who offered to be my guide. It became clear that an unaccompanied female tourist was fair game, so I asked the next guide who approached me how much he charged. "Oh, no charge," he assured me with a happy show of white teeth against his dark skin, "It would be a pleasure to show you my city." Not believing him for a moment, I took him on.

It turned out to be a good idea, because other would-be guides no longer bothered me, and Mohammed was a pleasant and knowledgeable companion. He easily engaged bicycle rickshaws and negotiated with the drivers. We saw both the old and new parts of the city; we dined in reasonably priced and quite pleasant restaurants and went to see the great Red Fort. Later, he took care of moving all my luggage (which had grown a bit) when my reservation at the YWCA ran out and I had to move to another hotel for a couple of nights.

Although I paid for all our trips and meals, I wondered if Mohammed was taking a commission because he never mentioned any fee for himself. He saw me to my hotel in the evenings and was waiting cheerfully outside my door the next morning. We took a train one day to see the Taj Mahal. I asked him to do something else for a couple of hours, since I wanted to be free to wander about that incredible building by myself. I found it more exquisitely beautiful than any photograph could show, or than all the admiration I'd ever read about it had conveyed.

When I left Delhi by taxi to catch my late night flight to Hong Kong, Mohammed insisted on accompanying me to the airport. On the way I gave him what I figured was a good tip; he seemed well pleased with it. I didn't know until later that someone (perhaps he) had pried the turquoise stone out of the ring Warren had given me when I left Bishop. It had been the only valuable item in my luggage.

One of the Chinese women I'd met at the ashram, who lived in the huge crowded city of Hong Kong, had made a hotel reservation for me. I was grateful to have a small out-of-the-way place with a view of the river for the two days I was in Hong Kong. The second day, I took a boat across the bay and then the tram up to Victoria Peak, where I stood with other tourists watching a wonderfully symbolic thunder and lightning storm play ominously over the hills of mainland China.

My plane landed at the new Tokyo airport at midnight; the airport was cavernously empty with only a handful of other passengers disembarking. Some travelers had limousines waiting to take them the twenty-five miles to their hotels in the city, but I had made no such arrangement. A hesitant young American woman, burdened with a backpack, discovered that the last train of the night was leaving for Tokyo a couple of floors down. Together we raced down the steps and reached it just before it pulled out, only to be told that we needed to buy tickets at the other end of the building. To our amazement, they held the train for us and we made it, flushed and happy and thoroughly awake.

It turned out that my new friend, Sarah, with a blessedly familiar American accent, was a schoolteacher from Arizona touring Japan on her own. Like me, she was much more interested in the temples of Kyoto than in the metropolis of Tokyo. When we got to the Tokyo train station at two a.m., we found that the bullet train for Kyoto left at six. It seemed foolish to try to find a hotel for a few hours, so we stayed in the station overnight. Their molded fiberglass chairs were not meant for sleeping, so all we could do was doze intermittently.

In the early hours of the morning, several Japanese people approached us in friendly fashion with the intent of practicing their English. I remember one tiny old woman in a long red dress, red hat and red high-heeled shoes who talked with us before wandering off. After my companion had fallen into a fitful sleep, an old man approached me and, struggling to find the right English words, asked, "No victor, no victim. What does it mean?" I thought it had been one of the American slogans for Japan after World War II, so I held up my hands side by side, one several inches above the other. "Victor," I said indicating the upper one, "victim" indicating the lower. I brought them level with each other. "No victor, no victim." He beamed, thanked me effusively, bowed deeply, and left. Considering the hour, I was proud of coming up with that, though I knew the question was probably his way of engaging a foreigner in conversation.

Just before six, Sarah and I gathered up our belongings, washed up a bit and boarded the bullet train for Kyoto. We had heard about its 200 mile-an-hour speed and were rather excited to be taking it, though we were too tired to be very impressed as it dashed through the green countryside. It was good to be with an American again, so I invited her to share the inexpensive dormitory room at the university that Gilda had arranged for me. Together we visited temples and the palace and massive figures of the Buddha. Language was not a problem. The restaurants showed colorful pictures of the dishes they offered, the street signs were in both Japanese and English, and we had only to open a map to have Japanese men and women crowd around us, eager to offer assistance in their broken English.

We went to the nearby town of Nara to see the original of a large photograph of a bodhisattva that Charlotte Selver displayed at all her workshops. The portrait was so serenely beautiful that when I found a copy of it in a coffee table book on Oriental art, I had it mounted for my wall at home. It looks like an infinitely knowing and peaceful young Buddha, but is a bodhisattva known as the Nyoirin Kannon. Kannon is the Japanese translation of Quan Yin, the Buddhist goddess of compassion. The small temple containing the statue had a heavy overhanging roof and was situated near a beautiful green park full of deer that mingled tamely with the people. The lovely, life-sized, camphor wood figure, carved 1300 years ago, didn't look quite as I remembered it from the photograph. A small sign in English said that the original halo-like headdress had been stolen.

Finally, I was with Marny in Kauai. She had been able to rent a small bungalow, part of the old plantation manager's estate in the middle of the little-visited public Ola Pua Gardens. Other than a couple of trips to the nearby beaches, we stayed in the gardens, talking, taking long walks and eating the ripe mangoes that had fallen from the huge tree near her home. The last week of my eighty days around the world passed in gentle friendship.

Chapter 11   Los Angeles

When I returned from Hawaii to San Francisco, I wasn't willing to go back to work for Bob; I no longer wanted to be involved in that level of dissension. I was sure that the Process could be converted to individual therapy, but I did not want to be in competition with the San Francisco Institute. It was time for me to return to my longtime home in the Los Angeles area, where I knew people and where both my adult children lived. My friend, Margaret Conway, wanted to move back to LA also, so we decided to share an apartment in Santa Monica.

Shevy Healy, a psychologist friend who had worked with me at the Neuropsychiatric Institute at UCLA, became my first individual Process client. The Process cleared up so many things for her that she sent a number of her friends and clients to me. They referred others and soon I had a busy satisfying practice, but still I felt at loose ends.

Mary Alexander, whom I had taken through a version of the Process in Bishop, was also in Los Angeles. She had been training in Canada in the therapeutic use of

LSD and Ketamine, and she offered to take me on a guided Ketamine experience which I accepted gladly. I was very willing to take Ketamine again to try to access a different, higher state of consciousness.

She set up her bedroom beautifully for the occasion, with flowers, candles, incense and soft music. We both expected an experience of transcendence, but immediately after the Ketamine injection, I lost consciousness. All I could remember afterwards was that it had been a very enjoyable vacation-like time, colorful and pleasant. We were both disappointed. She suggested that I go home, smoke some pot, and look into my eyes in a mirror for an hour.

I didn't have any marijuana, but I retreated to my bedroom at home to follow the rest of her instructions. I put a mirror on my desk, lit a candle, set the alarm for an hour and stared resolutely at my own image. After a while, what I had come to think of as my unattractive, aging face vanished from the mirror to be replaced by an unknown feminine face, gazing serenely back at me. She was a woman of about my own age, but her clear eyes were a different color and shape than mine and her hair was light brown, swept casually back from a smooth forehead. It was a face I couldn't remember ever having seen before, but one that seemed more familiar than my own. Her face was there for only a few seconds and then it vanished, and I saw only my own face reflected in the mirror.

Her face replaced mine again and again, each time for a little longer. Finally, she stayed in the mirror looking quietly back at me. When the timer went off, she disappeared. Stunned, I rose and wandered into the bathroom, where I discovered that my reflection in the bathroom mirror looked different to me. My customary visage had become a "good enough" face, more attractive, with better color and expression than before. Since this experience, I've never again seen my own face as ill-favored. That other face has stayed in my memory and I know I would recognize her if we were to meet. Or perhaps we do meet when I turn inside for guidance; perhaps she is the face of my guide.

I continued to "work on myself" on many levels. Over and over, I would reach the state of believing in the message of the Course in Miracles: "only God is real!" My joy and sense of inner peace would last for days, or even weeks. But into the midst of my belief, came bouts of questioning its truth. "Turn off your mind," the Course insisted, "let Me guide you. Surrender. What you really yearn for is rest." In some profound way I believed it to be the truth, but I couldn't accept it wholeheartedly, at least not yet. There was still too much else to explore.

Our apartment became the center of an active social life. Friends I'd made at UCLA, and Margaret's friends, came by. My clients were in and out. Warren spent a few days with me every month or so, and occasionally I drove to visit him in Bishop. My son and daughter lived in Los Angeles and, although they were busy with their own lives, we saw each other often.

Living with Margaret had its difficulties as well as its pleasures. She was messy and she ate the fruit I bought before it ripened properly. I was "rigid," unwilling to just "hang out" with her in the evenings. She would get angry and I would go silent. I disliked her smoking marijuana—I'd been wary of smoking pot since I'd taken the Arica training, and I didn't feel like drinking either. Our evenings together found me sober and serious, when she wanted to be relaxed and frivolous. I knew I was too serious. How could I stop being so serious and become the person I knew I could be?

In the individual Reichian bodywork sessions I was taking with a new teacher, I plunged again and again into numbness or hopelessness. More explicitly, the yearning I'd felt for so many years to die and get the whole thing over with, kept surfacing. I could not stand myself or the world we live in. I would watch a hearse in a funeral procession or notice the death notices in the newspaper, and assure myself, "I'll get to do that someday." At the same time, I was suspicious of the sincerity of my own wish for death. If I really wanted to die, surely I could have managed to do so by now?

What did seem true to me was that the Process was far from the panacea it was promised to be. If all this grief and anger underlay my own cheerfulness, then the Process was too superficial to be of any real value. Maybe there was no way to cure the "sickness" of being human. Natural disasters, disease, hunger and old age were bad enough, but what we do to each other and to ourselves is the real horror. I began to believe that the Buddha was right when he said that life is suffering. Was I giving my Process clients hope where there was none? But Shevy was obviously much happier, as were many of the others. I didn't understand any of this, but I wanted to.

I was ready to do something else, to try something new. I knew what to do to become happier and more effective, but that wasn't enough. How did what I was doing work? Freda and I took a five-day advanced workshop from a teacher named Gil Boyne, who used hypnosis as a way of influencing people into becoming happy and successful. I became so annoyed at his brash personality, and at his wife's eagerness to sell his books, that I was unable to learn from him. Later, I went to a hypnosis workshop conducted by Freda. I liked her non-directive and unobtrusive approach much better than Gil's; perhaps I could use her approach as one of my therapy tools.

At my next bodywork session I saw clearly how often I found it necessary to tell people how important I was, or I wished they knew I was important or I resented that they didn't know. Finally, I realized that I could now look honestly at myself without self-loathing. I had seen the truth about my inner thoughts and about some of my behaviors twenty years ago in Subud, and more recently in the Fischer/Hoffman Process. Yet it had taken me all this time to get to where I could stand still and look, even though I still heartily disapproved of myself.

As we got to know each other better, Margaret and I became closer. The pot-smoking, middle-aged party girl with her outspoken anger had given way to a lonely, unhappy woman, agonizing over the bad relationship she'd had with her mother who had died a year ago. After she let me take her through the mother part of the Process, she was able to find resolution and to mourn her loss with love and appreciation.

Later in the year I went to Berkeley for five days to see friends. Bob Hoffman was not in good shape, a little depressed and feeling his age, though he was a year younger than me. He was trying to learn to let go of his tight grip on every aspect of the Process and let other people take over, at least partially. He wanted me to come back and work at the Center. Freda wanted me to join her new business, the Hypnosis Clearing House, but I felt very leery of her repeated pronouncements that she intended to be "rich and famous," that this was her pathway to growth. I was sure it wasn't mine.

∞ ∞ ∞ ∞ ∞

Back in Santa Monica, when I reread my journals, I saw myself learning the same things over and over. Repeatedly running my "father deserted me" trip, and doing my mother's defensiveness, superiority, inadequacies, and criticisms, again and again. I knew that I didn't have to be this way, but I was being it anyhow. I went back and forth between softening and becoming more real, and running the same negative trips as before. I love. I hate. I have compassion. I rage. I feel connection with God. I feel lost and unhappy. My egocentricity overwhelmed me.

We are all sinners the Christian churches proclaim. Pride, lust, envy, anger, covetousness, gluttony, and sloth are the seven deadly sins that beset us. Human beings are taught that they must eradicate these sins in themselves, or at least acknowledge them and ask for forgiveness. Even though Freda and Lee and I had talked about this, I hadn't realized that I was wrestling with the same problems human beings have been trying to solve for thousands of years. I experienced these sins in myself in their full Technicolor horror. Set against the experiences of joy and love I'd had, they were all the darker.

I recognized what had bothered me about the current "me generation's" consciousness-raising trip— it was their self-importance, their damned, childish self-absorption. One of my clients, a therapist who intended to teach the Process, told me how he was changing, how he wanted more time for himself, more nourishment; how he heard a voice within crying "me!" I felt myself cringe inwardly. I taught people to love themselves—they must love themselves to be whole. Why then, I asked myself, did it bother me when they announced triumphantly that they do? It was a given for me that no one can truly love another until they love themselves. Yet inside, I reacted against that assertion. Surely there must be something more useful that I could do with the rest of my life than work on myself!

Knowing this, I still wasn't willing to give up on inner exploration. There was so much I didn't know. In my Reichian sessions I continued to find new depths in myself; I encountered rage over having accepted other people's versions of how I should be and disappointment at not knowing who I really was. I swore to myself that, cost what it might, I would find out.

Margaret returned from a month's vacation in a happier frame of mind than I'd ever known her, and Shevy was in a wonderful space. For the first time in many years, she had arrived at a new and loving relationship with her daughter and had decided that she wanted to teach the Process. I was crewing on a friend's thirty-two foot sloop, sailing to Catalina Island every week and loving being on the ocean.

∞ ∞ ∞ ∞ ∞

I took a weekend workshop in Silva Mind Control. They taught most of what was in the Course in Miracles, but I thought that they had missed a major point: the surrender to a higher force that I was battling within myself. "You must learn to give yourself orders," they

203

taught. That seemed like hubris to me. When I felt most at home with myself, my "orders" came from somewhere else, not from my conscious mind.

The final process of the Silva Mind Control weekend was to write a description of the physical illness or disability of someone you knew, then let another student attempt to read your mind, having only the name of the ill person. Surprisingly, about 70% of the students managed to do it successfully. When it was my turn to do the reading, I saw an obese woman sitting in a wheelchair because of troubles with her legs. My partner's card read "ulcerated varicose veins in her legs." The person my partner had in mind wasn't actually fat, but often complained about gaining weight because she could not exercise. I also saw a younger woman in the background, standing with her back to the ill woman. In reality, this person had a daughter who reluctantly took care of her. It appeared that, with practice, it was possible to learn to read another person's thoughts.

Margaret took me on several guided mind trips to help me decide whether to stay in Los Angeles or return to San Francisco. In one, I saw myself stylishly and expensively dressed, with perfect hair and nails, living in an elegant beautifully appointed home. It seemed that I had earned all this as a highly successful professional therapist somewhere in Los Angeles. "How did you feel there?" Margaret asked. "I felt nothing," I said "except admiration for how perfect everything was." There was no heart in it, no life.

When she suggested that I try again, this time I found myself in a comfortable, informal room with many trees visible outside the windows. A desk covered with books and papers filled one side of the room, and on the other side was a big deep inviting sofa, where I could imagine reading far into the night, or pulling a blanket over myself and going to sleep. I was seated at the desk, casually dressed in slacks with my feet up, and I was reading, making notes, and feeling completely at home. I saw myself lounging on the sofa, talking and laughing intimately with a couple of friends. This place could only be in the San Francisco Bay Area.

A week later we had a potluck dinner for all our graduates, and it was clear that the one-to-one Process was a success. Shevy and David Grill, another therapist who had taken the Process with me, were bursting with enthusiasm. Among us we had eight clients ready to go. There was the possibility of real success with the Process here in Los Angeles.

By the beginning of my sixtieth year, I had decided that "all is illusion" and "all is real" merely reflected the level on which you perceived them, just as seeing an object as a solid or as a swarm of molecules depended on the level from which you were seeing it. Trouble comes when we operate on the lower or solid level, while pretending we are on the higher one. Getting to the higher level requires intention, effort and grace.

What I said to our graduating students was "What matters is your intention. You've learned the tools, now you have the opportunity to use them on the major issues of your life—and none of your tools will make any permanent difference unless it is your intention that they will. Do you intend to use your tools to let go of grief, of anger about the losses in your life, of disappointment for the ways in which you have defined yourself so far? Are you willing to take on a new way of dealing with life?" I was really talking to myself—was I willing to take on a new way of dealing with my life?

I read John Blofeld's *Bodhisattva of Compassion; the Mystical Tradition of Kuan Yin,* and loved the part where Kuan Yin changes into a thousand other forms to show that they were all one. Marny brought me a little statue of Quan Yin and, when I felt distressed, I prayed to her. Suddenly my "face in the mirror," the other woman who was achingly familiar, gentle, whole, my unknown self, was an unseen presence. All my tension and fear and ready anger, all the frequent feelings of being threatened, left me. Blofeld had spoken of the need for the imaginative acceptance of some kind of symbol that was charismatic for me. I felt as if I had been searching for such an image of inner guidance all my life. When I turned to Quan Yin, my attention was no longer drawn inward to lick my wounds; I was no longer the naïve, self-disapproving imitation of a grown-up that I had created. I felt quiet and peaceful as I went about my daily work, enveloped in grace.

After a while, however, I began to fret. I had peace of mind, happiness, professional success, friends, kids, and a possible new male relationship. Yet it wasn't enough, because all offered only temporary satisfaction—wonderful now but not to be pursued year after year. I began to notice that I felt a subtle sense of wasting time no matter what I was doing. I felt good, I even did what seemed to be good, but I did not feel the rightness of my activity, or of my accomplishments. My life was like a dance in which I was trying to follow music I couldn't really hear. I had no sense of using my precious human capacity of choice.

I knew how to go into a state of inner peace and serenity, and I could teach others how to as well. I could create, as the Course in Miracles called it, "thinner, happier dreams." But that wasn't enough. There was more, I was certain, and I sensed that there were people somewhere who knew more. I began to think once again about getting my Ph.D. When I studied the offerings of various universities, the only one that seemed to teach what I wanted to learn was the California Institute of Integral Studies, in San Francisco.

Margaret took me on a guided imagery trip to find someone who could tell me what to do. In my visualization, I climbed a mountain path and met a wise man, shriveled and ancient, meditating in a cave near the edge of a cliff. When I asked to see his face, I got an impression of level eyes, not old, totally present but impersonal. Margaret suggested that I ask about the anxiety I had been feeling in my solar plexus since I had begun thinking of returning to San Francisco.

The guru rose and pushed me over the cliff. For an instant I was in free fall and scared, and then he reached out and grabbed me effortlessly, holding me safely. My momentary bewilderment and fear relaxed into enjoyment of swinging in space. I took it as a powerful statement that my inner guide would keep me safe, even though my situation might seem precarious. There was no longer a question in my mind: in the fall, using my remaining savings, I would return to San Francisco to enter the California Institute of Integral Studies as a doctoral student.

During the next month I went to visit Warren at his home in Bishop. As he came out of his mother's house to greet me, a voice within me said quietly, "he's dying."

Shocked, I promptly put the negative thought aside. Even though he was too ill to do much, we had a pleasant, friendly time together that weekend. On our last evening he held my hand and told me, "You know, you are my best friend."

In Santa Monica, I sent the same letter to everyone I knew in the San Francisco Bay Area, telling of my plans to return and asking if they knew of a place I could live. I got only one reply, a telephone call from Ron Kane, saying simply, "Come and live with me." I knew his big, old house in Berkeley; I'd attended Thanksgiving parties there several times. The two other young men with whom he had bought it, Hameed Ali and Raymond Biase, had both married and moved away, leaving him with a too-big house that he couldn't afford. I was delighted to share it.

I was so glad to return to the North Berkeley hills, with their greenery and views across the bay of San Francisco and the magnificent bridges. I'd decided years before that I didn't want to live in San Francisco; I wanted to live where I could look at San Francisco. When I arrived, Ron solemnly explained more than a dozen "rules of the house," mentioning how neatly things were to be kept, how expenses were to be shared, and so on. I sat there agreeing to everything, chortling inwardly, too happy to be back in the Bay Area to find anything he said objectionable.

Chapter 12   CIIS

Before I began my fall term at CIIS in San Francisco, I experimented with a new form of psychological work called Focusing. Focusing was created by Eugene Gendlin, a professor at the University of Chicago, based on his research showing that real psychological change occurs only when there is a "felt sense" of change in the body. The protocol he devised begins with a simple question, "What stands between me and feeling fine?" The questioner senses what has happened in her body in response to the question and welcomes whatever signals come up. She gets a "handle" for the bodily response. That is, she finds a phrase or image that relates to what she is feeling. Then she goes back and forth between the chosen "handle" and the "felt sense" in her body until they "resonate," i.e. they are fully connected to each other. At that point the personal issue underlying the problem usually becomes clear. She then asks herself (or is asked) a series of questions such as "What is so painful about this?" "What might it need?" "What might help?" or "What would it be like to have a good solution?" while checking how the answers feel in her body. She can tell by a bodily shift and sense of recognition, that she has reached resolution.

Using the Focusing procedure, I felt the loneliness of not having an active partner in my life as a vague discomfort in my chest. I looked for a name or image for that feeling. Suddenly I saw a brilliant circle, shooting out bright blue flames, descending through the evening sky to sink into the dark ocean stretching to the horizon. When I resonated that image with the feeling in my chest, I experienced a quiet acceptance of my own impending old age and death. This beautiful image was reminding me that my life was on its descending trajectory, and it was time to pay attention to what was really important.

Impressed, I decided to try Focusing on the sense of incompetence that so often plagued me. When I paid attention to my body, I noticed tension in my stomach. The image that came as a handle was my being in charge of the fast-growing Process Center for a month. Then I flashed on how unsafe I had felt when we hit heavy seas while sailing under another woman's leadership. Resonating to that, I came upon my childhood sense that the world wasn't safe when my mother was in charge—only the presence of my father would have made it safe. I continued to focus on my anxiety and asked what it needed. There was a sudden, consolingly clear message as my body relaxed and I got the answer: "To recognize that it is a lie." Focusing was clearly another valuable tool for inner exploration.

When I started my Ph.D. program in 1982, CIIS was located in three large private houses around Dolores and Church Streets in San Francisco. (One of them was almost a mile from the other two.) None of the well-known philosophers who had founded it (Haridas Chaudhuri, Frederick Speigelburg and Alan Watts) was still alive. It wasn't even clear who was running it, although Chaudhuri's widow Bina was still actively involved. I really didn't care. Its catalog offered philosophy, religious traditions and modern psychology, which were the exact subjects I wanted to study.

I picked three of the available classes that sounded interesting to me: "The Life and Literature of Contemporary Japan," "Buddhist Self-healing," and "The Theory and Practice of Mindfulness Meditation."

I was welcomed enthusiastically to the class on "The Life and Literature of Contemporary Japan." There were six students: two mature professional men in business suits, a couple who were strikingly casual in appearance, and a younger woman. The professor was a tiny, twinkly old Englishman who had taught Japanese literature to English-speaking students in Tokyo for twenty years, without ever learning to speak Japanese. Teaching this course at CIIS meant he was financially able to visit with his friends in America. The professional-type men were the president and the provost of CIIS; the couple and the single woman were the professor's friends and were guests in the class. I was especially welcome because I was the only paying student whose presence legitimized the course. The CIIS officials did not return after the first class, but the rest of us had a fine time discussing the works of modern Japanese authors. I thought the stories beautiful, but I had difficulty empathizing with their fatalism toward whatever happened. The famous author, Yukio Mishima, particularly disturbed me: not only did his characters commit hari kari (disemboweling themselves with a dagger) but so had he, bloodily and publicly.

The Mindfulness class was simple and clear. Using your breathing as an anchor, you watched whatever thoughts and emotions arose in your awareness while, at the same time, letting go of trying to do anything about

211

them. I argued with the earnest young instructor, John Welwood, that our expectations about meditation already constituted an interference with seeing things as they are. In my own attempts at this form of meditation, I'd never been able to achieve more than noticing my uncomfortable bodily sensations and my mildly drifting thoughts about everyday affairs. Distrust of anything good coming out of mindfulness meditation constituted my set of expectations.

Buddhist Self-healing was taught by a small brown middle-aged woman wearing black robes. Rina Sincar had been a nun in a Buddhist monastery in the Far East since her fifteenth year. She startled me by describing healing experiences she had had and assigning, as homework, a book written by an American chiropractor whose preface described exactly the same events as having happened to him. One of them had taken the other's story, but I had no idea which one. I didn't ask because she was so clearly revered by the young students who had studied with her before, and who saw her as a kind of saint.

She taught a Buddhist meditation on the "32 body parts," which sometimes used the customary names for bodily organs and sometimes used terms like "new food" for stomach and "bile" for spleen. I understood that this meditation was a way of disconnecting from one's body by thinking of its parts individually and objectively. Rina taught the meditation as if it would heal the parts. Though she didn't say so, I thought what she meant was that by seeing "body parts" objectively, we could remove our fearful, subjective view and thereby heal them. She explained that the ancient Buddhist sutras taught that, when free of fear and worries and tensions, the mind is full of positive healing forces. She herself was a center of peace

212

and compassion and seemed to be using whatever New Age ideas she found in this strange land to try to tell us how she had gotten to such peace and contentment.

Later that fall I got a telegram from Warren's sister, Josephine, telling me that Warren had died of a heart attack. I felt unable to grasp what had happened, although I had somehow known at our last visit that he was dying. I was grateful when Marny, visiting from Hawaii, offered to drive with me to Bishop to attend his funeral. It was only on seeing Warren's body lying in his coffin, his face made up and unreal, that the tears came and I felt almost unbearably sad.

I was grateful that Warren hadn't lived long enough to lose his eyesight or any more of his mobility because of his often-untreated diabetes, but I missed him deeply. In the coming months, I began to see what a gift his presence had been. My transition from never feeling complete without a partner to being a whole person on my own had become possible through my relationship with him. I found myself saying to my intimates that he had been my last lover, in all senses of the word. In my late sixties, I knew with only mild regret that this was the way it was going to be for the rest of my life.

Despite the peculiarities of the California Institute for Integral Studies, including their frequent lack of sound scholarship, I continued my doctoral program in Philosophy and Religion. (I probably felt more at home because of the peculiarities.) In the spring I chose among their rather limited offerings a couple of psychology classes and one on the Asian Foundations of the Integral Perspective. This was 1983, before Asian perspectives were endemic in western culture.

Group Dynamics turned out to be almost entirely experiential, using the dozen or so students in the class as the group whose dynamics we were to study. It was led by a large and confidant professor named Walt Voigt. He kept telling us that the group was to be entirely non-directive, but he was so strong a personality that his presence shaped our interactions. When I pointed this out to him, he agreed and said that his tendency to control everything was the reason he wanted a non-directive group.

I was the oldest person in the class and was only too aware of the likelihood of my again becoming an object of negative mother-transference. But I also recognized my lack of connection with the other students and my frequent annoyance with them. I seldom spoke, but since our homework assignment was to describe what happened in each session, I found that on paper I could quite ruthlessly analyze the other participants' behavior as well as my own.

The class on the Psychology of Feeling and Emotion was taught by a young woman who displayed little feeling or emotion, and it had little to teach me academically that I hadn't known before. The experiential exercises, however, were valuable in giving me new perspectives on human behavior.

The class on Integral Perspectives, on the other hand, had some intellectual meat. I learned about the history and practices of Hinduism and Buddhism, Taoism and Confucianism. I found their literature sometimes daunting, but I liked getting to exercise my mind. Words I could understand; it was the "background music" that continued to escape me.

The subjects I took in the succeeding two years were more academic than those first classes. In papers I compared either Christian Science or A Course In Miracles to the philosophies or religions we were studying, trying to understand how their ideas fit together. When I completed the required units in the fall of 1984, I was not sure if I was willing to undertake the writing of a dissertation, or what my subject should be. My dissertation advisor asked me why I wanted a Ph.D. in Philosophy and Religion. I told him that it was so I could understand the books I wanted to read, and so I could talk with people who were knowledgeable about such things. Both of these were true. It was also true that I loved being a student and learning new ideas, and also that I wanted the status of having a Ph.D.

Because I thought of CIIS as a rather flaky graduate school and myself as a rather flaky student, I never felt that I deserved the title "Dr," even though CIIS was a fully accredited university and my committee told me that the dissertation I eventually wrote was of far greater scope and scholarly detail than was required. In fact, looking at my dissertation now, it seems to me to be a sound piece of work. On the other hand, my faculty advisor kindly finagled the two-year foreign language requirements for me, and cheerfully accepted my life experience with Subud, Gestalt therapy, Muktananda and hypnosis as transfer credits.

I struggled with topics for my dissertation for more than a year, always circling around the major dichotomies in the truths I knew. Have we created the whole damn thing ourselves? Christian Science, Science of Mind and A Course In Miracles clearly had hold of some kind of truth. When I followed them, things went better for me; I was happier, there was less dissension in my life, and people were friendlier. Concrete things happened too: at sixteen I had found that ring in the bottom of a crowded swimming pool after I had cleared my thoughts; I could heal myself of the flu; and when I did nothing but turn my mind to having more clients, the phone started ringing. But I couldn't relate to the people I knew who followed those paths; they didn't feel authentic to me, and I knew I wasn't being genuine either. I didn't fully believe the teachings, I just used them.

I thought it might be useful to write about anger and forgiveness, so I read a lot of people's ideas about anger. One author pointed out that, in its essence, anger is the sense that a wrong has been committed coupled with the passionate intention of flinging oneself into battle to correct it. It is a commitment to act. That was appealing. The spiritual approach was to recognize that the whole thing is going on in your own mind and to correct it there. Even when it worked, where was the fun in that? There was something in me that objected to the idea of "it is all in your mind." And yet, at the same time, I believed that it *is* all in our minds. I was revolted at the thought that you should love other people because they are yourself as A Course In Miracles said; it sounded bloodless, solipsistic. What if you didn't love yourself?

I was stuck between these two realities, but not committed to either one. It felt like a form of mental constipation. I'd yearned for a cause that I could commit to heart and soul, yet I was always aware of the one-sidedness, the temporariness of everything we did and of how self-serving our every act is. Even when we appear to be doing things for other people, *we* are the ones who feel good about it.

I believed that my mind created my world, yet the spiritual perspectives I was drawn to, teach that you must let the Holy Spirit make your decisions. I'd certainly known relief when I turned to another, surer part of myself (perhaps it was the Holy Spirit) for guidance. But it felt like letting someone else take over my life while I went along for the ride. Why was there no satisfying sense of self-activity, of personal choice in any of this?

On one side, the world is complete, exactly as it is; there is nothing to do but recognize its perfection. We can get rid of the illusions of unhappiness, guilt, war, misery, and poverty simply by teaching ourselves to think differently, for it is all in our minds. On the other side, my intellect kept falling over the inconsistencies. The old inconsistency: God is Love and loves us all but created us with the potential to create misery for ourselves and others. A Course In Miracles presented new inconsistencies: the whole human trip happened because of a small error, made so long ago it should have been forgotten by this time, only it hasn't been. A Course In Miracles says that God is perfect, but He is lonely for his sons. It says that God has only one son, Jesus Christ—and you and me. But I didn't feel like God's child, no matter how much I tried to follow the spiritual teachings I knew. I felt like a confused and rather lonely woman, coming to fully integrated life only when I got to use my mind and emotions and skills as a therapist or as a student.

I took a class in Aikido, whose many variations are based on the idea of using the energy of one's opponents to overcome them. It was originally taught by a legendary Japanese man known as O Sensei; my Aikido master was a serenely centered young woman who taught Aikido as a psychospiritual discipline. It was not a combative practice; it was more like a dance of exchanging energy with a partner. It was lovely to experience the simple pleasures of being in my body, of directly tasting and touching and feeling the world. She urged me to forget the dissertation and the Ph.D., "You are so close to discovering how to simply be," she said. But I couldn't give up doing a dissertation and having a Ph.D.. There was still too much to learn.

I thought I might write a dissertation about the history and consequences of anger and forgiveness. After months of wrestling with the material, I decided that, together, they were too major a project; I would write only about forgiveness. It was certainly prominent in A Course In Miracles, and there were at least half a dozen popular books on forgiveness in the bookstores by people with various religious approaches. It felt like a fertile subject for investigation and it was—I used much of my time over the next year putting it together. Its rather weighty title is *The Nature of Forgiveness in the Christian Tradition, Modern Western Psychology and A Course In Miracles.*

At CIIS you weren't required to do a research project; the dissertation could be heuristic in form. I did a lot of reading about Christian forgiveness, and also about what Freud, Jung, Fromm, Maslow and Rogers had to say on forgiveness, as well as analyzing the use of the word in the Course. There was general agreement that forgiveness means that, after a relationship is broken because one party has apparently wronged the other, the second party extends love rather than vengeance or rejection, and thereby reconstitutes the relationship.

218

According to the works of well-known Christian theologians, however, I found that most Christian churches throughout the centuries had focused on the necessity of being forgiven by God for our on-going sinfulness, rather than on our forgiving each other. Jesus' clear instruction in the Lord's Prayer, "Forgive us our trespasses, as we forgive others," hadn't gotten much attention from these theologians. In fact, the idea of forgiveness being extended by anyone but God, or one of His earthly representatives, had been considered heresy for a time.

In order to relate forgiveness to secular psychology, it had to be stripped down to its simplest and most basic formulation. In Christianity the two "parties" to forgiveness are God (the Good One who has been rejected) and humanity (the sinful one who has rejected the Good). In psychology, the two "parties" might be said to be the better aspect or possibilities of a person, and the lesser and more painful aspects of the self (or of another person) that is now operating in one's life. The psychologists all dealt with a sense of wrongness in human beings, and the belief that there is something better available to them. In A Course In Miracles, on the other hand, all human beings are one; the world as we experience it is pure projection. Forgiveness of one's fellows is necessary to acknowledge that we are all one, but there really isn't anything to forgive.

I was still struggling with the dissertation when I was offered a better place to live. Dhiravamsa, the meditation teacher who had been living in the small studio apartment under the garage behind Ron Kane's house, decided to leave. It was further down the hillside, entirely private, surrounded by so much greenery that the large

219

windows seemed to open onto a wood rather than a suburban neighborhood. It even had a little fish pool outside its glass patio doors. Its ceiling was the unpainted wooden beams that held up the garage floor above. Its funkiness appealed to me and I was delighted when Ron offered it to me. After I moved in, I recognized how much it resembled the living space in the guided visualization that I had done with Margaret, before I moved back to Berkeley.

While in graduate school in San Francisco, I'd kept in touch with staff at the Fischer/Hoffman Center, who had been urging me to return. They seemed to be much happier, and Dorothea Hamilton, Kathie Tamm and Bob Hoffman all assured me that they were now working together harmoniously. I decided that I would begin teaching part-time at the Center. When I recently reminded Dorothea, still a good friend, what she and Kathie had told me about their working together in harmony, she answered blithely, "We lied."

At the Center the usual difficulties of putting up with Bob resumed, though the Institute itself was fairly successful. The classes were running to twenty-five people, as many as we had individual teachers for. As before, when it seemed that the Process wasn't working for students as well as was expected, Bob would come up with an exercise that he insisted would resolve all problems. His latest exercise was to have the client visualize him or herself standing on a seashore (their present position) with the intent to swim across a channel to the further shore (completing the Process). Obstructions encountered on the way symbolized any problems the client was having.

The staff was developing a publicity video about the Process. I thought that it wasn't a very good video, since they weren't showing the Process live but rather acted out by former clients, most of whom were not actors. One day I tried out Bob's new visualization on an image of the video and saw it sink in the channel before it reached the other shore. The video was completed, but the woman who produced it had kept all the copies in the trunk of her car and, when her car was stolen, the copies were never recovered.

Bob's new ideas worked until he would demand that the idea be used with every client at every session. Soon teachers and clients alike were bored with it. All staff members were now licensed therapists with private practices—we had to have our own practices because none of us ever made a living from the Process, though it was a source of referrals. Having Bob, who had no professional psychological background, try to control our every interaction with the clients became more and more bothersome. Our "non-guru guru," as he called himself, was off the wall in many of his decisions. He took to collecting the staff into a prayer circle before each meeting, during which he prayed aloud that we would all learn to stop resisting him and follow his instructions.

Although the latest edition of his book was called *No One is to Blame*, Bob announced that anyone who was still having difficulties after taking the Process was guilty and was to blame. This was too much for the staff. At our spring Closure, all the staff members were angry with Bob, while our clients, who were paying attention only to themselves, were joyful.

Between the Process and my academic courses, occasionally I was able to turn to other interests. Gilda Grillo had been urging me to come to Brazil as a consultant to the four different Fischer/Hoffman Centers flourishing there. They would send me a roundtrip ticket and pay me $1,500. Ron Kane assured me that the Brazilians treated guests royally and that I'd have a good time.

Between standing up to Bob at the Center, my classes at CIIS and my Reichian bodywork, I felt that I didn't want Jesus or anybody else telling me what to do. Somewhere within me was someone capable of following through with my own choices. I felt a burst of new energy: I decided I would go to Brazil, return to the Center in the fall as Clinical Director and complete my dissertation. Suddenly it all seemed doable.

In Brazil, Gilda was a generous and charming hostess, showing me the sights, taking me to delightful restaurants and insisting on paying for everything. She and her partner had a beautiful three-tiered home in the suburbs of Rio where I had a big, comfortable bedroom, with fresh flowers every day. She had arranged for me to lead a workshop with three dozen students. Several evenings, I was scheduled to teach the Rio de Janeiro Center staff, all of whom spoke English and were welcoming, eager students.

I had one really unusual experience. The week before leaving for Brazil I'd been picking wild blackberries near my Berkeley hills home, and inadvertently touched some poison oak. By my second day in Rio, my whole right arm was red and swollen, the skin broken out in a typical poison oak rash. I had read about Umbanda (a combination of Catholicism and native Brazilian voodoo faiths from before the Catholics arrived) so I asked to go to an Umbanda healing ceremony. Since Gilda's darkly handsome young cousin was both a Process teacher and an Umbanda healer, we were given seats at the front of the crowded room.

The impressive temple had been built and was run by a small, sturdy-looking Dutchman. Dressed in simple white pants and shirt, he mounted the lectern and blew a sharp whistle. About twenty healers in white robes filed in and took their places before the crowd. Another blast of the whistle and healers-in-training, also dressed in white robes, filed in and stood before one of the senior healers. Another blast and the trainees threw themselves full length on the floor. One more whistle blast and each trainee sprang to his or her feet, lit a cigar, and placed it in the mouth of a senior healer who gently wafted smoke of some kind into the room.

While I was watching all this with bemused fascination, I suddenly felt as if I'd stuck my right middle finger into a light socket. An electrical shock raced up my arm. Though each of us later got a chance to stand between a senior healer and one in training while they made passes in the air around us, I was sure that my healing had already taken place. By the next morning the running sores on my arm was drying up, and within days all marks of the poison oak rash were gone.

Rio and the area around it were breathtakingly beautiful. We climbed the famous rock guarding the city and paid homage to the huge figure of Christ towering above it. We drove into the lush green mountains and ate lunch outdoors, with flowering trees cascading over our table and a gurgling brook nearby. We visited a small peninsula with seventeen beaches; each one had sand of a different color, ranging from dazzling white to pink to almost black.

After a week in Rio, I flew to Bela Horizonte to meet with staff at their Fischer/Hoffman Center. It was run by another of Gilda's cousins (whom I knew from his San Francisco training) and his pretty, lively young wife. I'd been a strict vegetarian when he'd known me a year before and, driving to their home from the airport, she asked me hesitatingly what foods I ate. When I assured her that I'd be happy with anything they ate, she sighed with relief. "He said you ate only lettuce," she explained. After we quit laughing, I backtracked a little and admitted I didn't usually eat red meat. That night she set a big beef roast on the dining table. "Is not red," she assured me proudly, "I cooked it for hours!" I ate roast beef.

Bela Horizonte was also beautiful with wonderful old-town sections and magnificent cathedrals. The people could not have been more gracious or welcoming, and the workshops and trainings they had arranged for me were well attended and successful.

A week later, I flew to the newly-built capital city of Brasilia to consult at another center. I was greeted by a good friend of Ron Kane's whom I already knew, and I met others who were teaching the Process there. Brasilia was a peculiar city. It had been built from scratch on bare land and was intended to be an ideal city. Composed of a series of independent sections, each section contained its own apartment buildings, stores, churches and schools. Even though they were close to each other, there were no paths for walking from one of these localities to another; they were connected only by spiraling highways.

The huge government buildings at its center were architecturally impressive and a bit inhuman in their magnificence. I learned that hardly anyone considered Brasilia to be their home. Most government workers accepted two-year assignments (they were paid very well) but were anxious to get back to their "real lives" elsewhere. Even my hosts thought of themselves as only temporary residents. Other than the huge modern government buildings, the one thing everyone thought worth seeing was the avenue of the houses of foreign diplomats. Each was handsomer than the next, designed to show off the architectural style of the country it represented: Chinese pagoda-like roofs slanted toward a palatial red-brick British residence, which was next door to a Spanish hacienda.

When I returned, things seemed to have settled down at the Center and Bob was in a more conciliatory mood. I accepted the job of half-time Clinical Director (which actually meant three-fourths time with half-time pay). I did lots of reading and thinking, and noticed that the more I used my mind this way, the less emotional turmoil I experienced.

Things at the Center deteriorated when I became furious with Bob over his vendetta against Ron Luyet. He wanted me to agree that Ron, a warm, humorous, popular speaker, should not ever be a presenter. We were still arguing about what to do when Bob, suddenly and unexpectedly, fired Ron from the organization. All my years of resenting Bob's arrogance and lack of caring came to a head. I confronted Bob and told him that he couldn't fire Ron, that our Board of Directors had hired Ron, so only they could fire him. Bob saw me as betraying him and siding with "the enemy." This led to a tumultuous Board

225

meeting which was attended by many of our graduates. They attempted to kick Bob "upstairs," by giving him an even more prestigious, but less powerful, position. I knew that wouldn't work—Bob had often assured me that he *was* the Process. Nobody was going to take it away from his control.

The senior staff—Dorothea and Kathy, Ron Luyet and James Cusack and I—decided that the time had come to split with Bob. We wanted to continue doing the Process but we didn't want to put up with him anymore. Bob promptly copyrighted all the Process's materials and told us we could only use them by paying him half of the profit we made. Since the Center had never made any profit (Bob had personally bailed it out more than once) that was nonsense.

Bob finally admitted that we had a right to teach the Process, but we all agreed to vacate the quarters where we had taught together for many years. We called our new center The Pacific Process Institute and decided to run it by consensus. James let us hold night classes in a large schoolroom of the private school he and his wife ran. After a year of searching unsuccessfully for better quarters, the original Process building became vacant and we moved back. We had, we assured ourselves, fulfilled our agreement by moving out. This didn't feel terribly comfortable, but it was logical since we couldn't find another place that didn't object to the noise level of the bitch sessions. Someone told us that when Bob heard of our moving back into the building we had shared with him, he laid a curse on our whole operation.

Without the clashes with Bob, things were a good deal happier, if not completely smooth. The real problem was that all of us would have preferred to be doing therapy work with our clients, while someone else dealt with running the business and recruiting more clients. Nobody wanted to take charge, certainly not me. I wanted to focus on writing my dissertation and seeing clients.

After another year's work, my dissertation was officially completed in the fall of 1986. There was no question about its being accepted. My advisor, Paul Schwarz, told me to bring a bottle of champagne to the defense meeting. He also sent me a congratulatory card, quoting Martin Luther King, Jr., "Free at last, oh Lord, free at last!"

Chapter 13   Hameed

I first heard Hameed Ali (or H.A. Almaas, as he later signed his many books) speak publicly in the spring of 1986.   Larry Shapiro, a big, bewhiskered young psychiatrist, had set up an on-going Berkeley symposium called Melia to bring local practitioners of psychotherapy and of spirituality together— rather a new idea at the time.

I'd met Hameed when he had been briefly involved in our Fischer/Hoffman Center years before. He was one of the original members of Claudio Naranjo's SAT (Seekers after Truth) and had taught Claudio's version of the Fischer/Hoffman Process in Boulder, Colorado. I wasn't especially interested in hearing Hameed, but went because he was in Larry's series of speakers. For the first time, I was exposed to his composure, conviction and extraordinary verbal fluency. Nothing in his talk on "the spiritual path" struck me as unusual, however, until I heard him say, "There must be some reason for the ego. I've never known or heard of anybody, no matter how enlightened, who didn't have one." I thought this was a remarkably astute statement, since I'd spent years struggling to get rid of mine. "He's brilliant," I enthused to the attractive, blond young woman seated next to me who turned out to be his wife.   She, of course, agreed wholeheartedly.

A few weeks later, I got a letter inviting me to be part of his new group to explore the connections between psychological and spiritual work. At our first meeting, there were thirty of us in Hameed's big, casual living room, almost all professional therapists of some kind. I thought the group to be mature, intelligent and open-minded. We were all impressed by Hameed himself, as well as with his idea that by investigating our psychological experiences we could arrive at spiritual truths. It seemed an interesting approach to try, so I signed up for a three-month trial participation, as did most of the other therapists present. At the end of the three months, Hameed suggested that the group meet without him, to discuss the work we had been doing. We tried to figure out exactly what it was Hameed was teaching, but it wasn't clear to anybody, probably because he presented his ideas piecemeal as different aspects came to him.

Hameed was, and is, an incredibly persuasive teacher. Eventually, most group members discovered that the effect of his teachings on our lives was unquestionable, though for many of us it took a long time for the results to manifest. He often commented, "So, if we continue doing this for thirty years..." When I pointed out that at my age I didn't have thirty years, he only nodded in agreement.

Hameed called his primary method of group work "inquiry." He would sit quietly until someone brought up a troubling personal issue, whereupon Hameed would probe gently into the ideas, emotions and bodily sensations that were associated with the issue. This process could take forty minutes or more, as the person slowly went deeper and deeper in exploring and describing his or her own reality. Their interaction often resulted in surprising new

230

realizations and experiences for all of us, sometimes on an entirely different level of consciousness.

We progressed to a daylong meeting each month, and then two-day meetings, and then ten-day retreats each year. All these gatherings started with silent meditation for forty minutes, after which Hameed would give a talk on various facets of his worldview. Later we would break up into twos or threes to engage in interactional inquiry, giving answers in turn to such questions as, "What is your real purpose in life?" Occasionally, the question would be more devious, such as "What's right about *not* being compassionate?" Sometimes the assignment was for each participant to talk for five or ten minutes, without interruption, about our personal take on the question.

In private weekly sessions with Hameed he primarily did Reichian work with me, as I had done with Hal Streitfeld and Giovanna. His work differed from theirs, though, because he was not just helping me to explore my bodily reactions; he was looking for internal movement from my psychological problems to my spiritual experience. Often, the problem that was disturbing me would simply evaporate, leaving behind a sense of solidity or of lightness and happiness. Not insight, however, because I could never track the connection between my psychological problems and my spiritual experiences.

Sometimes I found myself plunging from my personal unhappiness to that of all humanity. My sorrow and guilt over not having been a better mother metamorphosed into the grief of all mothers, weeping for their children. Hameed never accepted this. "How you feel about the world," he told me, "is the way you felt about your own mother." Like much of Hameed's teachings, I

231

accepted this idea provisionally, but it seemed that my provisional acceptance of it prevented me from entering more fully into the work.

Hameed is an extraordinary human being. As a teacher, he was invariably kind, friendly, good-humored, objective, and totally present. Simply being in his presence was nourishing, not only because of what he modeled but also because of his ability to transmit his own state to his students. It took years, though, for him to realize that the rest of us might not always feel so kindly towards each other, that there might be interactive problems within the group. "For those on the Path," he taught, "any problem is given to us as an opportunity to learn." To me, that meant that people on a spiritual path can choose to turn any situation into a learning opportunity.

On one of our weekend retreats, the topic was "conscience." As usual on such occasions he began by soliciting our ideas. "What is conscience? How can we explore what conscience is, what it means." Nobody said anything. My thought, that "conscience is that which tells you the difference between right and wrong," felt so pathetically simplistic that I didn't offer it. Besides, that definition only tells what conscience does, not what it is. As no other ideas occurred to me, I listened to what the rest of the group had to say. Those few who always contributed ideas tried to tease out his meaning of the term. Someone suggested that it was more than superego guilt; that it had to do with what the present moment required, not just with a set of rules. Someone else thought that it was impersonal and had to do with the faculty of discernment. Others said that conscience had to come from the heart, not so much from thinking as from knowing.

232

Finally Hameed offered some clues to his thinking, "Yes, those are all good ideas, but we want to make it more specific. What does it relate to? How does conscience manifest, how is it connected with what you think, feel, and do?" Someone suggested that what was needed was clarity, before they could proceed with conscience. "But what if the clarity is not there?" Hameed challenged. "It seems to me that when you have no clarity is when your conscience is most needed." Embarrassed laughter ensued. "Even after you become clear about your choices, what makes you choose one over the other?" The group chewed on that for a while.

Hameed led us to his point: that your conscience depends on what you believe to be true about the universe, what you define as reality. "We believe many things about the world, but when we don't act in accordance with our own beliefs, it indicates an absence of conscience. We know there is conscience when we live our lives in harmony with the highest truth we know, when we always act in accordance with our beliefs—from daily situations to major life choices like jobs, friends and marriage partners, and all the way to self-realization. New realizations cannot change your life unless you have the will to live in harmony with them. That is conscience."

This new aspect of his work Hameed called "the Citadel," the true defense of our essential life. He explained that the Citadel was diamond-platinum, because it was a combination, not only of the gold of personal will and the diamond of objective truth, but of the platinum of universal will, which is where he lost me. Hameed explained that it was really very simple, very practical and down to earth: "Is my behavior leading me in the direction

I want to go? For instance, if I believe that meditating forty minutes a day will advance my awareness and security, why aren't I meditating forty minutes a day? The Citadel is not just guidance; it is the will to follow that guidance."

It didn't seem simple to me. I'd never known "will" to be golden, let alone platinum, nor experienced anything remotely like a Citadel inside myself. Nothing was impelling me to meditate forty minutes a day either, because the twenty minutes I did meditate each day led only to a brief period of quiet in my head. Like most of the group, however, I was fascinated by Hameed's confident ability to describe what the spiritual realms were like. I was also encouraged because my work with him sometimes produced an experience of expansion and possibility within me.

Starting in 1984, he wrote at least a dozen books under the name of H.A.Almaas, describing facets of what came to be called the Diamond Approach. His books were brilliant and wise, but I found them difficult to read. His exuberant, convincing, expressive flow of words, so fascinating and uplifting when he spoke, was often difficult to follow in print. Hameed said that we should be checking everything he taught us against our own experience, and it didn't check out for me. I was sure that somehow, someway, we were creating it all. If that were true, it meant that Hameed was creating these extraordinary spaces he kept assuring us were really there. It was obvious that they were there for him and for those who accepted his vision. There were times when I felt like weeping with frustration because I was sure that the extraordinary experiences he spoke of were available—I just couldn't find or recreate them.

Working individually with Hameed, however, often brought small gifts that seemed to mark permanent change. In one session, my oddly constricted solar plexus jerked spasmodically for a long time and then my breathing opened up. At another time I was aware of an almost scary sense of emptiness in my chest, and I heard Hameed's gentle question, "Who abandoned you?" in a new way. Something in my heart seemed to come alive, and I decided that maybe I could drop my envy of other people's rich imagery and accept my own path as plain and simple.

I had become conscious once again of a low-level bodily anxiety that I resolved to track down and root out. I worked on "letting go" in my sessions with Hameed, and began another attempt at practicing the Subud latihan. Slowly I felt my body relaxing, and sometimes I experienced a sense of joy arising. I brought my new sense of joy to Hameed and with his gentle guidance it deepened into my usual stillness, but then into an entirely new sense of self. When it faded, I didn't feel bereft.

The next time I worked individually with Hameed, however, I found myself back into personal unhappiness and then again into silence. I was beginning to feel peaceful, when I noticed that there was no place for initiative in this silent space. Hameed assured me that if you just hung out in the silence, it would change. It did change but to more and more peace. That didn't feel like enough to me—what use was it to the world if I felt peaceful? At work, I would go from feeling furious at the Center staff, to a new depth of compassion for all of us. Hameed pointed out that compassion was one of the Essential states. But when he said "Compassion is green and looks like a fountain," he lost me again.

235

Hameed spoke of "presence" and had us do dyad or triad exchanges on questions like "What keeps me from being present?" I would go from the devastating knowledge that I was sixty-five years old and had not been present for most of my life, to the joyous realization that I could be present now. I'd forget the whole thing until our next meeting, but my appreciation of Hameed and my gratitude for the privilege of working with him grew. I felt more relaxed than I ever had. Freda remarked that I'd lost "all those little prickles."

In 1990 I finally completed my book about the Fischer/Hoffman Process that I'd been working on for more than ten years. Those of us at the Center thought that the book I'd helped Dennis write for Bob was too much a reflection of Bob himself to use with our clients. We wanted something that would help people understand what the Process was like, something that would encourage them to take it. I personally felt that its material was important enough that it should appear in book form before Bob, or others in our group, changed it so much that its original straightforward approach was lost.

It was difficult to find a format that both explained the Process and was interesting to read. Several other would-be authors had tried and failed. When it dawned on me that I could follow a class through the various steps of the Process, using the students' and teachers' actual words from tapes of the sessions, it seemed simple. It wasn't. Interspersed between the quotations, I needed to explain the psychological basis for each step. The writing itself took me a year, with the help of a seasoned writing coach. I integrated feedback from a dozen other interested people, as well as a careful line-by-line editing by Steve Burton, a law professor with published books to his credit, who was my friend as well as the husband of my friend Serena Stier. The Institute gave me a grant of $5000 for financial support, so I would not have to work while I was writing. When the book was finished we published it ourselves as *Anger and Forgiveness: an Approach That Works*. When the printer delivered 2000 spanking new colorful copies of the book to me, friends stored boxes of them in their basements. The Center staff threw a wonderfully elaborate book-signing party that attracted more than sixty of our past students.

The week before the party, I attended a retreat on the desert near Joshua Pines, California, given by Stanislav Grof and Jack Kornfield, which was a mixture of Stan's holotropic breath work and meditation. I thought of holotropic breath work as "hyperventilating to music," but I had great respect for the depths to which it could take one. (Stan Grof had turned to this modality when the U.S. government would no longer permit his medical research on LSD therapy.)

At the end of the retreat, Jack led us in a visualization where we were asked to imagine facing a difficult situation in our everyday lives. As I was nervous about going public as the author of a book, I chose to visualize the upcoming book-signing party. In my imagination, just as my anxiety was at its highest point, I heard a knock on the door. Everybody in the scene froze while I went the door to find the being I most admired and relied on standing on the other side: my personal guide, Jennis. "Let me take over your body for a bit," she said cheerfully. In the visualization, as we returned to the party scene everybody came to life again. Jennis-as-me handled the entire event with grace, intelligence and aplomb.

A week later, when I had forgotten the guided meditation, I spoke at the book-signing party with a grace, intelligence and aplomb unusual for me. Everybody had a good time, and many stayed to socialize after my lighthearted speech and I signed many copies of the book. (Some people even bought copies for friends.) Gradually, most of the 2000 copies sold over the next two years. When the copies were almost gone, I revised the book, making it more of a "how to" manual and adding the name of our presenter, Ron Luyet, as co-author. (I had quoted him a lot and he wanted to use the book in workshops he was giving throughout the country.) This time a small commercial publisher took over, though most of the 3000 copies they printed were sold through our Institute or through Ron's work.

By the sixth year of our work with Hameed he seemed to be withdrawing, and he became almost passive in individual therapy sessions. He started to see his students every other week rather than every week and he raised his fees. Once every two weeks was enough for me until I realized that I was angry with him. I'd spent more than $20,000 and six years on what was now called the Diamond Approach and I didn't feel like I'd made much real progress. For example, I had never broken through to the colorful visionary states that he described so ecstatically. His experience of the world was not mine.

By mid-1991, Hameed began to change the structure of our Professional Group. He wanted some members of the group to train as assistant teachers of the Diamond Approach, and he wanted all of us to integrate with an earlier group from Boulder, Colorado, who were moving into the area. One of his most devoted students, a woman with whom I had no rapport, began to lead part of the training. Gradually, there were assignments of materials to study and tests to fill out. The plan was for the men and women in our group to become individual teachers of new students of the Diamond Approach, as Hameed had done for me and others. None of this felt like anything I wanted to do, or could do. I knew that leaving both Hameed and our group would be significant losses for me, so I decided to take a four month sabbatical from both my work with the Diamond Approach and my psychotherapy practice, leaving open the possibility of returning to either of them if it seemed right.

More recently, with my own broader views and also with the help of a book written by John Davis, *The Diamond Approach: An Introduction to the Teachings of A.H. Almaas,* the full thrust of Hameed's work has become clearer to me. Davis studied and practiced with Hameed for twenty-four years, and spread his teachings for many years afterwards. He admits that it was five years before he fully trusted Hameed's material; I quit after six years, feeling that I would never entirely trust it. I was too aware of our ability to create things in our minds and then experience them as real. I thought that Hameed had built the magnificent structure of his teachings out of his own remarkable mind and spirit. Any student who accepted his teachings whole-heartedly could rebuild them for herself, but I didn't want to rebuild someone else's ideas.

As I now understand them, Hameed's teachings differ from others because of the idea that had appealed to me the first time I heard him: "There must be some use for the ego, for everyone has one." His Diamond Approach maintains that each negative aspect of the human ego— arrogance, wanton sexuality, envy, anger, selfishness, greed, indolence and so on—enters our personality because we have lost our access to its analogous essential aspect of our True Natures. For instance, fear rushes in to fill the hole left by our being out of contact with Essential Courage; greed fills the gap left by the loss of Essential Satisfaction; dependence takes the place left by lack of Essential Love. Our Essence, then, while One in its highest aspects, has qualities that we can activate by seeing our negativities as indications of which essential qualities we lack. The Diamond Approach, Hameed said, was never intended to be a method of relieving emotional and mental suffering, but rather as a way to lead us back to our True Natures, whose loss, of course, is the reason we suffer.

There is another realm Hameed called the Boundless Dimensions, which other teachings refer to as non-duality, or no-self. In this realm there is only Divine Love, presence, awareness and the dynamic unfolding and pure mystery of Being. Hameed clearly experienced all of these states himself, and described them in eloquent, rhapsodic terms. He talked about the Absolute, our final home, the place that is beyond consciousness. I recognized that, again and again, I had been drawn to a space that might have been the Absolute, but it frightened me because it felt so empty. In meditation I would feel painful reactions to ongoing events in my life, then peaceful emptiness, and then back to longing for empathetic human connection—over and over again.

I awoke one morning wanting to give up the whole thing. I had completed my work—the book explaining the

240

Process—and nothing further was needed from me. I could just let go. Not sure that this idea was real, I did a visualization of jumping into the emptiness—and found myself wide-awake in the reality of my room and in the reality of my life.

Chapter 14   EMDR

Still searching, I took the transformed est training, now called the Landmark Forum. The Forum was different from other methods of personal growth I had studied, for it focused on taking action in the world. Action seemed to me to be the other half of an equation: you create beliefs that cause you to have certain experiences, or you create experiences that lead you to certain beliefs. In the Forum's approach, your behavior in the world generates the way you think and feel, and carrying out a commitment to act requires structure and practice and the sharing of goals with others.

"Arrange your circumstances," the woman leader said, "so that you can't help but act." Ways of encouraging yourself to act included identifying milestones for achieving your goals, making displays, (e.g., posters) of the goals you want to reach, and letting go of anything that stands in your way. "Your present experience," she stressed, "should not be based on your past, but on your expectations of the future."

She spoke rather severely in the beginning and wore a formal business suit, as if to emphasize the significance of what she was saying. By the end of the workshop she was more intimate, however, loosening her collar and unbuttoning her jacket to display a colorful blouse, and sitting on the desk. It seemed obvious to me that she was deftly manipulating us. When I asked a question, I was taken aback by the cold, disconnected, calculating look in her eyes, which reminded me of the way my mother sometimes looked at me. Even though it apparently could work, the new est was no more palatable to me than the old est had been.

∞ ∞ ∞ ∞ ∞

Late in 1991 I got a card in the mail offering an inexpensive lecture by a Francine Shapiro, Ph.D., about a new form of therapy called EMD (Eye Movement Desensitization). I added it to the other advertisements in my wastebasket. It kept nagging at me though, so I picked it out again and studied it. Eye movement? I knew that Reichian therapists sometimes had clients release tension by having them follow, with their eyes, a small penlight making circles and loops in the air. EMD might be useful, but probably not, so I threw the card away. Then Kathy Tamm, a long-time friend and colleague at the Process, called to ask if I wanted to go to the EMD lecture with her and Dorothea to check it out. Three nudges seemed like a message of sorts so I went, and learned a whole new approach to therapy so effective that I used it with most of my psychotherapy clients for years afterward.

Francine Shapiro was a tall, handsome, solid-looking woman in her forties. During her presentation, she told us that leading a person in emotional distress to shift their eyes laterally over and over again had astonishing psychological results. She said that she had been walking by herself in a park, upset about a personal matter, when she started rapidly moving her eyes from side to side. As she did so, new insights and calmness came over her, and soon her whole problem had melted away. Excited, she tried her new method on friends and they experienced the same results.

As a good research psychologist should, Francine set up a formal experiment to test her hypothesis. For participants, she chose ten women who had been raped, as well as ten men who were Vietnam War veterans suffering from flashbacks, sleeplessness and overwhelming anxiety. She asked each of her subjects to rate, on a scale of zero to ten, how upset they were feeling about the horrors that they had experienced. All of them rated their present upset at the top, a ten. After participating in a lengthy EMD session with Francine, each of them rated their anxiety level at zero. She told us that, six months later, all the subjects still rated their upset level at zero, except for one woman whose rapist had moved back into her neighborhood; her level of upset had climbed to six. "EMD takes away your unwarranted anxiety," she explained with wry humor. "It doesn't make you stupid."

She expressed such enthusiasm and assurance about her discovery that we were intrigued and signed up for a two-day workshop to learn more about this miraculous-sounding practice. Amazingly, it turned out to be as radically positive in its effects as she had promised, though more was involved, of course, than just eye movement.

During our two-day workshop, Francine explained and demonstrated in detail the entire protocol she had worked out: after taking a client's history and establishing a relationship with her, the therapist would make a list of ten of her core traumatic issues, one of which (usually the earliest) was targeted for immediate work. As part of the preparation for working on the chosen trauma, the client would describe her strongest image of the event, note the emotional and bodily feelings she associated with it, and identify a belief about herself that she carried because of what had happened to her. She was then asked to rate her feelings on the zero to ten scale, to represent how upset she was by the trauma (Subjective Units of Distress or SUDs).

After all these preliminaries were completed, the desensitization began. The client was asked to think of the image that represented the trauma, bring up the emotions and the bodily sensations she associated with the event, rehearse the negative beliefs about herself that had come out of it, and then simply follow the therapist's hand as it rapidly passed a couple of dozen times back and forth in front of her eyes. Every subject exhibited a change of some kind in the way the trauma was held, usually a shift toward more exploration and less anxiety. The subject would say out loud what she was experiencing and then, without the therapist saying anything, the whole thing was repeated, with the client again following the therapist's hand movement with her eyes. Again, the client would experience an inner shift of some kind, and the focus would move to that.

Francine showed us a video of a client whose feelings changed from fearful and defeated (a result of childhood sexual molestations by her father) to powerful, as she shifted responsibility to the perpetrator and gained an adult sense of compassion for her child self. "It's over," the woman declared quietly at the end of the session, "I can let it go now." Her anxiety level was zero.

During the afternoons, we gathered in groups of three or four to practice the procedures. When it was my turn to be the client, I decided to work on my painful feelings about Warren's death several years ago. Within a couple of sets of eye movements, I found myself sobbing uncontrollably. As soon as I was able, I assured my "therapist" that this was obviously a long-term issue requiring further work. (I wasn't willing to expose my feelings publicly using both a new method and an unknown, untrained therapist.) Other people in our group, who had chosen their targets more cautiously, were able to desensitize their issues. The power of the EMD method was demonstrable and real.

By our next workshop, Francine had added another step: before beginning the eye movement, the client was asked what belief about himself he would rather have than the negative idea that the traumatic experience had affirmed. For instance, if he felt that he was a coward because he ran away from a bully when he was a child, he was asked what he would want to believe about himself now. In this situation, he might want to think that he had done the sensible thing, considering the size of the other child, or if were to happen again, that he would respond courageously. The client was asked to rate, on a scale of one to seven, how strongly this new positive belief was held. Though clients weren't consciously aware of the mechanism at work during the desensitization phase, adding the goal of a positive belief seemed to reassure them that they would not only drop their painful reactions, but also that their positive belief would become real as their eye movements were continued.

I began to use EMDR with my own clients. (Francine had added the R to represent the reprocessing that was happening, as well as the desensitization of the traumatic material.)   As a therapist, I'd been reluctant to pin a diagnosis on my clients. It seemed to me that giving a person a diagnosis was like putting them in a box; afterwards, it was too easy to fit anything they said or did into the diagnosis we'd given them. Instead, I subscribed to the teachings of Carl Rogers, who said that a person's own inner knowledge was much more useful than anything a therapist could dream up, and that my role as the therapist was to help my clients to get in touch with their own wisdom. EMDR is a wonderful tool that permits people to find their own way to handle their problems, without a therapist deciding how they should do it.

Another thing I liked about this new method was that every session ended with the client feeling uplifted and positive about themselves and the work we had done. In the few cases when a client hadn't come to a positive resolution by the time the session was up, I would do a brief visualization of a warm, healing light entering whatever part of their bodies still felt contracted. When necessary, I added an image of their leaving the problem in a drawer in my office until our next session. Even at the beginning, when I had to keep consulting a list of the various steps to be sure I didn't miss any, EMDR almost always brought immediate long-term results to my clients.

A few months later, I was delighted to receive an invitation from the EMDR Institute to become a facilitator at their trainings, helping newly trained therapists use the method correctly. Being a facilitator included sitting in on morning lectures where I learned more about the method, as well as spending afternoons helping other therapists learn to use EMDR.

∞ ∞ ∞ ∞ ∞

Yet, no matter how successful I became in helping clients, my journals continued to reflect personal dissatisfaction, and questions like: "What's true?" and, "Why hadn't the methods that made such a difference in other people's lives made a permanent difference in mine?" or, "Had the lessons of my childhood been too deeply imprinted?" At times, I saw myself as being so like my mother that her uncertainties, her anxieties, her ineffectiveness continued to be reflected in me. I'd experienced radical shifts in consciousness, as well as states of incredible freedom and power, joy and love, but these experiences of "enlightenment" were infrequent. A counterproductive anger and despair was always part of my constitution. Although my Ph.D. was completed, the original and the second edition of my book on the Process were in print, and my private therapy practice was thriving, I found myself being more and more dissatisfied.

As I understand it, psychotherapy is about leaving the past behind and building a strong, healthy self with which to live in the present and future. If you wanted to go beyond this, you had to have a *self* before you could get to *no-self* (whatever that meant). As I saw it, this was exactly my problem: I couldn't find an ordinary, solid center in myself. I had repeatedly experienced a state of emptiness that was like the "void" spoken of by Buddhists, but the comfort of having a normal healthy self seemed beyond me. For many years, it had been clear to me that I could *make* myself happy if I wanted, but that wasn't enough—I wanted to *be* happy. I wanted to know that which made happiness possible. All the authorities were so confident in their individual methods, but each method was different and the common thread among them eluded me.

I was sure that we either create something we have consciously chosen, or else we create what some part of us unconsciously wants. But did that mean that nothing has value beyond what we assign to it? Hameed assured us that the universe has an "optimizing thrust," i.e., has intrinsic value. He taught, as did Bob Hoffman, that when you have completely dealt with your negative states, a wonderful "essence" would bubble up in you.

It seemed to me that every aspect of our being is available to each of us: loving/unloving, adoring/critical—we choose which of these aspects we want to manifest. When I thought about that idea, for a brief time my body felt quiet, until I began to notice (again) that internal calm and peace felt like stasis to me. Love was not enough; there had to be power, too. Love without power is dependency, even though power without love turns evil. I envied the import of one of Hameed's statements that had stuck with me: "Your life originates from a sense of meaningfulness, significance, preciousness, value..." If only his experience were mine!

I returned again to *A Course in Miracles*. Like Helen Schucman had said about the Course: "I might not believe it, but I *knew* it was true." The ACIM Workbook said, "I will learn to see this differently." I *will*, I promised myself aloud, I will. I could perceive the layers of anger and grief inside me alongside my eternal questioning, "Why are we like this?" What underlies my anger and grief?"

I attended an Anger Workshop with an East Indian psychiatrist, Lobsang Rapgay, who maintained that when you had gone through all the pain and anger that you carried (and everyone carries pain and anger) you reach a place of emptiness. It was necessary to put something—a positive vision—in their place, or the pain and anger would return to fill the space that had been left. This was exactly what we had learned in the Process; we had found that positive feelings rarely just bubbled up on their own in a student. In hypnosis, I needed to do this with my clients as well. EMD was now known as EMDR, because it had become obvious that clients were experiencing reprocessing as well as desensitization. In EMDR, it was necessary for a client to articulate a positive belief they wanted for themselves at the beginning of the session, so that there was something to replace the negative belief that was gone by the end of the session.

Having to create a belief for oneself didn't feel authentic to me. I wanted to reach the joy and peace and power that I knew (and that all spiritual disciplines taught) was inside me under the negative beliefs that I was letting go. Finding it would be proof positive that joy and peace and power had actually been there, beneath the negative stuff, all along. But it seemed that I had to go through a process that implicitly suggested such a result, before such deeply positive states could appear for me.

I decided to give up trying to figure out what it was all about and just do what was before me. I would rebuild my psychotherapy practice and take my financial situation more seriously. I felt a need to do some kind of service, so I began to see people who could not afford to pay my regular fees. I decided to move to a new apartment, to get a new car, and to simplify my wardrobe and my life. Maybe these changes would help me to drop the feeling I had that there was still something missing.

But months of solidifying the "doings" in my life weren't fully satisfying either. Questions continued to haunt me. A Course in Miracles says that what we see of the world is illusion; by learning to approach it with peace, acceptance, gratitude, and love, we can ameliorate our experience of it so that it is easy to step through to God. I felt the truth of the Course and applied myself to the daily lessons in the workbook, as I had done a half dozen times before, since I first discovered it in 1976. No matter how hard I tried, though, I could not accept its teachings "without question." And, as usual, it was the mental uncertainty itself that undermined my ability to accept its teachings without reservation.

Chapter 15   Avatar

L ate in 1992, I heard about another teaching called "Avatar." According to its founder Harry Palmer, Avatar is a Hindu word for an enlightened being who has chosen to become incarnated on earth, either to play [*lila*], or to bless all of humanity [*bodhisattva*]. I later learned that what Harry meant was that every human being is an Avatar.

I took the one-day introduction to Avatar with a dozen other people. I didn't care much for the intellectual male leader but I loved the quiet grace of the woman working with him, and was impressed that after twenty-five years of Buddhist meditation she had turned to Avatar. The day's teachings gave me a new understanding of an idea that I had accepted as true, but had never been able to live for any length of time: our beliefs create our reality.

Avatar maintains that human beings can learn to move from acting as *creatures*, helplessly living out our beliefs, to becoming the *creators* of the beliefs we are living, to knowing ourselves as the *Source* of all beliefs. I knew how often I had acted as a creature, following a path determined by my history, despite all the work I had done to the contrary. I also knew that, over and over again, I had chosen to create something better for myself. And I'd known a few moments when I'd been in contact with *something* so far beyond anything else I'd experienced, that

I could not give up trying to find my way back to it. Despite an appalling (to me) price of $2000, I registered for their next nine-day course.

I arrived at a house in the Marin hills at the appointed time to discover that only Steve was teaching the course. He told me that the quietly beautiful, youthful woman I'd admired earlier had not been able to come from her home in Arizona. I thought perhaps they had been lovers and had split up, or maybe it wasn't practical for her to come that far for only two students. I didn't know of anyone else who was teaching Avatar in the Bay Area though, and I had made an agreement, so I stayed. There was one other student besides me, a depressed-looking young man who spoke very little.

I learned later, after interacting with many other Avatar teachers who were well trained and very involved with their students, how much of an anomaly Steve was. He gave us very little guidance in understanding what we were supposed to do, other than handing out the printed explanations and instructions. I felt both confused and resentful of his lack of involvement with us.

Still, when I was following the written instructions as well as I could, I experienced powerful moments in which my perceptions of the world were changed. We were sent outside for hours to look at different objects and to experience their physical reality, without adding any story in our minds about the object. Viewed like that, those things I was observing began to stand out with heightened clarity and substance. At the same time, I felt more present and centered. After a while, we were taught to extend this new way of seeing to living things, and ultimately to our own thoughts, so that I began to see my thoughts as "thought-forms," with shape and size and density.

Later, we learned how to suspend judgments, first about things and then about people—although it didn't occur to me to apply this new knowledge to my judgments about Steve. We learned to create specific beliefs by identifying, and then eliminating, all contradictory ideas about the topic, so as to arrive at the belief we were creating. In the final two days we learned how to "discreate" beliefs whose effect we no longer wanted to experience in our lives.

Although I had done Avatar in what I thought of as a "half-assed" fashion, I was nevertheless sure that I could teach it. During the first years of the Process, none of us understood why we were doing each step. Even Bob didn't understand how each step worked—he just relayed what Fischer had "told" him and passed it on to us to do. I'd taught the Process for years while I slowly worked out a psychological understanding of what was actually happening. Since Avatar was a structured process like the Fischer/Hoffman Process, I thought I could learn Avatar while I taught it. Within a few weeks, I went to the Avatar headquarters in Florida to take the Master's Course (for an additional $3000).

Harry Palmer, Avatar's founder and developer, spoke a number of times, although his wife Avra and two other women, Mikan and Sue, led the Master's training. A big, casual, friendly man, he was a wonderful speaker: personable, intelligent and humorous. There were over 200 of us taking the Master's Course, almost all of whom were middle-class white North American and European men and women, with only a sprinkling of Africans and Asians.

255

In his daily talks, Harry described investigations he had done on his own consciousness. After immersing himself in an isolation tank for weeks and reaching the point where he was receiving no sensory input, he realized that the whole circus of life he thought was going on around him was actually going on in his own mind. When that drained away and left him with only his own awareness, he realized that he was free to create anything he wanted.

When the Master's Course was completed, Mikan told me that I would have to intern twice with an experienced teacher and take the Master's Course a second time before I could be licensed. I was indignant: I'd been a highly-thought-of Social Work Instructor at UCLA and a successful Process teacher for fifteen years; I'd even written a book about the Process. Why couldn't I teach Avatar now?

Back home and thinking more calmly, I realized that they were right. I could control my mind, turn off my judgments, and decide what I wanted to believe, but I hadn't fully integrated Avatar's teachings. Using the processes they taught had changed my life, but they hadn't created any fundamental changes inside me—I was still as lonely and self-conscious as I usually was in such gatherings, and I got as annoyed as ever at people who ignored me or felt supercilious to me. Obviously there was much I needed to learn.

I swallowed my pride and assisted at several courses with experienced Masters and gradually I began to understand Avatar better. The essence of the Course was set forth in the introductory two days, which are now called ReSurfacing. Resurfacing is defined as "disentangling yourself from (your) old creations and rising back into Awareness." The combination of profound information along with a series of well-designed exercises makes the learning experiential.

The first section of ReSurfacing teaches that both personal consciousness and the physical universe arise from pure Being, and that all human life struggles come from not realizing this fact. When you can identify the beliefs you hold, consciously or unconsciously, and know how to change them, you can change your life.

The second section teaches the skills necessary to control your attention, which includes the ability to see—without judgment—objects, people and beliefs as they are. It also allows you to fully believe what you choose to believe: by learning how to eliminate contradictory thoughts that interfere with your chosen beliefs, you can change your experience of life. The third section initiates you into a state comparable to Harry's experience in a sensory deprivation tank, when everything in his mind "went down the drain" and he was left with simple awareness. The remainder of that section teaches different ways of using your new abilities to discreate limiting beliefs that keep you from having a happy and functional life.

I went to Switzerland to take the Master's Course a second time that summer. I wouldn't have felt justified in spending my slim savings only to visit Europe, but having a professional reason to travel abroad was wonderful. I flew to Lucerne, where I could take a train through Switzerland. I visited Interlaken to see the grand Swiss mountains. I saw an outdoor production of *William Tell*, with real cows and sheep on a hillside stage and the audience in an enclosed arena.

At the large hotel in Geneva where the course was held, the individual rooms were simple and small but adequate. My roommate opened the door and greeted me with an easy, cheerful smile, taking my offered right hand with her left. (She had been one of the thalidomide babies born during the tragedy and her right arm tapered off at the wrist.) She was a married schoolteacher with grown sons, and she was very comfortable for me to be with. We took to each other immediately.

The room where the teaching took place was set up with round tables, each seating a dozen people. Those speaking the same language sat at one table so they could use the same translator. The trainers would deliver a sentence in English and then wait for the soft murmur of the translators. After the day's formal teaching was over, students did their printed assignments. Our table of American, English and Australian men and women became an instant community, and we often worked together and met later for dinner.

Immediately finding a buddy and becoming a member of an "in-group" was a new and pleasant experience for me. I felt so at home that I got deeper into the material than I had before. Again and again, new vistas of what life could be like opened to me. At the end of the course I was issued a license to teach Avatar.

Back home in California, I was eager to start teaching. David Curry, a longtime friend who had dropped out of Hameed's work a few months before I did became the only student at my first course, and it went very well. I began my second Avatar course with three students, great excitement and trepidation, and a nasty cold.   David participated a second time, both to review the course and to support me in giving it.

That night I tried to do a self-healing of my cold by first discreating the belief that I couldn't heal myself. Unexpectedly, I found myself in the midst of deep feelings of guilt over the deaths of my mother and brothers, of Jean, of Warren, and even of Ronn's dog, killed by a passing car when he was a boy. "Why should I be able to heal myself, when I couldn't heal them?" my mind was asking. Since I needed to be able to focus on my students and not on myself, I used Avatar methodology to discreate my guilty feelings by realizing that I had created them in the first place, and then I gave myself permission to stop creating them. I also created a belief that my students and I and all people are involved in a beautiful, mysterious cosmic dance. My cold subsided at once and the Course unfolded beautifully.

It was easy to follow the written instructions, step by step. The three students—Larry, who had been a long-term psychotherapy client of mine, his girlfriend, and a woman colleague who had briefly taught the Fischer/Hoffman Process—all loved it.   They were fascinated by both the brief theoretical explanations and by the experiential work. To my intense gratitude, the right clarifying words came to me each time someone got stuck. Larry came inside from one exercise with the delighted announcement that he had identified with a squirrel and found out how great it was to have a tail for balance. Eventually, he no longer believed he was stuck under what he called "a glass ceiling" in the corporation where he worked, and his girlfriend lost her fear of commitment.

They were married a few months later, and he got a work promotion about the same time. We had a wonderful nine days and were all radiant at the end.

David was interested in learning anything that might take him further along his path to personal growth and good health. Soon after reviewing my second Course, he went on to get his own license to teach Avatar and subsequently taught many courses with me. His presence and support were invaluable. David and his wife Joyce had rebuilt their home in the Oakland hills after it had been destroyed by the 1991 fire, so we had a beautiful location in which to teach our Courses.

After several years, David and I were joined by a psychotherapist who had taken an Introductory Weekend with us. Marianne Gerhart and I had become good friends long before she (and her husband John) took the full Course with us. She and I had had similar psychospiritual experiences in our lives, and had been immediately attracted to one another. She was close to my age and was open to learning anything that was potentially valuable. When she too became a Master and brought in students of her own, the three of us delivered our courses with great pleasure and clear benefit to our students, as well as to ourselves.

I had occasional misgivings about Avatar, however. Perhaps my inner difficulties were not caused by personal beliefs I hadn't routed out, but were instead justifiable anxiety about a planet gone mad and self-destructing. Rather than helping people, was I teaching them the irresponsible notion of "Don't worry, be happy?" Day after day I tried to work out this puzzle: if my beliefs were creating my difficulties and I had the tools to discreate my

260

beliefs, why didn't they stay discreated? In practice sessions with other Avatar teachers, I sometimes found that I had to create not only that I was a successful Avatar teacher but that I *wanted* to teach Avatar at all.

What I really wanted was to continue learning about Avatar; the teaching had become incidental. Yet surely it was my responsibility as an older adult to teach, and not just to be a student. I felt I should be "out there" helping the transformation of our collective human consciousness, and not just "in here" focusing on my own consciousness and relating to my students and clients. In my most self-questioning moments, it didn't feel like I was doing anything useful. When I found the statement, "Everything is all right, and it doesn't depend on me," it was comforting to know that "rightness" didn't depend on anxious, doubtful little me at all. The knowledge of this truth was so deep and sweet that I was awestruck.

How could I distinguish my own beliefs from those of the collective consciousness? Always somewhere in the back of my mind was a statement by John Lilly, renowned for his early work with dolphins. "Your beliefs create your experience, *within limits yet to be explored.*" "Yes," I would assure my students (and myself), "there are probably limits—few of us have been cured of metastatic cancer, for instance. But those limits are so much further out than we can imagine that, for now, we can act as if they didn't exist."

∞ ∞ ∞ ∞ ∞

I couldn't help but continue to check out other teachings. At a Fischer/Hoffman Process Center meeting, an ex-teacher, Jackie Zimron, was enthusiastic about

261

something called the Sedona Method.   Kathy and I immediately registered for a workshop.

In its simplest form, the Sedona Method consisted of asking a person if they could let go of their negative reaction to a current problem.   When they said they couldn't, they would be asked if they could let it go for only thirty seconds. Most people could do that, whereupon they would see that if they could let it go for half a minute, they could let it go for longer.   Eventually, they would discover that they could let their negative reactions go entirely.   The next question was, "Are you willing to?" That took them a little further, since it required their intention to let the negative reaction go. When they agreed that they were willing to let it go (not doing so showed them to be intentionally hanging on to it) the next question was "When?" At that point the whole thing became very real, because the only reasonable answer was "Now." Through this process, they learned that they had a choice in what they experienced. I tried it on a number of things that annoyed me, and found that I didn't have to go through the steps of discreating my reactions—it was possible for me to let them go by simply intending to.

The Sedona Method had been developed many years before by a man named Lester Levinson. Lester had been a high-flying stockbroker in New York, living fast and making lots of money. In his late thirties, he was felled by a massive heart attack. The only thing the doctors could advise was total inactivity. They told him that if he even ventured a step out of his apartment he would probably have another heart attack and die. Faced with an intense fear of dying, he began to review his life, asking himself when he had actually been happy. At first, he thought it was when he was loved. Going through the people who had loved him, including many women, he realized that being loved had never made him happy, because it didn't feel safe. It was too easy for the person to stop loving him, and thereby take away his happiness. He had been happy and secure only when he loved someone else, because then he had the choice to love them or not.

He began to review all his relationships, consciously letting go of any ideas that stood in the way of his loving everybody and everything. By the end of three months, he was feeling joyful and running five miles a day. Lester lived another fifty years, while teaching his ideas to anyone who would listen. He died in his late eighties, after living for three years with painful cancer. When he was dying, he told his chief assistant, Hale Dwoskin, "Don't feel sorry for me. I'm the happiest man on earth."

I went to the Sedona Method headquarters in Arizona for a weeklong workshop to further explore his approach. The setting was extraordinary: a desert in the midst of huge red rocks, clear skies, a sparkling river, and a town full of artisans and artists. Our rooms had been dug into the rock and were cool and cave-like after the heat of the day. There was more to the training than the simple questions I knew about, although everything was based on discovering experientially that you could chose to let go of whatever was bothering you. They had added a refinement of dealing separately with the three basic attachments that keep people hooked: a need for security, a need for approval, and a need to control.

It seemed an exciting new approach and I introduced it to my friends and personal clients. It was much easier than Avatar to learn, since it didn't require a nine-day course. I was fascinated to see how easily people could just drop their negative ideas. To my dismay, I found that it was equally easy to drop positive reactions, which also disappeared when I let them go. Like other methods I had learned, the Sedona Method continued to work for me only so long as my interest in it as a healing method remained strong.

It became obvious to me that Avatar had more complete answers than any other method I knew, as well as a more effective way of teaching those answers. I became excited again about its possibilities. Deliberately using the Avatar tools on a daily basis, I began to feel alive and joyous. When I chose, I could discreate my eternal doubts and questions, one by one, and thereby create the changes within myself that I had sought for so long.

It was also becoming clear to me that we are all in psychic connection with one other. Feeling appreciation toward the person you were working with was taught as part of the Avatar Master's course. At a small local Avatar meeting called Thoughtstorming, I became angry with one of the women who I perceived as being abrasively sure of herself. Without any intention on my part, my annoyance simply disappeared. I was sure that the other teachers had quietly turned their appreciative attention on me and dissolved it.

∞ ∞ ∞ ∞ ∞

Still investigating other approaches, I took the Advanced Landmark Communication Course (a further evolvement of est). The leader startled us by her first words, "Make no mistake; this is a course about love." She continued, "But to truly love, you have to give something up." The latter I recognized as a belief, resulting in a

264

customary behavior. The most useful attitude, they taught, was to assume that everything was empty and meaningless, and that you could give it any meaning you chose. This all sounded very familiar. "Giving up something" was the same as Avatar's "discreating" as well as the Sedona Method's "releasing." "Empty and meaningless" pointed to the same state as Hameed's "boundless" and Avatar's "Source."

Not long after I took the evolved est, I became aware of pain in my chest and numbness in my arms when I was taking my daily walk up the hills of my neighborhood. When I called my longtime physician, I was surprised to learn that I had symptoms of heart trouble. When he wanted to schedule diagnostic tests in a couple of weeks I objected, as I planned to leave for Holland the next week for an Avatar Professional Course. I was hesitant to go abroad with a possible heart condition, so he obligingly arranged my tests for the next day.

I took a whole battery of heart tests at a local hospital, starting with a stress test and an electrocardiogram, and including a thallium injection and a large rotating table. The specialist told me that I had coronary artery disease. He offered me a range of choices, everything from medication to angioplasty. I was appalled. It had never occurred to me that my body would actually do something like this.

I found the idea of having heart disease useful, though. Such a serious problem gave me an excuse to live my life differently—I could quit everything. I thought that it would be good for me to be given a six-month death sentence: I could rest more, not expend so much effort on everything and be satisfied with what I had—and I could

265

give up any responsibility for helping to save the world or even for writing another book.

I asked my doctor if he thought I should cancel my trip to Holland. He answered cautiously that he knew people in my circumstances who would go anyway. So I went, taking some nitroglycerin "just in case." I used the nitro only once on the trip, when running for a train and carrying my suitcase in Switzerland left me gasping for breath and feeling faint.

My heart problem turned out not to be so serious. I decided to follow Dr. Dean Ornish's well-publicized program for reversing heart disease, although I was already doing most of the things he considered curative: I didn't drink, smoke, or have a lot of obvious stress in my life. It was the low fat diet that I was lacking; I also thought that if I were to have a more emotionally open heart it would help.

I followed the Ornish system for a couple of years, using nitro when I felt the need, but eventually I relied on stopping any activity strenuous enough to make my chest hurt and my arms go numb. Re-testing five years later showed no signs of heart disease. Perhaps following the Ornish diet for several years and having a more "open heart" provided the cure. Or perhaps I believed they would, and so they did.

The Professional Course in Holland was delightful. This program was not about *teaching* Avatar, but about how to *be* an Avatar. It challenged us to try on new identities, often in front of the entire group. It gave us opportunities to confront our deepest fears, as in creating that we were inadequate or stupid or disliked, in order to learn if we were carrying around a related belief without knowing it. Since a basic theory of Avatar is that you can't get rid of a belief until you have fully experienced it, deliberately creating those feelings allowed us to let any related beliefs go.

Our hotel, with its simple, almost stark rooms, was located at the apex of huge tulip fields that stretched away from us in every direction, each section a separate, vivid color. We were surrounded by wedges of solid purple or red or yellow. Once again a friendly companion found me. This time it was a much younger man who had a girlfriend back in California and was not interested in looking for romance (as many of the other young people were). We often ate, walked and played ping-pong together.

Many of the Dutch people spoke English and were charmingly friendly. One day I was talking with a pair of Dutch women who were clearly lesbians. When I told them I was staying on after the Course, they asked me what I wanted to see in Holland. I said that I particularly wanted to see the dikes, since I'd heard a lot about them. There was a moment's startled silence while they stared at me in disbelief, and then one of them said carefully, "I – think that word is used rather differently over here." Startled too, I could feel myself flush as I gesticulated wildly, "No-no, I'm talking about the engineering projects that hold back the sea!" They both said "Oh," and we smiled sheepishly at each other and changed the subject.

Chapter 16   Forgiveness

It was several months before my next Avatar group gathering, and I had more free time than usual. I had begun to notice how many resentments I was carrying toward people who were no longer in my life. Home by myself one day, I started thinking of an incident involving my first husband, Frank. Five years into our marriage, I had designed and constructed a dramatically unusual shirt that he wanted. Rather than being grateful, he had remarked complacently that he "could make a good wife out of any woman." I resented his unfeeling arrogance then, and I resented it still. I resented many other of his behaviors as well, including his unfaithfulness during my second pregnancy. I couldn't discreate my reactions to each of the ways he had disappointed me during our seven years together. I needed to forgive both of us: him for behaving so badly and me for putting up with it for so long.

I turned on my EMDR light bar, which had a line of small green lights that appeared to move from side to side. Following the light back and forth with my eyes enabled me to clearly confront the inner workings of my mind and emotions, just as it did for my clients. It brought up an unpleasant scene between Frank and me. Within seconds I found myself raging and cursing at him, feeling the anger I had been too emotionally blocked to articulate when we were married. Scene after scene flashed through my mind of his arrogance, his certainty that he could handle other people's emotional reactions without getting emotional himself. His refusal to pay child support a couple of years after we separated came up—he had left me with the whole financial burden of raising our children. It took more than an hour before I began to have some understanding of how things had been for him, and what being married to my brittle young self must have felt like. When I was finally able to feel compassion for both of us, I felt so light that I found myself humming and taking a few dance steps. I wondered why I had allowed myself to carry such a burden of animosity for so many years.

When I thought about my second husband, Ernst, I went back to the eye movements. His memory seemed less defined than Frank's, and my anger at him resolved itself quickly. I wished I could have gotten to know him as he was, instead of through the lens of my infatuation. Within fifteen minutes I felt affection and loving forgiveness for both of us. This lifting of my emotional burdens was proving to be miraculous!

I could now think of both Frank and Ernst with friendliness and compassion, and I wanted to be able to do that with everyone else who had been important in my life, much like Lester Levinson (the founder of the Sedona Method) had done. For the next few weeks I spent two hours each day working with EMDR, reviewing my thoughts and images of people who had been important to me. My father was the next one I needed to look at. I had already worked, in many different ways, on his not being there for me after I was three years old. There didn't seem to be a lot of charge left on his absence, and I easily reached a place of sympathy for him and gratitude for the life he had given me.

When I shifted my focus to Bill, my lover at Textaxi, it brought a jealous rage to the surface, as I listening to him make love to another woman in a room down the hall. It reminded me of when I was six years old and I'd watched my mother, who was listening to my father make love to her sister. When I asked myself, "How was it to be Bill and who was he anyway?" the answer came back that he was basically a good guy who was very casual about sex, and who hadn't promised me monogamy. This session ended also with my feeling warm and accepting.

Then came George. He had almost ruined my Arica experience. I felt his cruelty as he probed for my self-deprecation and deliberately pushed every button he could find. Panting, I stopped using the lightbar and changed to the Avatar method for discreating "strong emotions." When I went back to thoughts of George while doing eye movements, I found only tolerance and quiet amusement.

There were other men who had been important to me: Ray at Lockheed, who had died of leukemia six months after he ditched me. Both events had been a shock—up until then, I'd always been the one to leave a romantic relationship. Had I hexed him with my affronted anger? My work ended with sweet affection for him and regret for his vigorous life cut short. I considered Tom, an unemployed minister whom I had let talk me out of a little ivory laughing Buddha that Ernst had given me, and who cheated at cards. I could let that resentment go. There was Hugh, whom I sent back to marry his lady in Seattle. And another George, my first serious (if chaste) boyfriend when I was seventeen who showed up briefly in my life seventeen years later, but never again. Affection for them came easily. When I thought about my current landlord, colleague and friend, with his attitude of generalized superiority, I felt my own judgments of him. When my feelings turned to warmth and friendliness, I could see that his advice was often sound and his intentions were always kindly.

Remembering Uncle Teddy, who had touched me "down there" when I was a child and insisted that I caress his penis, was much more difficult. Destroy! Sorrow for all little girl victims, for the negative effect he had had on my life. I had to discreate "strong emotions" once again, but I eventually arrived at forgiveness and a feeling of tenderness for this depraved, lonely old man.

I was amazed and appalled at how much anger I still felt toward people who were no longer in my life. I was dismayed too, by the small guilty flashes of pleasure I had felt when colleagues I actually liked weren't doing well. I found that I could let go of my jealousy and competitiveness and feel joy in their successes.

I had mixed feelings about Bob Hoffman: anger and disappointment certainly, but also love. Eventually I found that I could let all these feelings go and simply appreciate him. I felt my envy of another colleague, Dorothea, with her gracious style, charming husband, beautiful home, cultured background, religious tradition, and musical ability. Set against her wealth of advantages, the limitations of my own social and cultural circumstances and the poverty and paucity of my childhood and adulthood stood out starkly. I had to take a "time out" to use Avatar to discreate "deprivation." My sense of feeling deprived had been so huge that, when I let it go, my mind was silent and spacious. People who had humiliated me as well as people whom I had humiliated came up, and I was astonished once again at the power human beings have over one another. It became obvious to me that to speak anything but love and hope and joy to another person is a terrible misuse of power.

I remembered my brothers, Walter and Charlie, and I remembered Warren. Memories of all three of them brought up sharp unshielded grief, and then soft affectionate tears, with the honest realization of how much I missed each of them. Jean, my childhood girlfriend, was with me for a long time; I relived many scenes in which we clashed and many more in which we had been good comrades. I'd not been able to accept the slow decline that preceded her death, her years of drinking while sitting in a little house trailer, doing nothing. Eventually, I felt acceptance rather than judgment, and warm good wishes for her and the path she had chosen.

Each person whose image surfaced forced me to face my own attitudes and behavior. I found that I had to forgive myself for the difficulties I had caused other people, and that I had to let go of my shame over not having been more loving with each of them.

Even though I had done much work on my relationship with my mother over the years, when I brought her image up my whole body contracted and shook, and I found myself whimpering like a child waiting to be punished. Her punishment of me had never been physical but, instead, took the form of disapproval and blame. I remembered at sixteen, when I learned that my father had died of a heart attack, she said "God has finally struck him dead for abandoning us," just as she had foretold He would.

273

I went from feeling dismay at the way she had nursed her desire for revenge, to having immense compassion for the entire human condition. It had not been easy for her, dealing with the darkly unhappy sons and daughter she had been left to raise alone.

I returned to my "forgiveness project" with new interest each day. There were so many surprises. People whom I thought I had only mild feelings for sometimes brought up raw emotional reactions. People I thought I felt grumpy toward often brought up fondness. As the list of resolved relationships grew, I felt a continuous lightness and a joyful connection with everyone who was, or had been, in my life. I gained a strong sense of finishing things, of completion.

∞ ∞ ∞ ∞ ∞

At the same time, I was unsure of my next step professionally. A friend pointed out that I didn't show the enthusiasm for Avatar that I had shown for the Fischer/Hoffman Process. He was right, but I wasn't very enthusiastic about the Process any more, either. The work was good, but they weren't attracting many students. Avatar, on the other hand, was growing and spreading all over the world. Their method of having each licensed teacher set up his or her own course while, at the same time, being responsible for delivering the course properly and paying royalties to Avatar, was very successful.

I began to think about taking the advanced Avatar Wizards' Course in Florida, hoping to resolve all my remaining questions. Seventy five hundred dollars plus expenses was too costly for me though. On the other hand, after an Avatar teacher had taken twenty or more students though the Course, her cost for the Wizards Course became

$5000, which was doable for me. As soon as I started to focus on that possibility, things began to fall into place. Many ex-clients and friends became interested in Avatar and, by the end of 1995, I had taught Avatar to twenty-one students.

In 1996 I took the Wizard's Course for the first time. There were nine hundred Masters in my Wizards Course, most of whom knew other participants well, but none of whom I knew well. My assigned roommate, though friendly, hung out with her friends. Eventually I made a few acquaintances but none of them felt like the friends I'd made in earlier Avatar courses I had taken. On the other hand, the course itself was wonderful. Each carefully designed and presented segment led me to new insights and deeper understandings. Avatar's goal of "Creating an Enlightened Planetary Civilization" was on track to being the best way I knew to save the human race from its own collective idiocies.

On my return to San Francisco, I found myself questioning again: was Avatar only a compendium of well-known techniques, put together in a brilliant, expensive package? But my students loved it, and, more importantly, it changed their lives dramatically. For most people, it worked just as it said it would. Yet I couldn't figure out how to teach Avatar, or even how to do therapy, without leading my students and clients to believe what I thought they should believe. It felt to me like manipulation. I needed to be clear about my own truth before I could feel comfortable guiding someone else who was searching for theirs.

∞ ∞ ∞ ∞ ∞

I tried LSD once again, for the last time. A friend, whom I knew well and trusted, told me that she had often acted as a guide on such trips. I was interested in finding out where a drug-induced change in consciousness might take me after all the work I'd been doing. She started with a prayer and played lovely music all day. To our dismay, I was nauseated much of the time and sometimes went through violent body spasms. I experienced an incredible number of images, as well as vivid brief vignettes, all of which fled before completion. The scenes were colorful and interesting while I was seeing them, but I was left with no memory of them nor any sense of their meaning. At one point, I felt deeply sad because there seemed to be an impenetrable, almost physical, barrier between me and the experiences I was having.

Then I began to notice that even though all these experiences were passing very quickly, there was a rock-solid, unquestionable presence among them that I could sense and in which I could participate. I saw that everything about Avatar was true, and I was convinced that Harry had developed it while on a trip like mine. It wasn't that Avatar was the only reality. There were choices of reality and he'd said, "I'll take this one."

At the peak of my trip, I experienced a period of timeless beatitude. My friend took me outside and I wandered through her garden, feeling wise and serene and enjoying the brilliantly colored and exquisitely detailed flowers and plants. Later on, we had a delicately prepared dinner. The very small portion I ate tasted indescribably delicious.

∞ ∞ ∞ ∞ ∞

A few weeks later, I heard about a training called the Enlightenment Intensive which sounded so interesting that I signed up. In this work, members of the group would practice in dyads from six in the morning to eleven at night for four days. There were short breaks for food and rest only. One person in the dyad would speak for five minutes in reply to one of four questions asked by their partner, "Who are you?" "What are you?" "What is an Other?" or "What is Life?" The idea was that the conceptual, thinking mind would have gone through all of its ready answers and finally given up, allowing an extraordinary experience to surface. It reminded me of the "Who am I?" question that Indian sage Ramana Maharshi asked of his followers.

Until the end of the fourth day of questions and answers, my consciousness remained stubbornly ordinary, while a few others were bursting through to states of transcendence and joy. On that last afternoon, suddenly and inexplicably, I found myself in a cold rage. Without caring what effect it might have on the young man dutifully inquiring of me "What are you?" I described how loathsome I considered the human race to be and predicted its well-deserved and catastrophic end. I scared him—people were supposed to be happy by this time in the weekend and most everybody else was. He called over a teacher who wisely encouraged him to let me continue, since these were the first words that had come from my gut during the entire workshop. When I finished, I felt purged, energized and joyful, and quite astonished by my behavior.

Another time, friends took me to a talk by Susanne Spiegel, a tall, handsome, earnest woman in her late thirties. She explained that ten years earlier, while standing on a street corner waiting for a bus, all her feelings of being a "self" disappeared, and from that moment on she felt present but without any personal desires or aversions. She was afraid she was having a mental breakdown and sought advice from a series of psychiatrists, none of whom was able to give her any help.

Eventually someone sent her to Jean Klein, a well-known European spiritual teacher, who explained that she had unaccountably stumbled into a very advanced spiritual state. Susanne studied with Klein for years to try to understand what had happened to her. She spoke to us with such authenticity and wonderment that it was impossible not to believe that she was speaking her truth. She pointed out that since she didn't know how she had gotten to where she was, she couldn't teach anyone else how to do it. She told us that she saw her role as being a witness that such a state is possible for human beings. I recognized the state she was describing, as I had reached the feeling of "no-self" a couple of dozen times myself, though each occurrence had lasted only a few moments.

Some weeks later I returned a call from a man who lived nearby and was interested in Avatar. Ray Hix was very willing to talk, particularly about the "Lightbody" work he was teaching. I went to his introductory evening primarily because I wanted to continue our contact. Lightbody involved working with a spiritual guide and I'd had lots of successful experience doing that.

Six of us showed up at his small, undistinguished suburban house for the introductory evening. Ray was a slight, friendly, unassuming young man. He told us that he would begin by evoking his guide, Theo, and asked everybody to sit silently until Theo showed up. After a few minutes I was startled to feel an abrupt change in the atmosphere in the room, as if it had suddenly become charged. The woman seated beside me, who had introduced herself as a psychic, exclaimed, "Theo just came in, didn't he?" Ray, his eyes shining, nodded. That was enough for me. I signed up for four weekends.

The Lightbody course was mainly a series of guided visualizations, accompanied by evocative music, that were done while contacting different energy centers in the body. The energy centers were given complex shapes and functions, but with the ethereal music and Ray's chanting hypnotic voice, I had no trouble visualizing mine. During the course, there were also a series of interactions with guidance figures. None of this was new to me, but I was in an unusual state of overt happiness the whole time the course lasted. I had also discovered that the guided mind trips were much more intense if I put myself into a light hypnotic trance beforehand.

On the last day, our instructions were to meet and speak with one's future self. I encountered someone so wise and serene and adult that my spontaneous thought was "If this is my future self, it's worth all the trouble." Ray suggested that we ask our future selves for advice. Mine said only, "Hang in there." Again I had gone from grief and anger about the human condition to a place of deep peace and acceptance.

∞ ∞ ∞ ∞ ∞

One weekend I went with a friend to a four-day training given by Keith Varnum, a man whose name I recognized from his regular ads in the Avatar Journal. Since he had been a successful Avatar Master, I thought he must know something new to have gone off on his own. About twenty people, most of them Avatar graduates, met in the conference room of an office building. It was a good-humored group, made more so by a cheerful and ribald old man who would throw in a totally unrelated joke whenever there was a break in what we were doing.

Keith, a confidant, enthusiastic man in his forties who was balding early, was at ease with interruptions. He told us of astonishing psychic experiences he had had and taught us an inquiry technique that considered a personal problem to be a veil, which when penetrated exposed the deeper truths underneath. He believed that all relationships were eternal, and that each relationship challenge we encountered in this life was an opportunity to work things out with a being who had accompanied us for many lifetimes.

Following his lead, I found that having no feelings toward my mother was a veil over wanting to avoid her suffering, which was a veil over my love for her. My fear of losing Marny to her cancer was a veil over my loneliness, which was a veil over my profound sense of love for her. The process that Keith was teaching reminded me of the Fischer/Hoffman Light Journey and certain EMDR experiences, as well as some of Hameed's work.

The results were enough to encourage me to take his workshop in Kauai that summer. I had longed to visit the Islands again, even though Marny no longer lived there. She wasn't well enough to go with me, so I went with two other woman friends. The place we stayed in was small, comfortable, and open to the outdoors. It provided a delicious breakfast served in the lanai each morning by our friendly hostess. As usual, the soft air of Hawaii gave us its blessing. The workshop was pleasant, though the material was no longer compelling to me. There was one memorable night at 3 A.M., however, when I wandered out into the warm, sweet-smelling garden under a majestic full moon. Suddenly, both my brothers were standing beside me. It seemed that we were in a magic ring of love and understanding, and I *knew* that all close relationships were forever.

∞ ∞ ∞ ∞ ∞

That fall, I went to Carmel to visit Marny, who was still cheerful between her bouts of pain. Her urine bag, necessary after the removal of her cancerous bladder, repeatedly became infected at the entrance. It seemed to me that she was waiting for her spiritual master, Kirpal Singh, to let her know when she would be sick enough to die. It was not something we talked about, as I had never resonated with Kirpal Singh's teachings. Indeed, the very idea of surrendering to a guru was incomprehensible to me. Nevertheless, it was good to be with her, to take her shopping or just to go for a drive down the lovely Monterey shoreline or south to the redwoods.

At home that fall, my studies ranged among three very different approaches: Rudolf Steiner's works which teach that we need to think our way to a higher life; A Course In Miracles which teaches us to let go of thinking entirely; and Avatar, which teaches that thinking equals beliefs and that we can learn to create and discreate our beliefs at will.

I felt so sad to be experiencing the grief of another loss. I'd lost my mother, my brothers, Warren and Jean, and now I was losing Marny, my little "sister-in-love" these forty years. She spent Christmas in the hospital and then moved to a hospice. Her two sons, her beloved granddaughter and I visited often, but there was no room

281

for any of us in her inner voyage to the place she yearned to be. She could still be her sweet Marny-self with the kindly folk at the hospice, but not with those of us who had shared her life. I thought that perhaps she was afraid that her connection to us would hold her here on earth. She let me help her in practical ways, like adjusting pillows or assisting her with eating, but nothing more than that.

Finally, the day came when she cried out resentfully, "I want to die! Why can't I die?" I said sorrowfully that she was doing a pretty good job of it, but she muttered, "No, no, you don't understand." I heard a sudden new strength in her voice when she cried out, "I don't *care* what Kirpal says. I want to die!" After all these years of surrender to the authority of her guru, in her last hours she finally spoke for herself. Weirdly, it seemed like a kind of victory to me and I felt a little like cheering.

I stayed at her side that afternoon and evening, going out only once for something to eat. When I returned she said clearly, "Oh, you came back. Go home—you are interfering with my process." I kissed her forehead and assured her that I didn't mean to interfere with her process and left. Tears blurring my sight, I drove home. She died very early the next morning, on Valentine's Day. Her oldest son, Rocky and I met beside her still body a few hours later. After some silent moments, he said, "She isn't hanging around. She's taken off." I felt it too. Wherever home was for Marny, her spirit had gone there. She had the freedom she'd longed for and she wasn't hanging around her body.

Three days later Rocky called to tell me of an extraordinary experience he and his younger brother Andy had had the day before. They had gone to Marny's home in

Carmel to share their feelings about her death. Rocky was worried about Andy, who had had such a deep emotional connection with their mother. Yet Andy seemed to be accepting her death in a sort of good-humored way. They both had a sense of not having quite taken in the reality of their loss.

It was a beautiful day, sunny and clear, so they decided to drive to a nearby monastery which Marny had loved. As they were leaving, the sky turned black and rain started to pour down. In a few minutes the rain stopped and the skies whitened, and the most incredible rainbow Rocky had ever seen appeared directly over her house. As a commercial pilot, he had seen lots of rainbows, but this one was so magnificent as to be completely unreal. Rainbows usually end somewhere indistinct, but they could see that this rainbow touched the ground on both ends. "If Andy hadn't been with me," he said, "I'd have thought I was having a hallucination". By the time they drove away, the skies were clear again. The whole event had lasted less than five minutes, yet Rocky described it as the most extraordinary experience he'd ever had.

I wrote his story in my notebook, just as he had told it to me. A few years later I read an article in the *Journal of Noetic Science* describing research into the many stories of rainbows appearing in the sky when a great spiritual figure has passed. I told Rocky what I had read and he had never heard of such a thing. Perhaps our "spiritual bag lady" as she sometimes called herself, was a greater light than even we had realized.

Chapter 17   Options

I was hiking alone around Lake Anza in Tilden Park a couple of weeks after Marny's death, deep in mourning. It was about five in the afternoon and would soon be dark, so I was hurrying a bit. When I stepped on some damp leaves, I felt my feet skidding out from under me and I fell heavily backwards on the rocky path. I couldn't get up and I knew that my leg was broken, though I wasn't in any pain. I lay there calmly (my calmness may have been shock) assessing my situation. There was no one around and there might not be any more hikers this late in the day. I couldn't possibly drag myself the quarter mile down the rough and rocky path to the swimming area where there was a phone. I might have to stay there till morning. There might be a mountain lion during the night—I pulled a short, heavy branch closer to me so I could defend myself if necessary. I hardly noticed that I'd fallen into a patch of poison oak.

After a while it occurred to me that I could send out a mental call for help, so I concentrated on the image of someone coming by. Within moments, two hikers came along. The bearded young chap went off to phone 911, and the Chinese girl sat on the ground beside me, patiently answering my questions about her life as a UC-Berkeley student. After a while, she took off her quilted parka and covered me with it and held my cold hand in her small warm one.

Suddenly there were big men all around us, one of whom announced portentously into his cell phone, "We have located the victim." They wanted to know if it was all right to cut off my pants leg, which by this time could hardly contain my swollen flesh and I agreed. Somebody asked if I would like to be lifted out by the helicopter hovering over our heads. I imagined swinging helplessly far up in the cold air. (It didn't occur to me that the helicopter could descend almost to the ground.) I was sure that my medical insurance would never pay for it, so I said no. The men reluctantly carried me on a litter over the rough path to an ambulance waiting in the parking lot. Hazily, I heard one of them complain about carrying so much weight, and I tried to divide 140 lbs by 4 to see if his complaint were justified. When we reached the ambulance, the friendly attendant warmed me up with heat lamps, gave me pain medication, and explained, when I asked, that they didn't use a siren on non-critical deliveries.

At the hospital I was introduced to a doctor who told me he would be my surgeon. I knew nothing more afterwards, except that I heard ringing hammer blows from a great distance. What I was hearing, under anesthesia, was the doctor installing an orthopedic clamp that would hold together the triple break in my thighbone until it could mend. That metal clamp remains in my leg to this day.

In a time of short hospital stays, I was surprised when they kept me for almost two weeks. The surgeon visited me several times, saying that twenty years ago the accident would probably have been fatal at my age (nearly eighty). "I would have had to put you in a cast," he explained, "and you would have died of lung problems because you were immobilized."

After my first rescuers, the help and support that arrived from my family and friends left me astonished and grateful. Ron Kane, my landlord and friend, had been notified immediately because they'd found his name in my wallet. Though it was late evening by the time he heard, he called my doctor who was his personal friend, and together they conspired to call the best orthopedic surgeon they knew to do the operation.

I had full private nursing care during the first couple of days. I learned later that my friend Margaret Conway, a retired nurse, had come and simply taken over. Judith, another friend who called me her "spiritual mother," was there every day to do whatever I needed. My daughter flew up from LA and my son called every day. Notes and flowers appeared in my room; my phone rang often with calls from well-wishers. My friend Susan Reid offered me her college-bound son's room until I could safely navigate the stairs down to my place. Other friends took me to the theater in a wheelchair. My nephews built a railing beside the irregular stone steps to my studio apartment, so that I could return to my own place as soon as possible. When I was home and recovering, David traded his car with an automatic shift for mine with a standard shift, so I could drive before my leg was strong enough to push a clutch pedal.

My friends commented on how good-natured I was from the very first day. The truth was that I was content. I'm not a person who attracts sympathy— people assume that I can take care of myself, and rightly so. Yet, it felt wonderful to be taken care of and to discover that my

287

family and friends were glad to help when it was clear that I needed them.

Despite the loss of Marny, I was experiencing increasing moments of joy and serenity once I was home. I read a lot and listened to spiritual tapes. When I could use crutches, I went with friends to hear teachers like Richard Moss. His method of springing people into transcendence —by pushing them so hard psychologically that they had no place else to go—was too strenuous for me. One day I went to the beautiful Spirit Rock Meditation Center in Marin County, along with thousands of other people, to hear Thich Nhat Hanh, the gentle, widely-loved Buddhist monk and author.

When we learned that Bob Hoffman had died of the cancer he had held at bay for years, a mutual friend insisted that Bob had never forgiven me (or anyone else) who had chosen to thwart him. I didn't believe that. I had forgiven Bob, and when I remembered him I felt a loving, good-humored connection between us. Our battles were long ago and far away and no longer important.

∞ ∞ ∞ ∞ ∞

I heard of another human growth method whose ideas paralleled those of Avatar, but with a more heart-centered approach. The Options Institute, founded by Barry Neil Kaufman, was in Massachusetts. I felt ambivalent about spending the money to go east to take an Options workshop. To help decide, I tried a method I had read about in *Freeze-Frame; a Scientifically Proved Technique*, by Doc Lew Childre.

He teaches that each of us has another and wiser mind, located in our heart. His four-step procedure was easily learned: 1.) Identify the problem. 2.) Breathe into your heart. 3.) Relive a really happy occasion in your life. 4.) Ask your heart for a better solution to the problem. A very neat way, it seemed to me, of asking for guidance. As I got to the fourth step, a time years before came to mind when I had had a similar difficulty in deciding whether or not to take a trip I was considering. Then, the problem had vanished when I realized that whether I went or not wasn't important. Go or don't go —the world will not change. I chose to go.

The Options Institute was in the Berkshire Mountains in western Massachusetts, about thirty miles from Winsted, Connecticut where I had lived from ages six to nine. I rented a car and stopped at Highland Lake where my brother Charlie had driven us for picnic suppers in the summer. I expected feelings of recognition and nostalgia, but none came. It was just a pretty little lake, now ringed with vacation cottages. It was easier to relate to Mill River Falls, Massachusetts, since I had a photo of myself that had been taken there. I sat with my back against a rock and tried to enter the mind of the skinny little girl I had been then. I felt a great rush of tenderness for her and for my mother, who tried so hard to give us a good life, and for my brothers, and even for Uncle Teddy who was in the photo with a rose between his teeth. My tears felt sweet.

I loved the affluent countryside with its magnificent trees and beautiful big white wooden houses in the midst of great stretches of open lawn. It was March and the snows had melted and everything was as lushly green as I remembered. It would stay green until fall, I knew, not turn golden brown by the end of April like the California hills did.

The Options Institute was as handsome as its flyers promised it would be. Located on ninety-five acres of pastoral countryside, it was surrounded by carefully maintained buildings spread widely apart. The staff and other students were friendly, even loving, since love was what they were teaching and learning. "Happiness is a choice," said "Bears" Kaufman, who had founded the Institute with his wife, and everyone there had chosen to be happy.

Options was also like Avatar in its emphasis on choice, though its method was more unstructured, which meant that its results were more dependent on the skills of the mentors. Like Diamond Approach work, its basis was inquiry, but there was only one inquiry: "What stops you from choosing to be happy?" After identifying the unhappiness that a person wanted to explore, the mentor encouraged them to be more and more specific by asking, "What do you mean?" and, "Do you have an example?" and the therapists' eternal question "How do you feel about that?" Eventually the person would realize that if they had *chosen* to be so unhappy, they could just as easily choose to be happy.

The Options method asked mentors to acknowledge that they did not have the answers to the questions they were asking of someone else. Only the person being asked the questions could know their own authentic answers, which they would find for themselves as they engaged with the questions.

Learning their kind of mentoring led me to a painful awareness about how directive I still tended to be. After our teacher talked about the approach, we paired up to ask each other questions. My first partner was Harriet, an experienced mentor-in-training. I trusted her to direct her own work and our back and forth went beautifully. My second partner was Barb, a newcomer to the work, who wore an habitually pinched, worried expression. She started out by saying that she didn't have anything to explore. She was happy and peaceful and was handling everything in her life very well. I didn't believe her. From that point on, unwittingly, I had an agenda: I wanted her to realize that she was kidding herself.

The instructor came around with a tape recorder while we were working. Later she played a few minutes of several people's work for the whole group to listen to and comment on. She didn't play those dyads that went well; she played those that had not gone well, including mine with Barb. When I heard myself assuming that I knew more about my partner than she herself did, I felt my face flush with embarrassment, although I was able to laugh with the rest of the group.

I wholeheartedly agreed with the Options Institute's position that the person being questioned was the true expert on their own situation, and my role as mentor was to help them open up to their own knowledge. But with Barb, once I had decided that she was in denial, I had forgotten that my role was to help her find what was true for her, if she wanted to. I saw that I still had something to learn about listening to *all* people with an attitude of love and respect.

Options taught us to have the same open-minded curiosity about the person we were talking with as Avatar expected its Masters to have. Both taught us to appreciate everyone as the amazing creators of the human beings they were. Since loving-kindness was the overt goal of everybody there, the Options Institute was a pleasant and friendly place to be. Conversation was easy—your instructions were to ask a question of whomever you were having conversation with about the last thing they had said, and to ask yourself, "What is the most loving thing I can do right now?" At the end of five days I wasn't sure that I wanted to return to the noisy aggressive world outside, but I did.

Back in Berkeley, I did my own Options session on how to use a couple of big drawers-full of many years worth of personal journals and notes. At first I felt amusement followed by a deep silence, and finally I saw an image of myself throwing all my journals away, as well as all my books, decorations, clothes, and the rest of my "stuff." Underneath my vision, I sensed a sort of inner chortling and the felicitous realization that someday I would, indeed, get rid of it all

Chapter 18   Being Present

Marianne, David and I continued to give Avatar courses together until about 2005. We had a wonderful time with our students, and they had a wonderful time too. Before the students arrived each day, the three of us would meet to clear our minds and recreate ourselves as the source of everything we did. Each of us in turn would commit to being there to appreciate, support and empower the students and each other. Doing these rituals added special energy and joy to the day for all three of us.

In between giving courses, I was becoming concerned about my memory. I would find myself arriving at a store without my purse, or unable to remember words when I wanted them. I accumulated half a dozen books and tapes on how to improve your memory but nothing ever helped, so I would put the problem behind me until the next egregious mistake happened. Eventually, I thought about using an Avatar process for handling limitations, which a poor memory certainly was: I wanted a better memory and I didn't have one. When I "discreated" the whole thing— that I wanted what I didn't have—my memory improved because I was able to pay more attention to what I was actually doing or thinking. I found too that I was developing a kind of "external memory:" whenever I couldn't remember a word or couldn't find something I

293

wanted, a friend or even a nearby stranger would produce what I was looking for.

In the early 2000's, Marianne and I went to La Jolla (near San Diego) to attend an Inner Directions conference on non-duality. For the first time, I heard both Eckhart Tolle and Adyashanti speak. Tolle—who had written a book called *The Power of Now*—spoke with such authenticity about both his experience of Awakening and his understandings that, when he ended, the whole audience was silent for a moment and then rose as one and broke into fervent applause. Both his message that a profound transformation of human consciousness is possible now, not in a distant future, as well as his extraordinary assurance moved us.

Tolle's concept of "no-self" has been central to Eastern spiritual traditions for thousands of years. As I understood it, no-self means a state where you have no consciousness awareness of your individual self. When you look deeply enough, there is no "you" looking back; only the looking itself is happening. When I was in a certain frame of mind, the concept of no-self made sense to me.

Back in Berkeley, I attended Tolle's workshops and listened to his tapes. His message was the same as it had been at the Inner Directions conference. When you silence your ego-mind, you are with the Now. He was clearly in no-self and was able to take many in his audience with him part way. When I compared his teachings to Avatar's, it seemed to me that he was saying, "See the mountaintop? You can be there with me if you choose," while Avatar was saying, "See the mountaintop? If you use these flights of stairs that we have made for you, you can easily ascend from one level to the next, and we will both be on the mountaintop."

I heard Adyashanti speak almost every other Saturday in the Bay Area until his reputation spread across the country, and he was no longer available so regularly. I found him to be both remarkably wise and entirely down-to-earth. An enormously personable young American Zen teacher, he told wonderful stories that charmed his audiences. I thought he might be able to explain the phenomenon of "flat-lining" that I continued to experience when I meditated. (I was still suspicious of that neutral space I sometimes found in meditation, although I no longer considered it negative.) I made an appointment and drove to his Palo Alto office to talk with him.

Adyashanti listened respectfully and assured me that many people he'd spoken to had told him of a similar problem. He suggested that I ask the question, "What is deeper than this?" when my mind went blank during meditation. I left feeling no wiser than when I came, but a few weeks later I noticed that when I encountered the "neutral zone" in my meditation, if I stayed with it and asked "What is deeper than this?" it tended to morph into peaceful joy and quiet awareness.

Adya's "What is deeper than this?" was the same solution as one of the Avatar procedures, where the student lets go of one layer after another until all the layers disappear, leaving only the one who is letting go. It felt like the same approach as going down the levels in the Light Journey that Bob Hoffman taught us. It also felt the same as "Can you let that go?" from the Sedona Method; and "What keeps you from being happy?" in the Options Method; as well as "Inquiry" in Hameed's Diamond

Approach. They all seemed to be different ways of teaching that, as you go deeper into accepting your present experience, you become more "grace prone" as Adya called it.

Each time I heard Adyashanti speak—at a satsang, weekend intensive or five-day retreat—his words resonated more deeply with what I knew to be true. I found him to be especially understandable because he talks in a cheerful American voice and uses references familiar to us (he was brought up near San Francisco). He continued to remind his audiences, however, that it isn't his words that matter but the experience they point to. Avatar, too, points out that word lessons (verbal information) can be useful and interesting, but it is only world lessons (experience) that bring about change. Like all real spiritual teachers, Adya's very presence makes what he says believable. "The best way to become enlightened," he has written, "is to be with an enlightened teacher and to listen." That's how he got there.

"Let your mind go silent," he says, "and don't be afraid of the space that opens up." Something in my mind has wanted to go silent ever since I walked into that lake in Wisconsin when I was five years old. When I was younger, I thought of it as a yearning for death, but I know now that it is a yearning for inner silence. When I go beyond my ego-mind (the little me) there is a possibility of my entering into Big Mind/Being/Awareness/Source /God—not as if it were other than myself, but as if it is my very Self.

In his first book, *The Impact of Awakening,* Adya writes that "awakening is a never-ending process of opening and deepening, so that our lives become an expression of the mystery we've discovered ourselves to be." "Do not seek what you yearn for," he says. "Seek the source of the yearning." He counsels, "The need to be free does not come from limitation, but is an evolutionary impulse—we can choose to follow it or not."

I know many people who believe that we can consciously participate in our own evolution. Hameed said, "The ordinary self, the ego, constantly demands attention because the energy of attention is all that holds it together—it has no reality in itself." Avatar's Harry Palmer says that "an ego identity is a bunch of beliefs with a viewpoint." Avatar has many techniques, each of which is intended to take the student beyond the technique itself. Adyashanti uses no techniques. "True meditation," he says," has no direction, no goals or methods. Leave everything to its natural functioning and just be still. The purpose of meditation is to find the meditator. "

∞ ∞ ∞ ∞ ∞

I went to hear Hameed, whom I love dearly, at his yearly one-day meeting to benefit the Spirit Rock Meditation Center. All morning he spoke glowingly about the feeling of anger, under which he said was the glorious, beautiful, rich, warm, nourishing, luminous feeling of Power, one of the qualities of Essence. "Get in touch with your anger," he said, "let it enliven you!" Only toward the end did he throw in a few cautionary words, "Don't act it out, just feel it."

In the afternoon, Hameed turned his flowing speech and full charisma onto looking at "hurt," under which lay the essential quality of Compassion. The feeling of hurt is so delicate, so painful, so sweet, so tender and soft, and always so wrenching for humans to explore. He had us break into groups of three to share what hurt meant to each of us. I brought up the fragments of pain that I felt from Marny's last words to me, "Go home, you are interfering with my process." For the first time I felt a connection with her earlier words, "I don't care what Kirpal says, I want to die!" If even her teacher, Kirpal Singh, could not get in the way of her process, surely neither could I. My hurt dissolved into compassion for us both.

In meditation one day I felt the thought-form of a fatherly personal God, which had existed for so long in my mind, disintegrate. My world momentarily felt empty and a little scary. I could discern the edges of what it must feel like to be an atheist—nothing beyond oneself. (How fearful it must have been when humans lost contact with their old protective deity as the "Scientific Revolution" progressed.) I had often known guidance that had been absolutely and experientially real to me. I never knew if it came from outside, or from the deeply wise part inside me. I might have created those experiences, but surely *I was not the one who created that I could create them.* It seems to me that there is a much deeper Mystery of which we are all a part.

The critical voice that had persecuted me since childhood and had never ceased to weigh in with its derogatory opinions finally went silent one day. I can still be concerned about my lapses of memory, for instance, but my mind no longer intimates "you are wrong and bad for forgetting." Forgetting things occasionally is what is happening to me, so I do my best to deal with it. War and famine and human misery are happening everywhere, so I do my best to help in any way I can and I support those who are helping. I have learned it is all right for me to do what I can do and no more.

∞ ∞ ∞ ∞ ∞

Amazing new ways are emerging of teaching the old truths. My attention was drawn to an internet site called Sacred Awakenings, which featured interviews with forty psychospiritual teachers, many of whom I had never heard of. I learned of Byron Katie, who awakened out of a ten-year state of anxious depression to become a much loved and respected teacher who works with audiences all over the world. I read her first book called *Loving What Is: Four Questions that can Change your Life,* and I attended one of her workshops also.

Katie asks: "1. Is this true? 2. Can you really know that it is true? 3. How do you feel when you think this? 4. How would you feel if you could never think it again?" Then she turns the whole thing around and asks: "What if the miscreant was not the person you thought it was, but you?" Considering her questions can bring a person's identification with their inner misery to a complete halt, as well as open them to an entirely new way of seeing things.

When I meditated, sometimes I experienced the state of love that spiritual teachers describe: full and uninhibited, overflowing with sweetness, filled with love for all that exists (including me). Occasionally, I could stay in a state of complete alertness without a single movement in my mind, where I had no emotional reactions, nothing recognizable as bliss or joy or even the normal me—I had only awareness without content. Each of these moments was lovely but they were like vacations, because they were always temporary. They were windows looking into a

299

world I wanted to live in, but they were still not doorways through which I could walk.

One day in 2002, Freda told me about a book called *The Presence Process,* by Michael Brown. His style of writing was a delight: enormously intelligent, persuasive and good-humored. Each sentence was carefully crafted to deepen the reader's experience of the profound wisdom being conveyed. Michael had been a music journalist in South Africa who was leading an ordinary and happy life, when suddenly he was struck down by a neurological disease that left him writhing in pain by the side of a dirt road where he had been walking. For nine years the pain did not let up.

He tried to find a cure, even enduring cortisone shots in his face and having his wisdom teeth pulled, but nothing helped. When Michael consulted a top neurosurgeon he was told that there was no cure or even relief for the ailment, and there was a danger of his succumbing to narcotics or suicide. Alternative healers could not aid him either. Finally Michael realized that nobody else could help him—he would have to find his own cure. He studied and became a healer in several different native American traditions, always trying a method on himself first. He discovered that those methods that took him away from grief about the past, or anxiety about the future, reduced the severity and frequency of his pain. Eventually, being able to bring his consciousness fully into the present moment brought about his complete healing.

A crucial element of Michael's teachings is that the negative emotional reactions we learned in childhood are the roots of our negative adult attitudes. Learning to let go of these reactions, reified as the "pain body" by Eckhart Tolle, leads us to deeper and more secure contact with our own Inner Presence. Michael found that learning to be present required an experiential knowledge of the fact that neither shame nor grief about the past, nor fear or anticipation of the future, has any reality basis in the present. Those negative emotions are happening only in our minds.

The wisdom and the methods used in *The Presence Process* were very familiar to me, yet they seemed entirely new. I'd heard all of them many times before, yet I found his book to be like having a wise, loving, personal teacher who was always available. Each time I immerse myself in his writings, I am able to peel away more layers of myself, exposing and healing the emotions, attitudes and beliefs that have shaped my life. It was this "always available" book that finally resolved my slipping back into ordinary miseries as I had done before.

I can make my chosen beliefs part of my life and thereby recreate them in myself. Whether or not I have a "self" no longer seems important or even relevant to me. I am simply here. Whether I create my experiences internally or whether they are part of some greater wisdom than my own seems irrelevant too. What matters is that I am continuing to learn and grow each day: to love more deeply, to share what I have learned with others and, most of all, to be as present as I am able in every moment of my life.

I think that the auspicious state I am in now has come about not only because of the paths I have followed, but also because I have written these pages. Writing them has allowed me to see clearly that all my psychospiritual teachers have been saying basically the same thing: the more we are able to let go of the learned demands and fearfulness of our little selves to turn deep within, the more we are in harmony with the wondrous Self that is under the surface of all human life.

During the last couple of years I have retired from therapy work, or perhaps it has retired from me. I could no longer get up and down the stairs to my home in Berkeley, and I am no longer physically able to do much. My daughter and her family moved from Southern California to Washington State. They invited me to relocate with them and found me a perfect small condo looking out on the peaceful view shown on the cover of this book. I knew that this was the next step for me and so it has turned out to be. I have lots of time now to focus on the psychospiritual ideas that interest me most.

It has been my experience that if you earnestly use any of the processes I've described (or one of the myriad other sound methods offered today) you can control both your thoughts and your feelings. You can choose to drop fear, anger and delusion from your inner experience. But what of creating bodily and social changes, as some of these methods say we can? Can we deliberately affect what happens in our world? To misquote a sentence I used elsewhere, "Whatever you believe fully and consistently becomes your experience—within limits still to be explored."

Index

306

Made in the USA
Lexington, KY
31 May 2011